Learning to teach

Teacher education is currently the subject of widespread political debate and radical reform. There is, however, very little recent empirical evidence about what actually happens on teacher training courses and in the first year of teaching. The Leverhulme Primary Project reported here looks in detail at the experience of all the student teachers on one post-graduate primary teacher training course and of those responsible for them in their university and in schools. It tracks them as they work to acquire the appropriate subject and pedagogical knowledge and as their own attitudes and beliefs about teaching develop through the course. A final section follows some of the students through their first year as qualified teachers. The aim throughout the book is to define the basic teaching competencies and to show how these relate to the knowledge bases with which novice teachers enter the profession. More people than ever before have some responsibility, whether in higher education or in schools, for the training of teachers. None of them can afford to ignore the fresh insights into how teachers are made contained in this book.

Neville Bennett is Professor of Primary Education at the University of Exeter and co-director of the Leverhulme Primary Project. His publications include *Teaching Styles and Pupil Progress* (1976), *The Quality of Pupil Learning Experiences* (with Charles Desforges, Anne Cockburn and Betty Wilkinson, 1984), *A Good Start? Four Year Olds in Infant School* (with Joy Kell, 1989) and *Talking and Learning in Groups* (with Elisabeth Dunne; Routledge, 1990), part of the Leverhulme Primary Project *Classroom Skills* series of notebooks.

Clive Carré is coordinator of the Leverhulme Primary Project and editor of the Leverhulme Primary Project *Classroom Skills* series. His publications include *Language Teaching and Learning in Science* (1981) and *Visual Communication in Science: Learning through Sharing Images* (with D. Barlex, 1985).

Learning to teach

Edited by

Neville Bennett
and Clive Carré

ROUTLEDGE

London and New York

irst published 1993
y Routledge
1 New Fetter Lane, London EC4P 4EE

imultaneously published in the USA and Canada
y Routledge
29 West 35th Street, New York, NY 10001

© 1993 Neville Bennett and Clive Carré

Typeset in Times by J&L Composition Ltd, Filey, North Yorkshire
Printed and bound in Great Britain by
Mackays of Chatham PLC, Chatham, Kent

British Library Cataloguing in Publication Data
A catalogue record for this book is available from the British Library.

ISBN 0–415–08309–5
     0–415–08310–9 (pbk)

Library of Congress Cataloging-in-Publication Data
Bennett, Neville.
    Learning to teach / Neville Bennett and Clive Carré.
        p.   cm.
    Includes bibliographical references (p.   ) and index.
    ISBN 0–415–08309–5. — ISBN 0–415–08310–9 (pbk.)
    1. Teachers—Training of—Great Britain. 2. Teachers—Training
of—United States. sj10 10–05–92. I. Carré, Clive. II. Title.
LB1725.G6B46   1993
370.71′0941—dc20   92–37257
                                                          CIP

Contents

List of figures and tables

FIGURES

TABLES

Foreword

The nature and quality of teacher education is the subject of much concern in many countries around the world. In Britain, and elsewhere, change is being demanded, and generated, by political assertion rather than by careful evaluation highlighting the lack of independent evidence on the processes and outcomes of teacher training.

The three-year study reported here provides independent evidence in relation to the one-year Postgraduate Certificate in Education (PGCE) primary training route. The student-teachers' subject-matter knowledge for teaching and beliefs were assessed on entry to their course, and again at exit. Course processes, including those based in the institution and in schools, were recorded and analysed through the use of multiple methods (including student diaries, interviews and direct observations), and from multiple sources (student-teachers, cooperating teachers, tutors and supervisors). The role of knowledge and beliefs in teaching performances were carefully ascertained before following a group of these same student-teachers through their first year of teaching.

The analyses of these diverse data were designed to identify patterns and trends, not to make grand generalizations. Nevertheless the findings are clear, and supportive of the outcomes of other studies, and provide implications for teacher training in such areas as school-based work, teaching competences and course design.

The chapters of the book have been carefully sequenced to present the findings in a progressive and cohesive manner. Each chapter has been written by the members of the research team who took responsibility for that particular aspect of the study. However as director, and senior research fellow, respectively, of the Leverhulme Primary Project, the overall responsibility for the study, and this book, lies with us.

Neville Bennett and Clive Carré

Acknowledgements

The success of the Leverhulme Primary Project has been built on the cooperation and enthusiasm of many people. Pride of place must go to the student-teachers themselves, particularly to those who faithfully kept diaries through the course recording their reflections, evaluations and perceived development. These same students also gave willingly, if no doubt anxiously, their permission for extensive observation of their classroom performances. Particular acknowledgement must go to those thirteen students who allowed us to follow them through their first year of teaching.

Our thanks are also due to the tutors in the training institution studied, and to the schools and cooperating teachers with whom the students spent their teaching practices.

For parts of the study it was necessary to draw on consultants with particular expertise, and in this context we would like to express our gratitude to Richard Dunne, Paul Ernest, John Fox, Gareth Harvard, Christine Mitchell, Tricia Nash and David Wray.

A mountain of data were collected both by field workers and research assistants, many of whom were also involved in the collation and initial analysis of data. Our thanks in this regard go to Chris Burley, Carol Galton, Cathie Holden, Linda King, Louise Langston, Mary MacMullen, Joanna Marsden-Caulkett, Rosemary Turner-Bisset and Peter Willis.

The foundation on which every project stands or falls is dependent on the quality of the permanent research and secretarial staff. In this case we were particularly fortunate in having Elisabeth Dunne as research fellow, and Jo Small as project secretary, and special thanks go to both. Finally, the onerous job of typing drafts and re-drafts, and of assuring that we all worked to the same format, fell to Pamela Hoad, to whom we are all grateful.

Finally our thanks are due to the Leverhulme Trust which funded the longer research programme of which this study was part, and to Ted Wragg, who, with the first author, co-directed the whole programme.

Chapter 1

Knowledge bases for learning to teach

Neville Bennett

THE QUALITY OF TEACHER EDUCATION

The nature and quality of teacher education is the subject of analysis and debate worldwide. In Britain it is Her Majesty's Inspectorate who, in the absence of independent research evidence, has been influential in mapping the domain (HMI, 1987; 1988; 1991). In making their professional judgements they have tended to emphasize knowledge of subjects, of curriculum, of learners and of assessment.

In their survey of primary B.Ed. courses, HMI claimed that it is essential for primary teachers to acquire both an effective grasp of a broad curriculum repertoire and a deeper knowledge of some specialized aspect of it (HMI, 1987). However, most courses were not achieving this. Most institutions fell considerably short of providing adequate subject study, and the curriculum courses were failing to cover adequately several crucial areas of professional competence. Foremost among these were the ability to assess children's performances, to teach to those assessments, to provide for a wide diversity of pupils' needs and to plan for the progressive growth of pupils' knowledge, concepts and skills. Further, key issues such as multi-ethnic education and special educational needs were too often only offered as options. Finally, they argued that training courses were not always well managed, lacking strong leadership and clear goals, and were too often taught by those with no primary school experience.

In their recent commentary on inspections of twenty courses for the training of primary teachers, HMI judged the quality of each academic subject as well as aspects of professional skills and competence (HMI, 1991). They considered the English and mathematics courses to be the most satisfactory, although there were weaknesses in assessment and evaluation in English, and in progression and differentiation in mathematics. They complained that science courses were much too short to ensure that student-teachers understood the progressive development of children's scientific knowledge skills and attitudes, or to develop a knowledge base on which to work with confidence.

Time, too, was of the essence in the humanities; time devoted to history and geography generally being insufficient. Consequently student-teachers' knowledge base was poor, the matching of work to children's levels of understanding was inadequate, and the assessment of pupils' learning weak. As such, most of the humanities courses were felt to require considerable review and modification in the light of the demands of the National Curriculum.

In relation to the professional skills and competences needed, HMI emphasized knowledge of children's development, and of evaluation and assessment. In the former they believed there was a need to strengthen the links between the theoretical components of the courses and practical experiences with children. In the latter, they were considerably concerned at the inadequate levels of student knowledge, arguing that they need a more detailed and rigorous conceptual framework and knowledge base on which to examine the purposes, methods and uses of assessment in relation to all aspects of teaching and learning. Many found it difficult to distinguish between observation and inference, and needed considerable help in diagnosing learning difficulties. Not surprisingly, in the light of this, it was unusual for student-teachers to refer to children's learning in the evaluation of their teaching. A related finding was that some had great difficulty in matching work to the different stages of children in the same class, and had similar difficulties formulating questions to probe their pupils' knowledge and understandings.

These same deficiencies in knowledge are cited in HMI surveys of primary teachers in their first year of teaching (HMI, 1988). They judged that effective mastery of the subject was achieved in less than half of the lessons observed, and some insecurity was noted in another quarter. Several other areas were identified where these teachers were experiencing difficulties. These included classroom management and control, identifying and making specific the aims of the lessons, matching work to the varied abilities of the children, skills of questioning, and the use of marking work as an instrument of diagnosis to help pupils to improve their performance. HMI further argued that worrying proportions of new teachers were inadequately prepared to use computers, teach the under-5s, cater for children with special needs, and take on the administrative and pastoral duties which schools expected them to perform.

Finally, these teachers were asked to reflect on, and rate, their satisfaction with their teacher training. Two-thirds were well, or reasonably well, satisfied, but, nevertheless, were unhappy with the balance of the courses. Too much time was allocated to educational studies and too little to practical work, teaching methods and classroom observation. Many primary teachers in particular felt less than adequately prepared for classroom management, the teaching of reading, teaching more able children, the under 5s, and the use of audio-visual equipment.

The importance of subject-matter knowledge is reflected in its inclusion in the criteria to which all teacher education courses in Britain must conform. Primary student-teachers must thus study at least one subject for up to two years at standards appropriate to higher education (DES, 1989b). The assumption is that mastery of a subject and its application facilitate more effective teaching and learning. Indeed the most recent advice argues that newly trained primary teachers should have sufficient subject knowledge in the core subjects of English, mathematics and science to teach and assess pupils across the full range of National Curriculum levels, i.e. to the level which an able 11-year-old, or average 14-year-old, would be expected to reach. In addition they should have sufficient subject knowledge to teach the rest of the curriculum to the same level 'with the support and guidance of colleagues' (NCC, 1991).

Similar concerns about the content and quality of teacher education programmes have been expressed in the United States. Teacher education programmes have been criticized as brief, technologically impoverished, and lacking in conceptual clarity and programmatic consistency (Howey, 1983; Holmes Group, 1986); criticisms recently supported by Goodlad (1991). Goodlad is reported as arguing that 'The research we conducted points rather painfully to incoherent programmes not tied to a mission, with no basic principles of curriculum guiding them, no organizing themes or elements. . . . Teacher education, no less than the schools, requires reconstruction' (Brandt, 1991). Lanier and Little (1986) were similarly scathing, characterizing teacher educators as largely rigid, shallow, anti-intellectual and conforming, and criticized research on student teaching as desultory in nature, poorly synthesized and weakly criticized.

Subject-matter knowledge is also regarded as important in the United States. One of the propositions of the National Board for Professional Teaching Standards, for example, is that 'teachers know the subjects they teach and how to teach those subjects to students' (Baratz-Snowden, 1990). However, an equally pressing concern appears to be that most teacher education practices reinforce traditional beliefs and methods of teaching through the placement of student-teachers with supervising teachers without considering whether the aims and methods of the supervising teacher are consistent with the goals of the teacher education programme (Ashton, 1991). As Joyce (1975) argued, 'no better method has been devised for preventing change in a social institution than to apprentice the novice to his elder'. Goodlad (1984), with a more colourful analogy, argued similarly, 'if we were to set out to provide the most advanced preparation for future doctors, surely we would not intern them with those whose solution to every illness is bloodletting'.

Although these arguments must be interpreted in the context of a continuing debate about innovation and change from traditional practices in American schools, it is clear, as in Britain, that all is not well with teacher education.

There is a glaring irony here. In an era when teacher educators and researchers have been exhorting teachers to engage in action research on their own practice, and more generally to be inquiring, reflective practitioners, they have signally failed to heed their own prescriptions. Empirical research on teacher education is conspicuous by its very absence. Consequently there is very little evidence on the nature and acquisition of teaching skills and competences, or on what is taught and learned in teacher education courses. There is as yet little understanding of the domains of knowledge on which student-teachers should draw, or of the relationships between knowledge bases and teaching performance. These are the broad questions to be addressed in this study.

THEORETICAL PERSPECTIVES

The theoretical perspectives adopted for these purposes draw on, and integrate, two different traditions of research on teaching and teacher education, i.e. those which Zeichner (1992) identifies as the 'academic' and 'social efficiency' traditions. The latter draws on the empirical study of teaching–learning processes in classrooms, and the former on models of pedagogical knowledge and reasoning.

Teaching–learning processes

Our previous studies of teaching–learning processes in primary classrooms have taken a constructivist view of learning, which perceives children as intellectually active learners holding schemata which they use to make sense of everyday experiences. Learning in classrooms thus involves the extension, elaboration or modification of learners' schema, through a process in which pupils' actively make sense of the world by constructing meanings (Bennett *et al.*, 1984; Bennett and Kell, 1989; Bennett and Dunne, 1992).

The outcomes of such studies bear directly on the teaching skills required for effective practice, and indirectly on the knowledge bases teachers need to draw on and develop. A brief overview of these findings is presented below using a summary model of task processes (see Bennett, 1988; 1992, for full details).

Analyses of data have tended to centre on several indices of appropriateness:

(i) Of task to intention

Of particular interest in this category has been teachers' planning and preparation. Crucial issues in this area are the selection of content and the

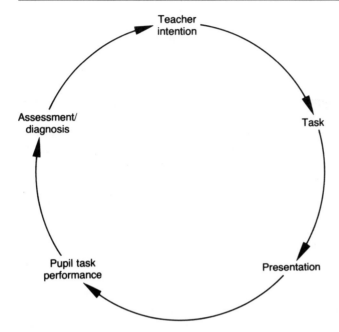

Figure 1.1 A model of task processes

design of tasks appropriate both to teachers' intentions, and to the range of pupils' capabilities. Empirical studies and observations by Her Majesty's Inspectorate have consistently shown that levels of matching tasks to children is generally poor, with high attainers underestimated and low attainers overestimated.

(ii) Of presentation

Lack of appropriateness in presentation can take many forms including lack of clarity, inadequate explanations, poor quality questioning and lack of necessary materials. Poor presentation by either teacher or text is not conducive to the construction of new understandings by learners, and poor task specification can actually undermine teachers' intentions.

(iii) Of implementation

Tasks are undertaken in learning settings largely determined by teachers. In organizing classrooms for optimal learning teachers need to ensure, among other things, that the setting is governed by a set of agreed ground rules, allows for high pupil involvement and incorporates pupil grouping arrangements that reflect task intentions. As a recent summary of evidence argued, 'The critical notion is that of fitness for purpose. The teacher must be clear about the goals of learning before deciding on methods of organization' (Alexander, Rose and Woodhead, 1992).

(iv) Of assessment and diagnosis

Ausubel (1968) asserted that if he had to reduce all of educational psychology to just one principle, he would say that the most important single factor influencing learning is what the learner already knows. Ascertain this and teach accordingly. In other words, for teachers adequately to take account of learners' schema in task planning then it follows that the diagnosis of those schema are a prerequisite, i.e. to gain a window into the learner's mind. Despite this the evidence is consistent in showing that diagnosis does not generally occur, for whatever reason. This has serious implications for planning and also for matching, since the root of poor matching appears to be inadequate diagnosis.

These findings strongly imply the role of teachers' subject knowledge. For teachers effectively to diagnose children's schema, to plan appropriate tasks, to present quality explanations and demonstrations, and to make curricular choices, all require knowledge and understanding of subject matter. This raises such important questions as 'how can teachers teach well knowledge that they do not fully understand?', 'how can teachers make clear decisions about development or progression in curriculum areas with which they are not thoroughly conversant?', and 'how can teachers accurately and adequately diagnose children's understandings and misconceptions without an adequate knowledge of the subject?'

Questions of this kind are not new of course. John Dewey argued in the 1930s that to recognize opportunities for early mathematical learning one must know mathematics: to recognize opportunities for elementary scientific learning one must know physics, chemistry, biology and geology, and so on down the list of fields of knowledge. In short, he contended that the demand on teachers is two-fold: a thorough knowledge of the disciplines and an awareness of those common experiences of childhood that can be utilized to lead children towards the understandings represented by this knowledge (Cremin, 1961).

Knowledge bases for teaching

Research on teaching has raised useful questions, but has provided few firm answers. As Shulman (1986b) pointed out, 'In their necessary simplification of the complexities of classroom teaching, investigators ignored one central aspect of classroom life: the subject matter'. He characterized this as the 'missing paradigm' problem, arguing that typical studies had treated teaching generically. Missing were questions about the content of the lessons taught, the nature of the questions asked and the quality of explanations offered. Although arguing that mere content knowledge is as likely to be as useless pedagogically as content-free skill, it is nevertheless important that as much attention be paid to content as has previously been devoted to teaching processes.

Shulman (1987a) delineated seven knowledge bases that identify the teacher understanding needed to promote comprehension among students. These are:

1 Content knowledge: referring to the amount and organization of knowledge in the mind of the teacher. This includes both substantive and syntactic structures of a subject, i.e. the variety of ways in which the basic concepts and principles of the discipline are organized, and the ways in which truth or falsehood, validity or invalidity, are established.
2 General pedagogical knowledge: with special reference to those broad principles and strategies of classroom management and organization that appear to transcend subject matter.
3 Curriculum knowledge: with particular grasp of the materials and programmes that serve as 'tools of the trade' for teachers.
4 Pedagogical-content knowledge: that form of content knowledge that embodies the aspect of content most germane to its teachability. It includes, for any given subject area, the most useful forms of representation of those ideas, the most powerful analogies, illustrations, examples, explanations and demonstrations. In other words, the ways of representing and formulating the subject that make it comprehensible to others.
5 Knowledge of learners and their characteristics.
6 Knowledge of educational contexts: ranging from the workings of the group or classroom, the governance and financing of schools, to the character of communities and cultures.
7 Knowledge of educational ends, purposes and values, and the philosophical and historical grounds.

These categories have unknown, and by no means clear, *a priori*, relationships between themselves or to teachers' classroom performances. They undeniably cloak complexities and, according to Leinhardt and Feinberg (1990), artificially split knowledge bases. Nevertheless they provide a useful starting point in conceptualizing students' learning to teach.

Shulman himself views teaching through a model of pedagogical reasoning and action, represented in Figure 1.2, which has many similar features to the task model discussed earlier. 'Given a text, educational purposes, and/or a set of ideas, pedagogical reasoning and action involve a cycle through the activities of comprehension, transformation, instruction, evaluation and reflection. The starting point and terminus for the process is an act of comprehension' (Shulman, 1987a).

Briefly, the argument underpinning the model is that the teacher must first comprehend the ideas to be taught and the purposes to be achieved.

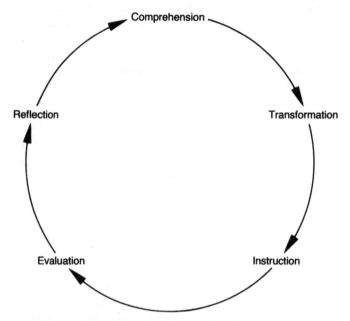

Figure 1.2 A model of pedagogical reasoning

These must then be transformed into forms which are pedagogically powerful, yet adaptive to pupil understandings. Such transformations require a combination of: (a) preparation – critical scrutiny and choice of materials of instruction; (b) representation – a consideration of the key ideas and how they might best be represented, in the form of analogies, examples and the like; (c) instructional selections – choice of teaching approach; and (d) adaptation – often called differentiation, i.e. the tailoring of input, whatever its form, to pupils' capabilities and characteristics. Instruction, i.e. the teaching act, then takes place within a system of classroom management and organization. The process of evaluation includes in-flight checks for pupil understanding as well as more formal assessments and feedback – a process which, Shulman argues, requires all the forms of teacher comprehension and transformation described above. Reflection requires a reconstruction, re-enactment or recapturing of events and accomplishments, and is the analytic process through which a professional learns from experience. This leads back to comprehension – a new beginning.

Few claims are made for the quality of fit of this model across primary and secondary teaching, or for the invariance of the steps or sequence in the cycle. Shulman does argue, however, that a teacher should demonstrate the capacity to engage in these processes when called upon, and teacher education should provide student-teachers with the understandings and performance abilities they will need to reason their ways through, and to produce a complete act of pedagogy, as represented in Figure 1.2.

Some tentative evidence on these processes, and their inter-relationships, is emerging from recent research. Grossman, Wilson and Shulman (1989), for example, report from their case studies of secondary student-teachers that content knowledge affects both what teachers teach and how they teach it. Depth of knowledge also appears to influence pedagogical choices. Student-teachers with specialist knowledge were more likely to stress conceptual understanding and syntactic knowledge, whereas non-specialists simply taught the content as it was represented in the text without discussion. Organization of knowledge also emerged as influential. Those who understood the larger map of their subject, and who understood the relationship of individual topics or skills to more general topics in their fields, may also be more effective in teaching their subjects. Knowledge of syntactic structures was also important. Student-teachers who did not understand the role played by inquiry in their disciplines were not capable of adequately representing, and therefore teaching, that subject matter to their pupils.

Borko *et al.* (1988) claim clear support for a relationship between subject knowledge and planning. When student-teachers had strong content area preparation and had confidence in their knowledge, they planned in less detail and were more responsive to pupils in their teaching.

McDiarmid, Ball and Anderson (1989) focus on the role of representation in pedagogical-content knowledge. They take the constructivist view that no matter how clearly teachers present material, pupils' understanding of it will be based on their prior assumptions and understandings. It follows therefore that teachers cannot simply deliver knowledge, and expect pupils to know it. It is the teacher's role, they argue, to connect children to 'the communities of the disciplines'.

Teachers do this by constructing instructional representations of subject matter through the use of activities, analogies, questions, worksheets and textbooks. Through the representations they select, and the ways that they use them, teachers convey messages, sometimes implicit, about the substance and nature of the subjects they teach. The nature of a subject is made known to pupils through the tasks they undertake, the problems they examine, the ways in which answers are sought and validated, what counts for an answer and on what basis. It is through these that pupils come to know what it means to do science, history or mathematics.

Recent research has highlighted the critical influence of teachers' subject-matter knowledge on decisions regarding representation, albeit at secondary school level. McDiarmid *et al.* (1989) report that a teacher's capacity to pose questions, select tasks, evaluate their pupils' understandings and make curriculum choices all depend on their understanding of subject matter. Teachers are better able to help pupils develop flexible understandings of subject matter if they understand the subject well. Moreover, their understandings enable teachers to develop a variety of ways of representing them to children of varying experiences and knowledge (cf. Leinhardt and Feinberg, 1990).

Evidence of the relationship between teacher knowledge and action is also available from research which has compared the performances of experts and novices. In general it is apparent that the rich and highly interconnected conceptual frameworks employed by experts are markedly different from those of novices. In the specific case of teachers, experts notice different aspects of classrooms from novices, are more selective and efficient in their use of information during planning and interactive teaching, and make greater use of instructional and management routines (cf. Ben-Peretz, Browne and Halkes, 1986; Berliner, 1987; Borko and Livingston, 1989).

Kennedy (1991), in setting out an agenda for research on teaching, defined the teaching task as that of connecting important substantive ideas to diverse learners. Teachers, she argues, cannot teach what they do not know. In choosing a task, for example, teachers need to have enough understanding of the subject to know which ideas are central, which are peripheral, how different ideas relate to one another, and how these ideas can be represented to the uninitiated.

TEACHERS' SUBJECT KNOWLEDGE

Despite the importance currently afforded to subject (and pedagogical subject-matter) knowledge, the evidence available indicates that experienced and student-teachers have only limited understanding of some subjects. For example, in Britain, the Department of Education and Science has asserted that 'the greatest obstacle to the continued improvement of science in primary schools is that many existing teachers lack a working knowledge of elementary science' (DES, 1985), and this has been supported in a set of studies on primary teachers' understanding of science concepts (e.g. Kruger and Summers, 1989). They reported that the majority of teachers' views were based on a 'mixture of intuitive beliefs and half-remembered textbook science from their school days, sometimes with incorrect or imprecise use of scientific language'. Another, smaller, group of teachers seemed not to possess any theoretical understanding of phenomena presented. This group had received little education in science at school and of necessity were able to explain the instances only at a perceptual level, or not at all. They concluded that the scientific thinking of many of the teachers studied resembled that of children, being limited to perceptual and observable entities.

Two recent national surveys reveal clearly that experienced teachers feel insecure with their subject knowledge in several areas of the curriculum (Wragg, Bennett and Carré, 1989; Bennett *et al.* 1992). When asked to what extent they felt competent to teach the subjects in the National Curriculum, in only English and maths did more than half state that they felt competent with their existing knowledge, without additional help from colleagues or in-service training. In both surveys less than 35 per cent of teachers felt competent to teach science, music or technology without substantial in-service support. In the case of technology only 14 per cent perceived themselves competent.

When questioned about their competences within subject areas they claimed particular difficulty with things electronic or related to information technology. Thus the area in which they felt least competent in mathematics was entering and accessing databases. In science it was the use of power sources and the use of micro-electronic kits. And in information technology itself less than a fifth felt able to add to a database, or use graphics to present work or to develop ideas (Bennett *et al.*, 1992).

Similar findings are represented in the United States. Ball (1990b) and McDiarmid (1990) report that in the areas of writing and mathematics the majority of teachers and student-teachers, including those who had majored in the subjects they would be teaching, had only a limited understanding of the two subjects. Moreover, in following teacher candidates through pre-service programmes, and practising teachers through induction and in-service programmes, it was found that despite the diversity of approaches to teacher education that were studied, many of those programmes were unable to alter substantially the ideas teachers held when they arrived. Many teachers perceived school subjects not as bodies of knowledge that might be uncertain or worthy of debate, nor as relating to everyday life. Instead they perceived the two subjects that the research team studied, i.e. writing and mathematics, as 'collections of fixed rules and procedures with few connections among them and even fewer connections to events or purposes outside the classroom' (Kennedy, 1991).

Grossman *et al.* (1989) report that student-teachers' beliefs about teaching and learning are related to how they think about teaching, how they learn from their experiences, and how they conduct themselves in classrooms. They identified two types of beliefs about subjects, one about the nature of the content taught and the other, which they termed an orientation toward subject matter. These beliefs appeared to influence what content was chosen to teach, their goals for instruction, and choices of activities and assignments. They concluded that prospective teachers' beliefs about subject matter are as powerful and influential as their beliefs about teaching and learning. As such, teacher educators should provide opportunities for their students to identify and examine their beliefs, otherwise they are unlikely to be radically changed by professional training (cf. Barnes, 1989).

IMPLICATIONS FOR TEACHER TRAINING

Grossman *et al.* (1989) identify three main implications for teacher education of the apparent influence on teaching of subject knowledge. Firstly, student-teachers must understand the centrality of content knowledge for teaching, and the consequences of lack of knowledge. Secondly, they need to learn about the central conceptual and organizing principles of a subject matter, and, since they cannot know everything before they begin to teach, they need to be aware of a responsibility to acquire new knowledge through their teaching career. Thirdly, they must develop the ability to reflect on, and learn from, experience.

Nevertheless, as Calderhead (1988) argues, the nature of teachers' knowledge is not well understood. Yet its complexity and the ways in which different types of knowledge are developed are crucial to explore in efforts to understand and improve teacher education. Barnes (1989) similarly argues that the need to build more powerful teacher education programmes raises serious questions about how teachers learn to teach. For example, how in the process of becoming teachers can novices be helped to replace simplistic notions about teaching and learning with grounded understandings of subject matter, learners, context and learning that can inform their teaching judgements and actions?

SUMMARY

Teacher education in Britain, as elsewhere, appears to be in a state of crisis. It has been the subject of continuing criticism from both the Inspectorate and the Department of Education and Science. The basis of this criticism is that new teachers lack the appropriate subject-matter knowledge to implement or deliver adequately the National Curriculum, and have insufficient knowledge about learners, and about evaluation and assessment.

Theoretical models of professional knowledge bases for teaching indicate that these areas of knowledge are important constituents of competent teaching, and the limited empirical evidence lends support to this. To date, however, this body of evidence is largely confined to the United States, and is mostly derived from small samples of secondary student-teachers. As such the generalizability of the findings to the training of primary teachers in Britain must be treated with caution.

THE STUDY

Drawing on the 'academic' and 'social efficiency' traditions of research on teacher education the following broad questions were addressed:

- To what extent, and how, do knowledge bases for teaching develop through training, i.e. knowledge of subjects, of pedagogy, of children, curriculum and educational beliefs and attitudes?
- What is the relationship of these knowledge bases to teaching performance (defined in terms of levels of competence or capacity – see Chapter 10)?
- What impact does training have on the development of knowledge bases and teaching performance?
- How does teaching performance develop through the first year of teaching, and what influences that development?

In order to answer these questions the whole population of fifty-nine students entering the one-year Primary Postgraduate Certificate of Education (PGCE) in one institution were invited to participate. All agreed.

The students were recruited into one of four overlapping strands specializing in mathematics, science, music and early years (the teaching of 4- to 8-year-olds). All were graduates and, with the exception of early years, required a qualification in the specialism chosen, although not necessarily at degree level. For example, a psychology graduate with a biology subsidiary could join the science strand.

The major difference in course structure for the four strands was that each followed a more extensive curriculum course in their own specialism, which incorporated preparation as a curriculum coordinator in school. The rest of the courses were common, as was the timing and duration of teaching practices. In term 1 they worked in schools for one day per week in groups of five or six; they then experienced a five-week block practice in term 2, followed by a final seven-week block practice in term 3. The whole programme conformed to the British accreditation criteria which stipulate the minimum numbers of hours to be devoted to each section of the programme.

Thus the assumption of programme developers, and indeed of the national criteria, is that graduates will enter with appropriate levels of subject knowledge for teaching, that the specialist curriculum courses will prepare them adequately for curriculum coordination, and that the general curriculum courses will provide the knowledge and pedagogical expertise necessary for their generalist class-teacher role. The overall design of the study is presented in Figure 1.3.

KNOWLEDGE AT ENTRY

Student-teachers were assessed at entry on subject-matter knowledge, pedagogical subject-matter knowledge and educational beliefs and values.

(a) *Subject-matter knowledge*
Since these students were preparing to become primary school teachers

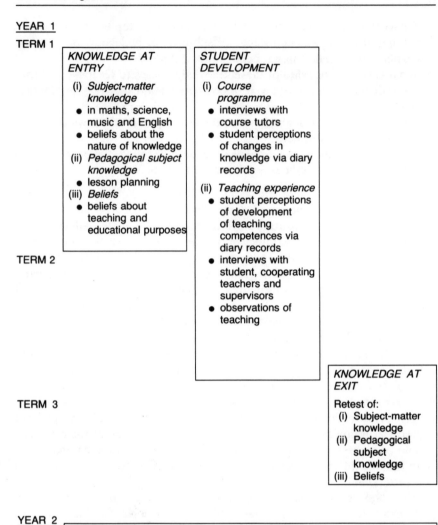

Figure 1.3 Research design

subject-matter knowledge was defined as that knowledge that is required to be taught in the British National Curriculum to level 6, i.e. that which an able 11-year-old or an average 14-year-old should be capable of understanding, hereafter called subject knowledge for teaching. Separate instruments for maths, science, music and English were developed from the content of the National Curriculum, in consultation with subject experts. In addition, instruments were developed to ascertain beliefs and attitudes about the nature of knowledge in these subjects.

(b) *Educational beliefs and attitudes*

A questionnaire was developed comprising Likert items on aims and opinions, together with a series of vignettes of classroom events to which students had to respond to indicate their preferred approaches to teaching and learning.

(c) *Pedagogical knowledge*

Statements of attainment in maths, science and English were taken from the National Curriculum on which lesson plans had to be constructed and justified, including decisions concerning classroom organization.

Each instrument took approximately one to one-and-a-half hours to complete, although no time limits were set. In general, therefore, a minimum of seven hours was required to collect data on knowledge bases at entry. It became apparent that this amount of time would not be available to repeat these assessments at the end of the programme. Accordingly they were reduced in length, to some four hours, via factor and item analyses of the pre-tests. (Copies of the assessment manuals are available from the authors.)

COURSE PROGRAMME

Attempts to identify reasons for student development or lack of it, required factual evidence on course content and aims, teaching approaches adopted, and their perceptions of the content and value of their courses. These data were acquired via in-depth interviews with the course tutors, and analyses of diaries in which the student-teachers were asked to reflect on each teaching session and assess its impact and value. They continued writing their diary entries throughout the thirty-six-week programme.

TEACHING PRACTICES

Teaching practices typically consist of a school experience phase in term 1 where students work in classrooms in groups with cooperating teachers in a system overseen by a supervising tutor. Thereafter teaching practices take place in terms 2 and 3 consisting of twelve weeks in all.

The impact of these teaching practices on the development of students' teaching performances, and on how subject-matter knowledge for teaching related to these developing performances, were assessed as follows:

1 Observation by trained observers on two days in the first teaching practice, and two days in the second, i.e. four days per student. Students were observed teaching their specialist subject and other, non-specialist,

subjects. They wore a radio-microphone throughout the observations so that a complete recording of the lesson could be acquired for later transcription.

2 Prior to each observed lesson the student completed a task protocol. This required details of the intention(s) for the lesson; the task chosen to fulfil the intention(s) and its rationale; the materials required; the presentation planned; the classroom organization; how the children's learning would be assessed, and so on. Immediately following the observed lessons the students were interviewed to ascertain their perceptions and reflections on their performance, and the extent to which their plans had been realized. In addition, the observers wrote their own evaluations of the lesson.

3 The cooperating teacher and the supervising tutor were also interviewed to ascertain their expectations of their roles, and the extent to which these had been fulfilled, together with their judgements of the students' teaching competences.

Further details of these data, and their analysis, are contained in Chapter 10.

The population of students participated in the pre- and post-testing of knowledge bases, but the in-depth investigation of course processes and their impact was carried out with a random sample of twenty-four students, six from each of the four specialist strands.

THE FOLLOW-UP

Thirteen of the observation sample volunteered to participate in a follow-up study through their first year of teaching. The aims of the follow-up study were to ascertain if, and how, their teaching developed through that period, and the role of induction and school support in that process.

Data were collected each term. The thirteen teachers were first interviewed by telephone at the end of their first week of teaching, relating to such matters as settling in, planning and relationships with their class and their peers. Thereafter they were interviewed each term, in addition to which an interview was carried out with their headteacher on such issues as progress, induction practices, mentoring and modes of assessment.

A final telephone interview was carried out a few weeks before the completion of their first year in teaching in which they reflected on the whole year and their professional development.

ANALYSIS

Schon (1987) has argued that the area of professional practice consists of the high hard hill of research based knowledge overlooking the soft, slimy swamp of real life problems. Up the hill simpler problems respond to the techniques of basic science whereas down in the swamp complex problems defy technical solutions. Thus the educational practitioner faces a rigour or relevance dilemma. Should he remain on the high ground where he can solve relatively unimportant problems according to prevailing standards of rigour or shall he descend to the swamp of important problems and non-rigorous enquiry?

Considered on the basis of this analogy we have had one leg on the hill and one in the swamp! We have utilized quantitative statistical techniques for the construction of tests and the analysis of their results, and have carried out both qualitative and quantitative analyses of diaries, interviews and lesson transcripts. Such multi-method approaches are necessary to adequately characterize both the processes and outcomes of complex teaching–learning settings. Schon's dichotomy is thus a false one; both rigour and relevance can, and should, be sought and achieved. Without either, the transformation of findings into implications for practice would be invalid.

The chapters which follow set out to answer the research questions posed and to assess their utility. The findings are presented in four sections. The chapters in the first section identify the knowledge and attitudes that the students entered the programme with, and how they changed. (Constraints of space have forced a concentration on the 'core' National Curriculum subjects in the knowledge chapters. However, analyses of music knowledge and its change are considered in Chapter 10 and in the Appendix.) Those in the second section record the teaching–learning processes to which they were exposed, and interacted with. The third section deals with the relationship of knowledge bases to teaching competences, and the final section addresses the first year of teaching and its contribution to professional development.

Chapter 2

Performance in subject-matter knowledge in science

Clive Carré

INTRODUCTION

Much recent debate on the development of teaching competences emphasizes the importance of a teacher's knowledge. Research in Australia and
the USA has indicated that when teachers taught outside their field of
expertise, there was evidence of non-exemplary practice. For example, the
importance of understanding science content for teaching has been demonstrated by Neale and Smith (1989). They showed that primary teachers,
when given the opportunity to construct knowledge in a training programme, could then facilitate changes in their classroom practice.

Grossman, Wilson and Shulman (1989) highlighted the importance of a
teacher's knowledge, of both content and process (syntactic) aspects of
science, in determining not only what, but how, student-teachers taught:

> Novice teachers who lack knowledge of syntactic structures of the
> subject matter fail to incorporate that aspect of the discipline in their
> curriculum. We believe that they consequently run the risk of misrepre-
> senting the subject matters they teach and seriously limit prospective
> teachers' abilities to learn new information in their fields.

In an overview of what teachers need to know to teach science effectively
Anderson (1991) argues for the central importance of content; the socially-
constructed conceptual knowledge of science which their pupils need to
modify their understanding. In contrast, Lawson (1991) sees the task of
teaching science as helping learners with enquiry skills: about scientific
reasoning and about experimentation, knowing what to do and how to do
it. It is through this procedural knowledge that concepts are generated.

The aims of the study, as described in the previous chapter, are
essentially about the processes of learning to teach: how and in what ways
do student-teachers change, in knowledge and beliefs; and what is the role
of knowledge in teaching? In order to fulfil this latter aim, and considering
the perceived importance of content and process in science teaching, it was
necessary to assess their subject-matter knowledge of both aspects of
science.

ASSESSING SUBJECT-MATTER KNOWLEDGE

What is 'subject-matter knowledge' that teachers are supposed to have to teach effectively? Although it is claimed to be of central importance, there is little agreement about what it means and, more importantly, how to tell whether one has it or not. Grossman *et al.* (1989) claim that recent research acknowledges a fundamental difference between subject-matter knowledge that scientists have and subject-matter knowledge for those teaching science. The essential difference is that teachers need to know their subject, but also understand it in ways that will help their pupils learn. For example, teaching electricity to 10-year-olds involves amongst other things, conceptual understanding of a simple circuit and several ways of representing electric current flowing round the circuit.

Subject-matter knowledge for teaching includes content knowledge, substantive knowledge, syntactic knowledge and beliefs about the subject. The terms substantive and syntactic require explanation. Substantive knowledge includes facts and concepts, but in addition the explanatory and organizing frameworks which are used to guide enquiry. Schwab (1964) referred to such organizing frameworks as, for example, the systems of classification of the elements and living things, or the use of models; both are ways of reducing an object or a theory to a manageable form, a purposeful abstraction to aid explanation.

Besides the two aspects of substantive knowledge, science knowledge includes a syntactic component, which is the basis of enquiry, how science is investigated and findings justified. Teachers should be familiar with enquiry skills such as suggesting questions which can be tested, formulating hypotheses, recognizing that conclusions may be invalid unless a fair test has been carried out and interpreting experimental evidence critically.

In creating the instrument to assess subject knowledge in science, it was thus important to test student-teachers in both substantive and syntactic knowledge in areas which they might be expected to teach. It was decided therefore that questions demanding a conceptual level of understanding up to that expected to be achieved by the most able 11/12-year-old, that is up to level 6 in the National Curriculum (DES, 1989d; 1991a). Questions were selected from the Assessment of Performance Unit (APU)* as there was no appropriate instrument for testing understanding of science of children at age 11 years prior to its first survey in 1980 (Harlen, Black and Johnson, 1981). The Assessment of Performance Unit in science carried out a series of national surveys in each of the years 1980–4, to monitor science performance in schools at the ages of 11, 13 and 15 (DES, 1989c). They were based on an assessment framework of six categories of

---

* The author gratefully acknowledges permission from the APU to use their science test items.

scientific activities, mainly process-oriented, which reflected the two inter-linked facets of science: those of experimental (syntactic) aspects and those requiring conceptual (substantive) understandings. Development of the assessment framework of the APU was the outcome of extensive consulta-tion; as such it represented the corporate opinions of science educators and science curriculum developers at that time. Thus the APU was seen as representing principles and consensus viewpoints about science education in a particular historical context; reflecting the aims in vogue in developing primary science in the UK in the early 1980s. It was from this validated bank that questions, and associated mark schemes, were selected for this study in the light of the demands of the National Curriculum.

Fourteen out of the sixteen questions in the instrument were of substantive content and one question required an application of particle theory. One question offered an opportunity to express understanding of syntactic knowledge (i.e. process or procedural understanding); con-sequently planning a whole investigation was chosen rather than a set of individual skills questions. The task was in an everyday context so that no particular science concepts needed to be recalled. The question, 'which kind of paper will hold most water?', involved planning an experiment and deciding which variables to change, which to keep constant and what had to be measured.

All sixteen questions required written answers and required recall of science concepts to explain or predict. No straight recall of facts was asked for. There were questions relating to both physical and biological sciences, and attempts were made to provide representative cover of topics from the National Curriculum, covering levels 2–6. The broad concept areas which composed the instrument were:

Units of measure	Variety of life
Processes of life	Forces
Energy	Structure of matter
Chemical change	Kinetic theory
Process of investigation	

KNOWLEDGE AT ENTRY

The performance in science of all student-teachers, and the subject groups, is shown in Table 2.1, where it can be seen that the average score overall was 56.9 per cent. The maths and science groups did better than this by achieving very similar scores of 63.4 per cent and 63.3 per cent respectively. The mean scores obtained by the music group (50.7 per cent) and the early years group (50.8 per cent) were also very similar, but significantly lower.

As might be expected, performance on individual items reflects this science/arts gulf. Highest scores were obtained by the maths and science groups in all but two questions.

Table 2.1 Science pre-test: mean percentage scores

Subject groups				All students
Maths	Science	Music	Early years	
63.4	63.3	50.7	50.8	56.9

Which questions did student-teachers find easy and which ones were difficult? In assessing difficulty, item analyses were carried out. Content validation was assisted by judging item facility and calculating discrimination indices.

The easiest question (see Figure 2.1) demanded an understanding of the relationship between an applied force, the area over which it acts and the resulting pressure. The average percentage score for this question was 97 per cent. A typical answer was:

> The ladder offers a large surface area and therefore the weight does not produce a large pressure on one point. With skates, all the weight is transferred into pressure on the small surface area of the blade.

The second-easiest question asked for the five parts of the lifecycle of the horse chestnut to be placed in sequence. Eighty per cent of answers were correct.

Six-year-old Peter put on his ice skates and skated out to the middle of a large frozen pond. The ice gave way and Peter fell in. Peter's mother, who was watching, rushed off and found a wooden ladder. She crawled along the ladder without breaking any more ice and managed to rescue her son.

Can you suggest a reason why the ice gave way under Peter's weight but not under his mother's?

I think the reason was because ....

....

....

Figure 2.1 'Thin ice'

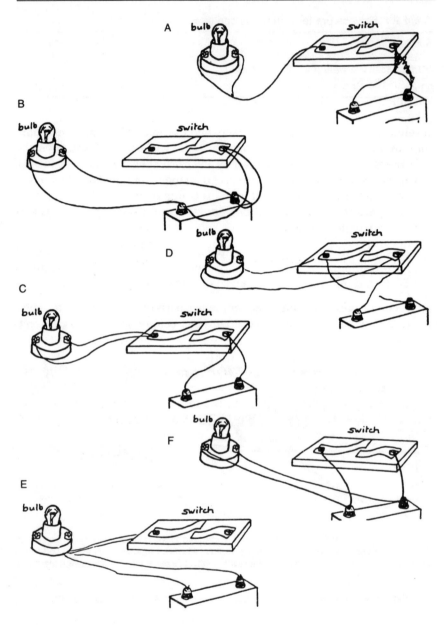

Figure 2.2 Some responses to completing a simple circuit

Of intermediate difficulty were two questions of a practical nature. The first, testing syntactical knowledge, was planning an investigation which asked, 'which kind of paper will hold more water?' The average score was 50 per cent. Introductory text showed pictures of apparatus that could be used in the investigation, and the word 'hold' had to be translated into a variable that could be measured, i.e. the amount of water the paper could take up in a given time, until saturated, or until water started to drip through, or whatever was thought convenient and effective. Some relied on ideas on absorbency, some on permeability.

Many did not have experience of practical work in science and it was not surprising that they were unable to be systematic in their approach, i.e. give operational practical details for the investigation, think of repeating the test or interpret their findings. On a positive note, more than half were capable of writing about the apparatus they would use, the factors they would measure and how they would measure them, making the test 'fair', and thinking of methods of recording results.

The second practical question found to be of intermediate difficulty, involved a simple circuit. When asked to draw in the wires between the terminals of a battery, a switch and a bulb so that the latter would light when the switch was closed, only half were able to do so. Examples of misunderstandings about the concept of a simple circuit can be seen in Figure 2.2.

The components in the series could be in any order; 'A', 'B', 'C' and 'E' are attempts to wire in series, but the circuits are incomplete. In 'E' the wires are not even connected to the terminals of the switch and bulb, but attached to the supporting blocks; 'D' and 'F' are parallel circuits and with the switch closed would short out the battery.

The two most difficult questions involved understandings about gravity and about energy. The first question asked about a spaceship which had planned to use up all its fuel when still only one seventh of the journey back to earth. Student-teachers needed to apply their understanding of gravity and lack of friction in space to explain the lack of any need for fuel (see Figure 2.3).

The average score was 30 per cent; the question produced statements which illustrated their thinking about there being an 'up and down' in space, and gravity having the consistency of treacle. The following are examples:

The [space] ship is no longer having to force itself up through gravity but is 'falling' down and therefore does not have to use so much fuel.

Fuel is not necessary when going downhill.

Suggesting the misconception about 'up and down' raises the interesting point as to whether the phrase was used relatively or absolutely. Children

In 1969 two Americans were the first people to land on the moon and return safely to earth.

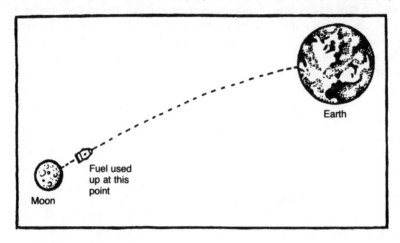

As planned, they had used up all their fuel when they had completed only one-seventh of the journey back to earth.

Why do you think the spaceship needed only this amount of fuel to get them back to earth?

....

....

....

Figure 2.3 'Spaceship'

often think in absolute terms and might think of falling 'down' off the bottom of the earth. The student-teachers' words could be acceptable, if they were thinking in terms of 'downhill' and 'falling down' being relative to the earth. Clearly the analysis of such responses is difficult when the language for communicating meaning is limited to short written statements.

The second most difficult question asked about a sledge which slid down one side of a slope and up the other side (see Figure 2.4).

They were asked to give a reason for choosing a position where the sledge had most energy. Their conceptual understanding of energy was poor, and the average score for this question was only 17 per cent. Over half stated that the sledge had most energy when at the bottom of the slope (position C) when it was going fastest. For example:

Because the most energy will be generated at C because the speed is greatest.

They realized that the greater the speed, the greater would be the kinetic energy. However, many failed to take into account the gravitational

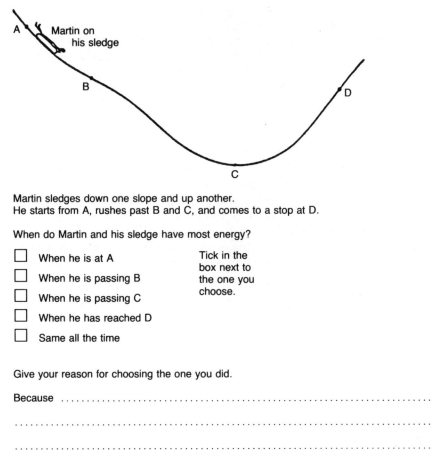

Martin sledges down one slope and up another.
He starts from A, rushes past B and C, and comes to a stop at D.

When do Martin and his sledge have most energy?

☐   When he is at A

☐   When he is passing B

☐   When he is passing C

☐   When he has reached D

☐   Same all the time

Tick in the
box next to
the one you
choose.

Give your reason for choosing the one you did.

Because ....

....

....

Figure 2.4 'Martin's sledge'

potential energy at the start, and the fact that some of this energy would
be lost in the descent through friction. One thought that the sledge would
have the same amount of energy all the time and misapplied the idea of
the principle of conservation of energy, albeit in a seemingly plausible and
logical way:

> Potential energy when he is stationary is converted into kinetic energy
> when he is moving. Where would extra energy therefore come from?

In summary, responses indicated that many did not have a bank of
concepts from which they could confidently apply their knowledge to make
sense of everyday phenomena. Besides those already described, other
confusions existed. For example, when asked about the weight of an ice

cube after melting, 20 per cent of the group thought that the mass either increased or decreased, instead of staying the same.

A quarter had misconceptions about explaining everyday events in terms of the kinetic theory. When asked why a football did not feel so hard in the evening when the temperature fell, as it did when it was warm during the day, answers revealed misconceptions about particles and their behaviour. Examples included ideas about particles changing size and particles moving apart.

Clearly, the 'alternative frameworks' which have been described for children by various researchers (e.g. Driver, Guesne and Tiberghien, 1985; Gilbert and Watts, 1983), persist into the adult population.

Given that all the questions were developed within an everyday context to represent just the sort of world of science which primary children might well wish to discuss, it would appear that many student-teachers would have difficulty doing so, within accepted adult science frameworks of understanding. A similar concern is expressed by Kruger, Summers and Palacio (1990) reporting on the lack of understanding possessed by primary teachers of forces, energy and the nature of materials. They concluded that in these three areas many primary teachers were:

> likely to have views of fundamental science concepts which are at variance with the 'accepted' scientific view . . . prevalence of non-Newtonian views of force . . . vitalistic views of energy . . . [and] non-molecular views of matter.

There is a concern that if student-teachers and experienced teachers have a low level or lack of understanding of science concepts, they will be unable to plan activities appropriately to guide children's conceptual development.

CHANGE IN SCIENCE SUBJECT-MATTER KNOWLEDGE

It was necessary to reduce the total number of questions in the science instrument by half because of the more limited time available for testing at the end of the course. This was achieved via factor and item analysis. A correlation between the total scores of the full form and the shortened version at pre-test was high (0.93).

In considering change, i.e. the difference in scores between pre- and post-test, the comparison is made between student-teachers who did *both* tests, i.e. a reduction from 59 to 49. The drop in numbers was accounted for through such things as absenteeism, illness, on interview, drop out, visiting schools, etc., on either test.

Table 2.2 shows the results of the pre- and post-tests based on the common items. It can be seen that the scores overall show a modest yet positive shift, but these are not statistically significant.

Improvement in the subject groups also is very small. Although all four

Table 2.2 Change in science knowledge

	n	Pre-test mean %	Post-test mean %	Change	Paired t-test prob. 2–tail
All students	49	43.9	46.6	2.7	0.16
Maths	12	48.8	51.3	2.5	0.58
Science	12	50.4	52.8	2.4	0.57
Music	12	38.2	44.2	6.0	0.12
Early years	13	38.5	38.9	0.4	0.92

Table 2.3 Performance of all students on individual items in science (mean raw scores)

Question	Pre-test	Post-test	Change	2–tail prob.
4	1.5	1.5	0	–
6	0.9	1.0	0.16	0.19
8	0.5	0.8	0.22	0.06
9	0.5	0.8	0.31	0.0001
12	0.8	0.7	−0.08	0.68
13	2.3	2.0	−0.31	0.08
15	1.4	1.1	−0.27	0.13
16	4.0	4.7	0.69	0.03

groups improve, none is statistically significant. The music group improved the most, but its starting point on the pre-test was much lower than that of the maths and science groups. However, although the early years group also started at a similar low point it hardly showed any improvement.

So, where did change occur? In Table 2.3 change in individual questions is given for all student-teachers in order to detect areas of improvement or decline.

Two aspects of their performance are worthy of note. The first is that on three questions they decline, i.e. questions 12, 13 and 15. At the end of the year they did worse on a question dealing with sound (applying their ideas of vibrations to the workings of a string telephone and a speaking tube), another on physical change (melting ice) and a third concerned with explaining, in terms of the behaviour of particles, why a football felt soft when the temperature fell.

The second point is that on two questions improvement is impressive, and change statistically significant. The change in question 9 (applying knowledge of a complete circuit) and question 16 (investigating which of two paper towels holds more water) is interestingly associated with questions which they had dealt with *practically* during the course.

COMPARISON WITH 11-YEAR-OLDS

The APU collected data nationally on pupils' performance at age 11, in six different categories of science activity. So, how did the performance of student-teachers at the end of their course compare with the performance of these 11-year-olds? It was possible to make a comparison in the category of applying science knowledge on five questions.

All four subject groups performed better than the 11-year-olds on four out of the five questions compared. In the question about the workings of a 'string telephone', the 11-year-olds achieved higher scores than the music and early years groups. Compared with the most 'able' 11-year-olds (ie the top 20 per cent), the student-teachers performed less well. The science group achieved higher scores on four questions, whereas the most 'able' pupils did better than the maths, music and early years groups on two (questions 12 and 13).

CHANGE IN ATTITUDES IN SCIENCE

The National Curriculum in science (DES, 1991a) identified a number of attitudes which teachers are expected to develop in their pupils. There is an expectation that student-teachers will have already acquired similar attitudes in their first degree, or will develop them through training. Although there is little attempt to monitor attitude change in teacher training, there is a body of literature which has emphasized the important relationship between teachers' attitudes and beliefs and the implemented curriculum.

Although Clarke and Peterson (1986) recognize in their extensive review of research of teachers' thought processes, that it is difficult to synthesize any clear set of conclusions, they say:

teachers do seem to hold implicit theories about their work and that these conceptual systems can be made more explicit through a variety of direct and indirect inquiry techniques.

They go on to argue that teachers' belief systems could be thought of as

a set of moderating contextual factors that could influence substantially the outcomes of teacher effectiveness and curriculum effectiveness studies.

If there is conflict between personal theories and beliefs and those of curriculum developers, implementation of innovations or uptake of government directives may be impaired. Analysis of teachers' thinking patterns, and the influences which school and courses may have to develop them is therefore of fundamental importance. In science Tobin, Butler Kahle and Fraser (1990) described the 'mindframes' of secondary teachers and the way their beliefs affected important aspects of classroom action, in planning, management and assessment. In part the belief set was about a teacher's role, about how learners learn, about using resources and also about the nature of science.

A positive attitude towards the nature of science is seen to be vital at primary level too, for the impact on classroom behaviours of teachers. The dangers of children acquiring inert bodies of content knowledge are well known and even though the National Curriculum emphasizes the importance of process or procedural knowledge, there is still a temptation for the unsure teacher to neglect enquiry approaches.

It is reasonable to suppose that if student-teachers have ideas of the tentative nature of science, a belief that there is no absolute knowledge and no one right answer, and above all that science is a very human activity, then these attitudes will affect the way they plan their lessons. It is hoped that they would include strategies enabling children to discover for themselves the way things are, the inexact nature of the material world, and also to allow for their unexpected answers. Finally, Crowther (1978) concluded that science self-concept was an important factor affecting a teacher's style and effectiveness and that it could be modified by pre-service training.

With these ideas in mind a three-section instrument was used in this study to measure attitudes in science. The sections were:

- attitude towards the nature of science
- attitude towards science in modern society
- attitude towards science teaching.

ATTITUDE TOWARDS THE NATURE OF SCIENCE

The pre-test contained sixteen assertions about important characteristics of science against which to measure differences of opinion. Each assertion was in a positive or negative form and required a response on a five-point Likert scale. Although there are obviously many orientations which could be taken to represent student-teachers' beliefs about what science is and how science as a discipline is established, it was decided to limit it to four. In the post-test, after item and factor analysis, the number of orientations was reduced to three, and the number of statements reduced to eight. The orientations were:

1 Science as a scientific method, process approach (the hypothetico-deductive view: Hyp-Ded).
2 Science as confirming organized bodies of knowledge (the naive-absolutist view: N-Abs).
3 Science as personal and social construction of meaning (social and personal constructivism/a relativist view: Soc-Con).

It is clearly naive to believe that these three orientations operate in some discrete fashion. There is no intention to imply that one view is more valid than another, for it is likely that the nature of scientific activity is best represented by the interaction of elements from all three orientations.

Table 2.4 Change in attitude towards the nature of science (mean raw scores)

Dimension	All students		Maths		Science		Music		Early years	
	Pre-test	Post-test	Pre-test	Post-test	Pre-test	Post-test	Pre-test	Post-test	Pre-test	Post-test
Hyp-Ded	6.4	6.7	6.6	7.2	6.1	6.3	6.3	6.5	6.7	6.8
N-Abs	10.6	10.0	10.6	10.4	11.9	10.5	10.2	10.3	9.5	8.8
Soc-Con	6.2	6.7	6.4	7.5	6.8	6.9	5.5	5.9	6.0	6.8

Table 2.4 summarizes the mean scores for the three orientations on the Likert scale where 1 = strongly agree and 5 = strongly disagree (maximum per orientation: Hyp-Ded = 10, N-Abs = 20, Soc-Con = 10).

The general trend for all student-teachers and for all four subject groups is for the change in the hypothetico-deductive view and social/personal constructivist view to be positive. With the exception of the music group, all other groups show a decrease in the naive absolutist view; i.e. an increasing disagreement with the notion that science is fixed and rigid and without the subjective influence of human investigators. However, all changes are small and not statistically significant, with the exception of the social dimension change for all student-teachers.

ATTITUDE TOWARDS SCIENCE IN MODERN SOCIETY

The second section of the instrument was concerned with the concept 'attitude towards science in modern society'.

There is a general awareness of science issues through newspaper reporting and representations of scientific matters on television and media in general. In addition, various documentaries and fiction-based entertainments portray the work of scientists and the field of scientific research. The borderline between reality and fantasy is often blurred; the confused image of science may provoke little more than a 'good' or 'bad' thing, as a simplistic value judgement.

Because of the ubiquitous influences of science, the diversity of situations in which reference is made to a scientific idea and the obvious benefits and disadvantages that result from scientific activity, everyone has an opinion about some aspects of science. Attitudes towards science and about science may conflict with common sense, but these are moulded when science appears to affect our lives in ways ethical, social, political and economic. The media heighten this awareness in forms of reporting which at times are sensationalist and often misleading.

As previously mentioned, there is a hope that student-teachers after training would impart positive attitudes about the role of science in society, communicating the benefits and achievement of science in a way that would motivate pupils' learning.

These attitudes were measured using the semantic differential technique of Osgood, Suci and Tannenbaum (1957). The technique required that the concept 'science in modern society' was rated on a number of scales each of which was a bi-polar adjective; with a seven-point scale for each bi-polar.

In the pre-test there were twenty bi-polars, examples being 'pleasant–unpleasant', 'moral–immoral', 'constructive–destructive'. They were selected from an instrument used by Crowther (1978) in his study on a similar population of student-teachers.

The change in attitude towards the concept 'science in society' was small and not statistically significant, although there was a slight shift towards the positive end of the scale for nine out of the eleven bi-polars. All but music indicated a positive shift. The science group indicated a marginally more positive view than the others. In general student-teachers did not alter over the year, and the course would appear not to have influenced their attitude to this dimension.

ATTITUDE TOWARDS SCIENCE TEACHING

It was thought likely that a student-teacher's orientation towards science teaching might result from two sets of influences, fundamental ideas about the nature of science and assumptions about how learners learn. In order to achieve an indication of these orientations they were asked to react to three teachers' imaginary 'portraits', each one comprising ideas about the nature of science and about learners.

A number of studies influenced the development of this part of the instrument, even though the nomenclature describing preferred approaches to teaching science is confusing. The typology used by Hacker (1984) was of considerable interest, because observational studies in science at primary level are almost non-existent. For example, although Galton, Simon and Croll (1980) reported on a large-scale study of fifty-eight primary school classrooms, science was not in any substantial way represented within the curriculum of these schools.

The portrait of teacher A corresponded with Hacker's 'concrete problem solver', a practical hands-on orientation. Teacher B corresponded closely to Hacker's 'verifier', where although practical work is organized, pupils rarely interpret their findings; experiment verifies information rather than being used for inquiry. Teacher C, with a strong personal and social orientation, has no direct equivalent in Hacker's typology; it is closest to a 'personal and social' category used by Smith and Neale (1989). It was necessary for the student-teachers to project their ideas and intentions about their future pupils learning science, to identify with one or more of these three 'portraits'.

Teacher A

Science is 'hands-on' practical work, discovering the world around using all five senses. Initiatives are by pupils; they pose the questions and I encourage them to work independently. I refrain from giving them clues or science information to help their enquiry. I don't mind if the pupils use descriptive, non-scientific language.

Teacher B

Science is a collection of laws, an accurate and organized body of knowledge. I present content very clearly and direct practical work to prevent aimless activity. Essentially the children gather essential information and confirm for themselves what is already laid down as core concepts. We always use correct scientific language.

Teacher C

Science is a creation of human mind; truth is formed in the mind of the observer. I assume that pupils have extensive knowledge about their world and I help them apply and relate what they already know to new problems. I challenge them to reject, reshape or extend their ideas and to justify why they think the way they do. I encourage them to use scientific language when explaining.

The three orientations towards science teaching were thus classified according to different beliefs about the nature of science and teaching behaviours.

Teacher A was seen as a 'problem solver' and Teacher B having a teacher-dominated style, acting as a 'verifier'. Teacher C, the 'personal and social' would have a belief about the value of a constructivist approach to learning.

The three 'portraits' were offered for comparison, and student-teachers were asked which statement best described their *intention* as a primary teacher of science. They were not asked to make a choice between the three, but rather to indicate how they might represent their intended feeling, by giving each descriptor a score out of ten points (10 = most of the time, 0 = never). In this way data provided an idea of balance of intended teaching strategies and approaches.

Table 2.5 summarizes the average scores obtained for each of the three teacher descriptions on pre- and post-test. The table shows clearly that the *balance* between A, B and C changed little over the year. Orientation was towards teaching as a mix of A and C, a problem-solving approach with strong leanings towards constructivism and child-centredness; the intended role for a teacher-centred approach (teacher B) was limited.

Table 2.5 Mean scores for attitude to science teaching

	Teacher	Pre-test	Post-test	Change	p
All students	A	7.2	7.1	−0.1	0.77
	B	3.2	2.3	−0.9	0.02
	C	6.7	7.0	0.3	0.49
Maths	A	7.7	7.1	−0.6	0.38
	B	2.1	2.0	−0.1	0.92
	C	7.2	8.1	0.9	0.42
Science	A	6.9	6.3	−0.6	0.57
	B	3.2	3.0	−0.2	0.73
	C	6.5	6.4	−0.1	0.94
Music	A	6.3	6.5	0.2	0.68
	B	3.9	3.3	−0.6	0.43
	C	6.2	7.1	−0.9	0.40
Early years	A	8.0	8.5	0.5	0.21
	B	3.4	0.7	−2.7	0.001
	C	6.9	6.6	−0.3	0.66

However, it is evident that all groups became more negative towards 'teacher B', and this change was large and statistically significant for all students and the early years group. They left the course feeling less inclined to be teacher-centred and less directed to see primary science in terms of investigations with 'right answers' as products, as so many had experienced in their own secondary teaching.

SUMMARY

Although there was no intention to suggest that the three orientations towards the 'nature of science' operated separately, the general outcome showed a decline in naive absolutist views. The tentative nature of investigation was appreciated and a strengthening of attitude towards the hypothetico-deductive and social/personal constructivist view. These results would be in keeping with the intentions of course tutors in science.

Attitudes to the role of science in society were in general stable and they remained positive throughout the year, with a slight decline recorded for the music group.

On the 'attitude towards science teaching' instrument, even though the changes were small, they showed a low and declining one for teacher B. The general picture which emerged was that student-teachers were favourably inclined towards a practical, problem-solving approach to science teaching and to a constructivist stance. These findings are particularly interesting in the light of the discussion document by Alexander, Rose and Woodhead (DES, 1992a). In reviewing available evidence about the quality of classroom practice they emphasized that too often the debate about practice was conducted in terms of a simplistic dichotomy, between 'traditional' and 'progressive', or 'formal' and 'informal'. The *balance* between different organizational strategies to which they made reference were not mutually exclusive; effective science teaching can result from a mix of the approaches described by teachers A and C, with some use of the teacher-directed strategies of teacher B.

CONCLUSION

The major finding in this section has been that graduates, on entering the course, have limited understandings of substantive and syntactic knowledge in science that is necessary to teach at primary school level. Science and maths groups perform better than the arts groups. Further, there is evidence that many have understandings of fundamental science concepts which differ from accepted consensus scientific views. These alternative conceptions are similar to those described elsewhere for children and with these student-teachers have persisted into adulthood. On those questions where comparison was possible, results showed that 'able' 11-year-olds performed better than the majority of student-teachers. This may reflect a gender effect in the predominantly female-student group. When comparison is made at age 11, in the application of physics concepts, there is a statistically significant performance difference in favour of boys (Johnson, 1989).

Comparison of pre- and post-test results have indicated that, in general, change in knowledge scores were modest and on three questions the whole group performed worse at the end of the course. This could reflect no more than end-of-term malaise! However, there were statistically significant changes shown on two questions; both were associated with questions dealing with practical and procedural (syntactical) aspects of knowledge, and both had been dealt with during the course. Given opportunity within course structure, student-teachers are capable of making considerable gains.

Overall, changes in attitude towards the nature of science, the role of science in society and towards science teaching altered little during the year. There were indications of a slight decline in seeing science in naive absolutist terms and in keeping with a strengthening of the hypothetio-deductive view, a more positive inclination towards a practical, problem-solving approach to teaching, based on a constructivist approach to learning.

These results have important implications. If teachers are to employ their knowledge to ensure that their teaching stretches pupils' thinking, and 'not merely keep step with it' (Alexander *et al.*, 1992), then steps must be taken to enhance understandings of subject knowledge for teaching in in-service and pre-service provision. Research-based INSET materials could be employed to help teachers realize what their misconceptions are and develop conceptual understanding to at least the level of bright children at the top end of the primary school, along lines suggested by Kruger *et al.* (1990) and Russell *et al.* (1992).

Chapter 3

Performance in subject-matter knowledge in mathematics

Clive Carré and Paul Ernest

INTRODUCTION

There is a growing recognition that subject matter shapes the way teachers teach, (e.g. Stodolsky, 1988), indeed Shulman (1986a; 1986b) has suggested that research on subject matter in teaching is the missing paradigm. Nowhere has this been more widely accepted than in mathematics. Researchers have focused on teacher and student-teacher knowledge, and in particular on their ability to deploy a variety of representations of mathematical knowledge in teaching (Lampert, 1985; Ball 1990a; Cohen and Peterson, 1990). In an overview on teaching mathematics for understanding, Ball (1991) argues for the three specific criteria of correctness, meaning and connectedness, for teachers' substantive knowledge. In addition, a number of researchers have extended the field of enquiry, to consider the breadth of teachers' knowledge of mathematics, as well as their attitudes and beliefs concerning the discipline (Ernest, 1989; McDiarmid and Wilson, 1991; Thompson, 1984).

There is an increasing awareness that student-teachers arrive for teacher training after inadequate experiences and with limited mathematical understandings that are frequently rule-bound. Ball (1990b) draws attention to those who, 'had difficulty working beneath the surface procedural level of so-called "simple" mathematics'. As an illustration, consider a student-teacher in the present study who was asked to express £18 as a percentage of £120. This graduate's difficulty of recall of simple procedures can be judged in Figure 3.1.

Her answer of 21.60 per cent is incorrect. As this chapter will show we cannot assume that graduate student-teachers will arrive with adequate subject-matter knowledge in mathematics.

RATIONALE FOR THE INSTRUMENT

What knowledge of mathematics do primary teachers need? There are three different aspects of that knowledge to be considered. Firstly, there

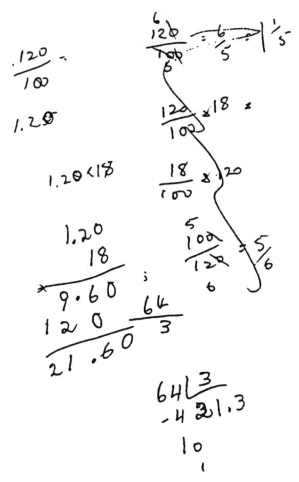

Figure 3.1 A graduate's struggles to recall maths procedures

is knowledge of facts, skills and concepts of primary school mathematics delineated by the National Curriculum (DES, 1991b). In part, this content is what Shulman (following Schwab) termed substantive knowledge of mathematics; it includes such things as the fact that 1 km = $\frac{5}{8}$ mile, the skill of decimal division and the concept of geometric reflection. But in addition to facts and central concepts there is a further element in substantive knowledge, that is the relationship between the basic parts of mathematics. For example, the notion of place value, the nature of zero, the powers of 10 (i.e. the column values), and the relationships between these parts, together contribute to the conceptual framework for decimals.

Secondly, there is a syntactic component (Schwab, 1978) which refers to those processes of mathematics by which mathematicians generate and test new mathematical knowledge.

Thirdly, there is the application of subject knowledge in teaching, and in particular its use in diagnosing pupil procedures and errors in their work.

The focus on all three of these domains in the instrument provides a broader picture of knowledge than traditional content alone. Consequently, the performance of student-teachers was assessed in each of these domains.

SUBSTANTIVE KNOWLEDGE–CONTENT

In testing knowledge in this area it is appropriate to consider knowledge up to a level to which higher attaining pupils in primary schools might aspire. Thus, most of the items in this part of the test, eighteen in all, were drawn from levels 4, 5 and 6 across the full range of attainment targets for mathematics in the National Curriculum. The topics chosen, and examples of the items, are shown in Figure 3.2.

No. of Items	Topic	Example from Instrument
4	Number	What does the figure 3 in 0.23 represent? ___
3	Algebra	Solve the equation $x^3 = 64$, $x =$ ___
2	Measures	Express 2.4 kg in grammes ___
3	Geometry	Which of these shapes tessellate?

a)   b)   ___

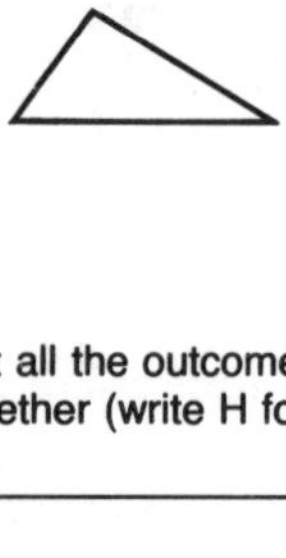

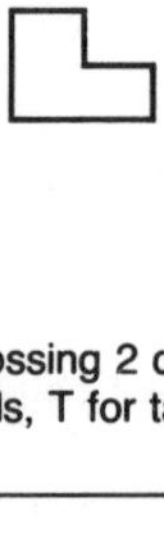

4	Probability, Statistics and Computing	List all the outcomes of tossing 2 coins together (write H for heads, T for tails)

_____

_____

2	Problem solving	Here is a pattern:

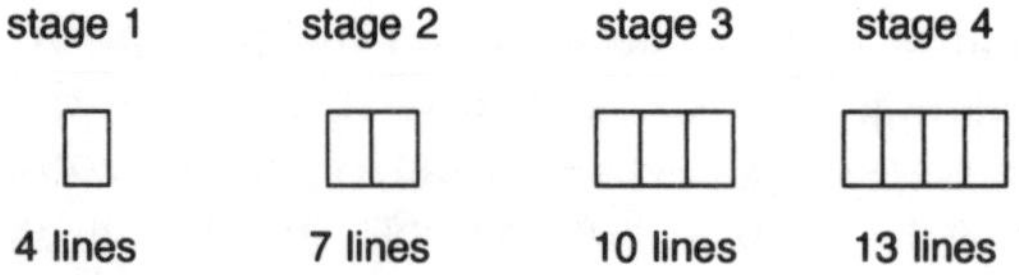

stage 1   stage 2   stage 3   stage 4

4 lines   7 lines   10 lines   13 lines

What is the number of lines for

(a) stage 5 ___   (b) stage 100 ___   (c) stage N ___

Figure 3.2 Items and topics from the mathematics instrument

KNOWLEDGE AT ENTRY

The average score, expressed as a percentage score for all students and for the four groups, is given in Table 3.1.

Table 3.1 Mathematics pre-test: mean percentage scores

Subject groups				All students
Maths	Science	Music	Early years	
67.4	63.4	49.6	50.4	57.6

The maths and science groups both performed better than the average of 57.6 per cent, in contrast to the music and early years groups. This difference between the science and maths, and music and early years groups was statistically highly significant, and parallels a similar dichotomy in the science knowledge test. Performance on individual questions in this content section reflected this dichotomy. Highest scores were obtained by students in the maths and science groups in thirteen out of the eighteen questions.

In the content section, the easiest question was about mirror reflections and 98 per cent answered this correctly. Almost as easy, with an average score of 89 per cent was a question on number sequences:

What is the next number in the sequence?

2, 5, 10, 17, 26, _____

Of intermediate difficulty, was a question on percentages:

What is £18 as a percentage of £120? _____

Six out of ten were able to answer this correctly. The two most difficult questions in this section were about shapes (and subsets, in one case). One asked which of two shapes tessellated (see Figure 3.2) and only 14 per cent managed to give a correct answer. Most failed to appreciate that both shapes tessellated, the 'L' shape in a chevron pattern. The question they found most difficult was about relationships between sets of shapes (i.e. quadrilaterals, parallelograms, squares and rectangles).

Only 12 per cent were able to do this. The commonest error was not to appreciate that 'squares' was a subset of the other *three* sets of shapes. It is interesting to note that the questions which they found easiest and most difficult were taken from the National Curriculum level 6.

EVIDENCE OF STUDENT-TEACHERS' THINKING

Beyond the bald numerical data, a closer look at the way they arrived at their answers told another story; elaborating on the distinction between

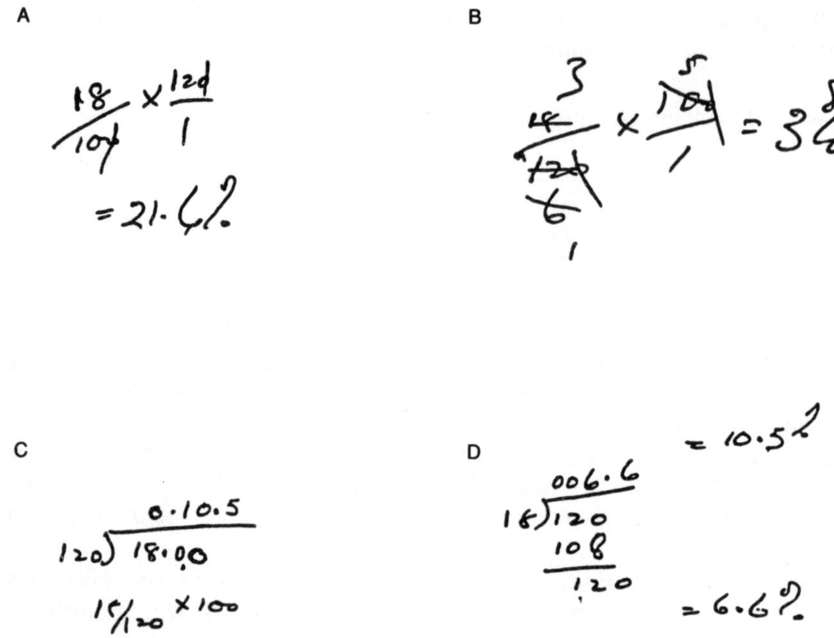

A

$$\frac{\cancel{18}}{\cancel{10}1} \times \frac{12\cancel{0}}{1}$$

$$= 21 \cdot 6\%$$

B

$$\frac{\cancel{18}}{\cancel{12}0} \times \frac{10\cancel{0}}{1} = 36$$

$$\frac{6}{1}$$

C

$$\begin{array}{r} 0.10.5 \\ 120\overline{)18.00} \end{array}$$

$$\tfrac{18}{120} \times 100$$

D

$$= 10.5$$

$$\begin{array}{r} 006.6 \\ 18\overline{)120} \\ 108 \\ \underline{120} \end{array}$$

$$= 6.6\%$$

Figure 3.3 Attempts at solving the question on percentages

procedural and conceptual understanding briefly mentioned in the introduction. A good example is provided by the variety of 'working-out'
scribbled on the inside cover of the answer-book in response to the
question on percentages. Figure 3.3 shows some of the procedures used:

(A) shows a rule has been dredged up from memory and used in the
wrong way, the roles of 100 and 120 reversed in error.
(B) shows a correct relationship, but the error is in simplifying the
answer; the student has not used common sense to check that the
answer is a reasonable size.
(C) shows the relationship is understood, but also shows an inability to
carry out long division and use place value.
(D) shows that division procedure is known, but the relationship is not
understood and hence the wrong calculation carried out.

These were the most common errors and show that many student-teachers
recalled correct or incorrect procedures, but applied them in an incorrect
way; they were unable to make sense of their answers to check and self-
correct. Answers to this question varied from 3 per cent to 666 per cent!
This suggests that even knowledge of elementary mathematics is often rote
learned and applied without real understanding.

SUBSTANTIVE KNOWLEDGE – ORGANIZING FRAMEWORKS

Substantive knowledge of mathematics includes an awareness of the different branches of mathematics and how these are related, the central ideas in different mathematical topics, and so on.

Questions from the instrument chosen to test such knowledge included:

List the main branches of mathematics.
Draw a diagram to show how they are linked.

This was difficult and only 20 per cent of the whole group gave acceptable answers. The aim was to elicit understanding of the *global* (macro-level) nature of mathematics and not disparate school topics, such as 'arithmetic and trigonometry', 'algebra, geometry, tangents and things' or the operations of, 'addition, subtraction, division and multiplication' (quotes from student answers). Answers which were acceptable specified fields such as: 'number, set theory, statistics, topology', or even 'pure maths, applied maths and stats' (the latter representing university entrance maths in the UK).

Another question in this section was:

What is the most important concept in the topic of decimals?

Answers to this question showed more than a cursory knowledge of local (micro-level) concepts of mathematics, but the brevity, confused and ill-expressed nature of the responses suggested that they did not have easy access to substantive knowledge of mathematics. Although 70 per cent gave sufficiently satisfactory answers to be scored as correct, the way they expressed understanding of the vital concept of place value was limited.

It might be inferred that much of the learning student-teachers bring to the course is surface knowledge and lacks conceptual depth and an awareness of interconnections.

SYNTACTICAL KNOWLEDGE

Four questions in this section were chosen to test syntactical knowledge. These were novel and quite difficult questions, testing vital aspects of knowledge *about* mathematics: the nature and means by which new mathematical knowledge is generated and the nature of truth and falsity in mathematics. In other words, the processes used by mathematicians in solving problems, testing generalizations and establishing the validity of an answer. As an example, a question, and an acceptable answer, about the nature of proof is given in Figure 3.4.

Only two responses indicated an understanding that a finite set of instances can never prove a numerical generalization. In all four questions in this section the maths and science groups performed better than the music and early years groups. Maths and science groups have had a

Arati (age 11) wrote the following:
'I have discovered a formula for prime numbers ($n^2 - n + 11$). This table proves it works.'

Number	1	2	3	4	5	6
Formula value	11	13	17	23	31	41
Prime?	Yes	Yes	Yes	Yes	Yes	Yes

(i) Do you think that Arati is right in her claim?
(ii) Justify your answer.

Six generations of primes is not sufficient to prove a formula. Strictly she needs to prove that the formula never generates a non-prime, either by theorem, e possibly some other guarantee that there are no counter examples. Her formula doesn't in any case generate all primes – it has missed those less than 11, also 19, 29, and others

Figure 3.4 The question and one answer about the nature of proof

training from which one might expect them to be more able to understand the nature of proof and falsification. Both groups achieved 53 per cent, compared with the music and early years groups which scored 35 per cent and 33 per cent, respectively.

Variation in response was particularly noticeable in a question (see Figure 3.5) on the *methods* used to solve a problem. This question involved identifying those *strategies* needed to solve a mathematical problem. The maths group was dramatically superior. Their average score was 80 per cent compared with the other three groups which achieved 20 per cent (science), and 10 per cent (music/early years). Presumably it is the maths student-teachers who bring this unique facet of syntactical knowledge to the course with them. It is clear that many student-teachers do not have a clear understanding of the syntactical nature of mathematics, the processes of mathematical thinking. Given the weight attached to mathematical processes in the National Curriculum (i.e. Using and Applying Mathematics) this is an important result.

PROBLEM The diagonal in this 5 × 3 rectangle passes through 7 squares. How many squares would the diagonal of a general n × m rectangle pass through?

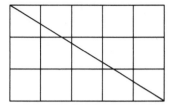

DO NOT TRY TO SOLVE THIS PROBLEM

Tick the METHODS you would try to help you solve the problem.

(i)   Remember the rule ___

(ii)   Draw rectangles of different sizes ___

(iii)   Write down the answer n + m − 1 ___

(iv)   Guess a rule and test it with a new rectangle ___

(v)   Draw more 5 × 3 rectangles ___

(vi)   Write down the answer (n × m) − 2 ___

(vii)   Draw 2 × 3, 3 × 3, 4 × 3, 6 × 3, 7 × 3, . . . etc. rectangles ___

Figure 3.5 A question on strategies used to solve a problem in maths

APPLICATION OF SUBJECT-MATTER KNOWLEDGE

It has been reported by McDiarmid (1989) that prospective teachers tend to assume that, to find out if pupils have learned, they need only ask them to re-state or perform what they have been taught. In mathematics there are many routine problems which fall into that category. They are the sequential procedures of which children have seen many similar examples and have been taught one or more procedures for tackling. For example, children learn to subtract two 3-digit numbers or learn to divide a 3-digit number by a 2-digit number in specific ways.

In this section two questions were given on routine tasks; problems which had been tackled by children. Each task depicted three children's attempts at solving the problem, using different methods. Student-teachers were asked to identify the errors in the children's answers. Figure 3.6 shows one question, illustrating three children's routine procedures.

Similarly two questions were set on non-routine tasks, again providing problems which had been tackled by children. A non-routine problem is one in which children are not able to recall a procedure; rather, they bring together parts of their mathematics knowledge in a novel way to solve it. For example, a question illustrated children's attempts to solve this non-routine problem:

You can choose vanilla, chocolate, strawberry, lemon or tutti-frutti flavour ice-cream. How many different two-colour cones are possible?

Three eight-year-olds were doing subtraction. In each case identify the children's errors, if any. Describe the errors in words.

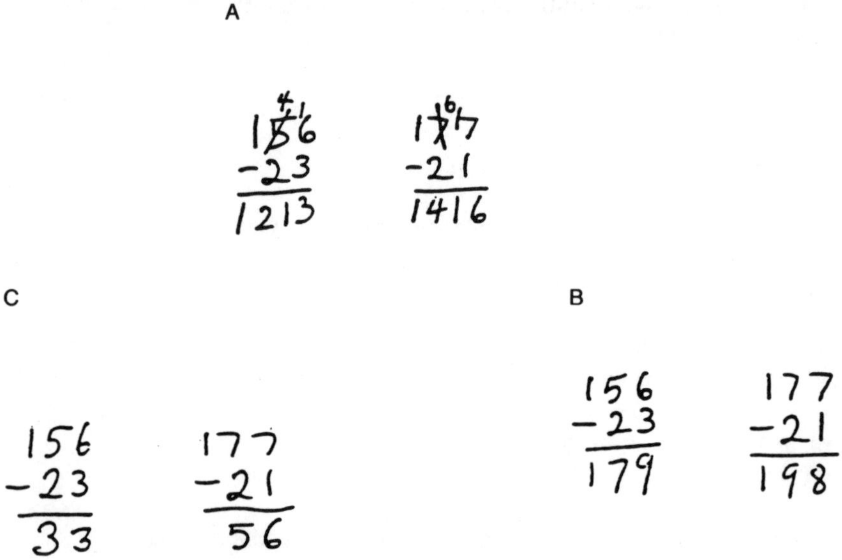

A

$$\begin{array}{r} 1\overset{4}{\cancel{5}}\overset{1}{6} \\ -\,2\,3 \\ \hline 1213 \end{array} \qquad \begin{array}{r} 1\overset{6}{\cancel{7}}7 \\ -\,2\,1 \\ \hline 1416 \end{array}$$

C

$$\begin{array}{r} 156 \\ -\,23 \\ \hline 33 \end{array} \qquad \begin{array}{r} 177 \\ -\,21 \\ \hline 56 \end{array}$$

B

$$\begin{array}{r} 156 \\ -\,23 \\ \hline 179 \end{array} \qquad \begin{array}{r} 177 \\ -\,21 \\ \hline 198 \end{array}$$

Figure 3.6 A question on a routine problem

Being asked to identify errors in the children's work involved more than an application of mathematical subject-matter knowledge. It required an understanding of procedures in mathematics and also an ability to view the subject through the eyes of the pupils. An ability to diagnose error involves what McDiarmid (1989) has described as 'a bifocal consideration of subject matter and pupils, framed by teachers' own understandings and beliefs about each'.

On this section the maths group did marginally better than the other groups on the routine tasks. However, when questions concerning non-routine problems were considered, the mathematicians did appreciably better overall; somewhat better than the science group, and much better than the music and early years groups (see Table 3.2).

One possible reason for the better performance of the maths group may

Table 3.2 Average percentage total scores for application of subject-matter knowledge

	Maths	Science	Music	Early years	All students
Routine questions	72	68	70	65	68
Non-routine questions	77	63	48	48	58

be that the routine questions are in the main numerical examples, utilizing standard methods with which all the student-teachers could be expected to be familiar. Non-routine questions could not be approached using standard procedures and required some ingenuity. Diagnosing errors in these tasks required the comprehension of a non-routine and unfamiliar child-invented method, with which non-mathematicians might be less familiar and less confident in analysing.

Being able to diagnose errors in the way that these questions demand is an important application of teachers' knowledge. Although all of the student-teachers are reasonably able to diagnose errors in *routine* mathematics, in *novel* mathematical situations subject-matter knowledge apparently makes a big difference.

CHANGE IN MATHEMATICAL SUBJECT-MATTER KNOWLEDGE

In constructing the post-test, the number of questions was reduced in each of the three sections; selection involved both factor analysis and item analysis.

Table 3.3 shows the results for all student-teachers and for the subject groups in the pre- and post-test. Only those forty-nine student-teachers who took both pre- and post-test were included in this analysis.

Table 3.3 Overall results in maths pre- and post-test

	n	Pre-test mean %	Post-test mean %	Change	Paired t-test prob. (2-tail)
All students	49	48.7	52.6	3.9	0.07
Maths	12	61.4	69.3	7.8	0.08
Science	12	55.7	53.8	−1.9	0.7
Music	12	40.3	49.7	9.4	0.04
Early years	13	38.2	38.8	0.6	0.69

Amongst the subject groups, the greatest gain is shown by the music group. It increased its score by 9.4 points, a change which is statistically significant. The changes in performance of all student-teachers in the three sections of the maths instrument is shown in Table 3.4.

Interestingly, the improvements are in content knowledge and in its

Table 3.4 Performance of all student-teachers in the three sections, pre- and post-test

Section	Pre-test	Post-test
1. Substantive: content	52.9	58.0
2. Substantive: organizing frameworks and syntactic	40.4	39.6
3. Application	49.4	56.3

pedagogical application, and not in the higher level substantive/syntactic knowledge. This is examined below.

Mathematical subject-matter knowledge is not taught specifically on the course. It is therefore perhaps understandable that there was only a marginal improvement for all students in the content section. With the exception of the question – solve the equation $x^3 = 64$, x = _____ – where there was a negative score, change was positive but small. The greatest improvement was in the question on probability:

> The probability of an even score with my loaded die is 3/5. What is the probability of an odd score? (note: die is a singular of dice)
> _____.

The 14 per cent change in this question was statistically significant. The most difficult question was the one on tessellation, and this showed the smallest change. Only 16 per cent of the student-teachers managed a correct answer at the end of the course, despite covering it, in curriculum terms, on the course.

In the maths group, although small gains were made on all questions bar one, these were not statistically significant. Thus, on leaving the course, half of the maths group still did not know that 8 km is approximately 5 miles, in common with half the music and early years groups and a third of the science group.

With the exception of the question on probability, change on individual questions in this section was small and not statistically significant. Perhaps it is no longer possible to assume that National Curriculum mathematics is easy, and Ball (1990b) has indicated that this implicit assumption about basic traditional maths needs to be challenged. A second assumption she also finds questionable is that courses prepare student-teachers to teach this level of mathematics. The courses studied in this research clearly did not; student-teachers therefore have to rely on recalling their own tenuous school learnings in the subject to plan and teach it, or study it 'on the job'.

In the substantive: organizing frameworks and syntactic section, three out of five questions showed negative scores, and overall there was little change for all student-teachers. The substantive questions were about the organization of mathematical knowledge as a discipline. The negative change scores and very low scoring was in part due to the responses describing branches and relationships of *school* curriculum maths and not those of the maths-subject discipline (i.e. set theory, group theory, analysis, etc.). The decline in scores in this section is therefore not necessarily a sign of weakness. It is rather that the focus of student-teachers at the end of the course was towards school-based study, rather than on the discipline of mathematics itself.

In the application section, Table 3.4 shows that the positive overall change score was small and not statistically significant. However, in this section the one question dealing with a *routine* task, where student-teachers were asked to diagnose an error in a child's subtraction, the percentage change for all student-teachers was 51 per cent and was statistically significant. *All* groups did very well and there was a universal pattern of gain of between 42 and 58 per cent.

It is possible that the influence of the course played a part in this change, where theoretical studies of children's errors were discussed. Their practical teaching experiences might also have been influential here. Whatever the source of improvement this is one area of gain for the student-teachers, which could potentially enhance their effectiveness in maths teaching.

However, they performed poorly on the rest of the section. When faced with diagnosing a child's error to a *non-routine* problem there was very little change – if anything the student-teachers get worse! It might have been expected that they would have excelled in this section because of the influence of methodological studies on the course. They did improve their performance dramatically in their ability to answer the questions on diagnosing children's errors in routine tasks. The lack of success for all student-teachers, including mathematicians, in dealing with non-routine questions is difficult to explain. It is possible that for all, mathematics is perceived as discrete units of procedural knowledge, a framework carried over from their own learning. This could account for their inflexible thinking in these non-routine problems, an inability to make connections from different aspects of mathematical ideas. Whatever the reason, it would seem that they have not had extensive experience either on the course or in practice in schools of trying to understand children's work on non-routine problems.

ATTITUDES TO MATHEMATICS

It is recognized that attitudes are important for the teaching of mathematics (Battista, 1986; Ernest, 1988; 1989; Schofield and Start, 1978). These authors, among others, distinguish between a number of different components of attitude to mathematics, and include:

1 teacher liking, enjoyment and interest in mathematics (and their opposites);
2 teachers' confidence in their own mathematical abilities (or its opposite, i.e. lack of confidence);

Both orientations are seen as vital in teaching mathematics, so that negative attitudes are not communicated to children. In addition it is plausible that lesson planning and reflection on lessons will be enhanced if student-teachers are positive in these two orientations.

The instrument used in the pre-test contained nineteen items, with a similar number for each orientation. The items were in positive and negative forms, with approximately equal distribution. In the post-test a subset of the items was used, the original items having been subjected to item and factor analysis, to give a total of nine items. The constructs were as follows:

(L) *Liking* (including interest and enjoyment) of maths;
(C) *Confident* (i.e. in own mathematical ability and in doing maths).

Table 3.5 summarizes the responses to the two orientations to mathematics, where 1 = strongly agree to 5 = strongly disagree. To make items comparable, all items had their scores adjusted so that high scoring indicates a positive attitude.

Table 3.5 Attitudes to mathematics (average raw scores on pre- and post-test)

Construct		All students	Maths	Science	Music	Early years
'Liking'	Pre-test	3.1	3.6	3.3	3.3	2.3
	Post-test	3.6	4.2	3.4	3.6	3.4
	Change	0.5	0.6	0.1	0.3	1.1
'Confidence'	Pre-test	3.2	4.0	3.4	3.2	2.4
	Post-test	3.5	4.0	3.5	3.3	3.4
	Change	0.3	0	0.1	0.1	1.0

Table 3.5 shows interesting differences in attitude at entry amongst the groups. The maths group, not surprisingly, shows the highest scores for both liking and confidence, and the early years the least, at both pre- and post-test. However, the latter show the biggest shift, reflecting a significant move towards liking and being confident in the subject.

Within the 'liking' scale there is some variation in responses which are hidden in examining the overall means for the construct. By way of illustration the results from two items (13 and 16) are examined in Table 3.6.

In response to 'I find mathematics very interesting' (item 13) the means are generally high, particularly so for the mathematicians. On leaving the course there is a strong agreement with this statement across all subject groups. In contrast, item 16 which stated 'I like mathematics better than most other subjects' showed low means, indicating that student-teachers

Table 3.6 Responses to two items on the attitude to maths dimension

		All students	Maths	Science	Music	Early years
Item 13	Pre-test	3.5	3.9	3.8	3.9	2.7
	Post-test	3.9	4.4	3.8	3.9	3.7
Item 16	Pre-test	2.4	2.9	2.3	2.7	1.8
	Post-test	2.9	3.3	2.8	2.7	2.7

in all groups preferred other subjects to mathematics; definitely so in the case of the early years group.

BELIEFS ABOUT THE NATURE OF MATHEMATICS

Research over the past decade has shown that teachers and student-teachers hold very different beliefs about the nature of mathematics. The importance of these has been noted by a number of authors, such as Thompson (1984) and Ernest (1989; 1991). A general model for the development of adult belief systems in mathematics, proposed by Perry (1970), was drawn upon and a simplified version of his classification used to devise the pre-test instrument. Nineteen items reflected two opposing orientations, thus:

Absolutism: Mathematics is right or wrong, certain, exact and is made up of facts, skills and fixed methods which are either correctly known or not.

Relativism: The variety of mathematical structures, forms and contexts allow differing sorts of analyses, comparisons, evaluations and approaches. This perspective incorporates a process view of mathematics and admits multiple problem-solving approaches.

The importance of these views is that absolutism is closed with regard to multiple methods and answers in mathematics. The other view admits these types of diversity. The result, in the latter case, is to encourage a more open, enquiring view of the subject in children. Such a view of mathematics has been promoted in official publications such as the Cockcroft Report (DES, 1982; HMI, 1985a), and is reflected in the inclusion of the 'Using and Applying Mathematics', Attainment Target 1 of the National Curriculum in Mathematics (DES, 1991b).

In the post-test, a subset of 11 of 19 items was used. High scoring on the scale for absolutism represents *disagreement* with statements about absolutist views. It can be seen from Table 3.7 that perceptions of student-teachers in all groups show an increase in scores for this dimension by the

Table 3.7 Beliefs about the nature of mathematics (average scores for totals on two dimensions, pre- and post-test)

		All students	Maths	Science	Music	Early years
Relativistic view	Pre-test	10.4	10.8	9.8	10.0	11.1
	Post-test	11.3	12.2	11.2	10.9	11.0
	Change	0.9	1.4	1.4	0.9	−0.1
Absolutist view	Pre-test	27.0	28.9	26.9	25.5	27.3
	Post-test	30.9	33.0	29.2	29.9	32.1
	Change	3.9	4.1	2.3	4.4	4.8

end of the course. There is a shift away from absolutist views, an increasing disagreement with the view that mathematics is right or wrong, certain and exact. These differences are statistically significant.

On the relativist dimension there is a shift towards relativism; the change is positive and statistically significant for the whole group and for the mathematics, music and science groups.

CONCLUSION

In general, change in knowledge of mathematics is small and not significant. Since Stoessiger and Ernest (1992) have argued that the National Curriculum does not represent a radical change in content from the traditional primary mathematics curriculum the low scores cannot be attributed to the introduction of new topics. On content knowledge most showed only a basic understanding of the topics likely to be taught by them in primary school.

Teacher education courses should include provision of learning basic content in mathematics to remedy an obvious deficiency. There is a risk that should teacher training become more school-based, the necessary teaching of content knowledge will be minimalized. Content knowledge is a too important knowledge base for teaching to be acquired incidentally through classroom experiences.

Content knowledge was not the only area of knowledge found wanting. That aspect of substantive knowledge dealing with knowledge about mathematics was clearly not understood, neither was their understanding of syntactic knowledge adequate. Both are thought necessary to teach mathematics well, for flexible understanding as opposed to teaching routine procedures. The data also suggest that by the end of the course student-teachers appeared to understand children's learning in routine tasks and could diagnose errors, but they did not show that they could coordinate content knowledge and children's thinking to deal with non-routine tasks.

Changes in attitude to mathematics, and in beliefs about the nature of mathematics for all students have been shown to be statistically significant. At the end of the course the general trend is to show a more positive attitude to liking and confidence towards the subject. The early years group not only started with the lowest scores, but recorded the greatest increase in feelings, on both scales. This is a desirable result considering the aims of the course. Also student-teachers leave the course feeling that mathematics is a more open and creative subject, allowing flexible approaches to solving mathematics problems. This is a shift away from a restricted view of maths, always having single 'right' answers or routine procedures. Given that modern expert opinion favours a relativistic view of mathematics (Ernest, 1991; NCTM, 1989) and that this orientation is one of the aims of the course, these results are important.

Chapter 4

Student-teachers' knowledge and beliefs about language

David Wray

INTRODUCTION

Knowledge about language has become a focus of some interest following the publication of the Kingman Report (DES, 1988b) and the subsequent setting up of the Language in the National Curriculum (LINC) project. The LINC project was charged with producing materials to assist with the in-service training of teachers who had to implement the requirements of the National Curriculum *vis-à-vis* language. For all the recent controversy surrounding this project and the embargo placed upon its materials by the government, the issue of knowledge about language does not seem likely to disappear from the educational landscape. One dimension of the issue which has not been investigated very fully, however, is the extent to which students training to be teachers are in possession of the requisite knowledge about language themselves. It could be hypothesized that in order to help children develop their knowledge about language in accordance with the analysis of the Kingman Report, prospective teachers of primary English should have, or acquire during their training period, a suitable level of personal knowledge about language. Yet little is known about the extent of this knowledge among students training to become primary teachers and still less about the effects upon this knowledge of these student-teachers' experience during their initial training period.

It could also be hypothesized that student-teachers' beliefs about the various aspects of language and literacy might strongly influence their approaches to teaching these areas and that, therefore, a course of teacher-training, to be effective, would need to have some effect upon these beliefs. Yet there is very little evidence pertaining to this, and what evidence there is (cf. Wray, 1988) suggests that training courses have little effect upon student-teachers' beliefs about literacy.

In this study student-teachers were asked to complete a series of assessments concerning various aspects of their knowledge and beliefs about language and literacy at the beginning and at the end of their course.

The particular questions which guided this aspect of the study were:

- What was the extent of the knowledge about language of the student-teachers beginning this primary postgraduate training course?
- In what ways, if at all, did this knowledge about language change over the period of the training course?
- What beliefs did the student-teachers hold about language and literacy education and how did these change during the course of their teacher-training?

THE EXTENT OF KNOWLEDGE ABOUT LANGUAGE

Design of the instrument

According to the second Cox Report (DES, 1989a), work on knowledge about language should cover the following material:

1 Language variation according to situation, purpose, language mode, regional or social group, etc.
2 Language in literature.
3 Language variation across time.

This classification follows from the model of knowledge about language put forward in the earlier Kingman Report (DES, 1988b) which included four components: forms of English, communication through and comprehension of language, acquisition and development, historical and geographical variation.

As argued above it could be hypothesized that in order to assist children to develop their knowledge about language in accordance with these analyses, now translated into National Curriculum requirements, prospective teachers of English should have, or be helped during their training period to acquire, a suitable level of personal knowledge about language. For teachers preparing to teach primary/middle school children an ability to perform satisfactorily themselves at levels 6 and 7 of the National Curriculum might not be considered unreasonable. Following from the specification in the Cox Report (DES, 1989a, paras. 6.22–6.24) of statements of attainment relating to knowledge about language, particularly relevant statements of attainment in the final National Curriculum English document are as follows. Pupils should be able to:

- show in discussion an awareness of grammatical differences between spoken standard English and a non-standard variety;
- show in discussion an awareness of the appropriate use of spoken language, according to purpose, topic and audience;
- show in discussion of their reading an awareness that words can change in use and meaning over time and demonstrate some of the reasons why;
- show in discussion or in writing an awareness of writers' use of sound patterns and some other literary devices and the effect on the reader;

- demonstrate, through discussion and in their writing, an awareness of grammatical differences between spoken and written English;
- show in discussion and in writing an awareness of what is appropriate and inappropriate language-use in written texts.

These statements formed the basis of the knowledge about language instrument. The sections cover:

1 knowledge of grammatical forms;
2 an awareness of the changing nature of grammatical 'rules' over time and according to purpose;
3 knowledge of the differences between spoken and written language and the demands of audience;
4 an appreciation of geographical and cultural variation in English;
5 the ability to discuss literary devices.

The sections were designed as follows:

1 While a 'parts of speech' approach to grammatical structure is somewhat dated and is not specifically demanded by the National Curriculum (although it figures more prominently in the Kingman Report), grammatical knowledge has traditionally been seen in this way (Bloor, 1986). Recent official documents have also suggested that children should be taught parts of speech explicitly, as, for example, *English from 5 to 16* (DES, 1984b) which recommended that 16-year-olds should know the names and functions of nouns, verbs, adjectives, adverbs, pronouns, conjunctions, prepositions and articles. Research reported by Chandler, Robinson and Noyes (1988) suggested that student-teachers themselves were not completely confident about the use of these terms and this section of the instrument was an attempt to replicate this part of their study. It should also be pointed out that, while not explicit in the National Curriculum, the use of a grammatical language is certainly implicit since, in order to discuss grammatical differences, for example, teachers and pupils alike need some way of referring to items of grammar.

   The format of this section was a simplified version of that of Chandler *et al.* (1988) in which respondents were asked to provide their own sentences containing particular parts of speech. It is generally agreed that the generation of parts of speech is significantly harder than their recognition and, accordingly, in this instrument respondents were asked only to underline particular parts of speech in the following: 'The tolerant teacher listened patiently to her whinging pupil and then politely clipped him around the ear.'

2 The Chandler *et al.* (1988) study also used a set of statements about language in order to gauge their respondents' general language awareness. As well as tapping knowledge about language rules, it was also felt that the inclusion of these statements in the present investigation would

allow informed respondents to comment upon the fact that language is dynamic rather than static and changes over time and according to purpose and mode.

3 This section was designed to ascertain respondents' knowledge of two aspects of language: firstly that spoken language uses different forms to written, and secondly that the nature of the audience determines the choice of language forms. In addition to allowing them to demonstrate that they could make the necessary alterations to a particular piece of language, this section also invited respondents to explain their reasons for making these changes, thus tapping their meta-linguistic as well as linguistic knowledge.

4 This section focused specifically on respondents' awareness of accent and dialect variation and upon their ability to describe the differences between a dialect, in this case Jamaican English, and standard English in terms of grammatical structure.

5 The final section of the instrument invited a use of literary language in order to compare two pieces of children's poetry. Respondents were marked according to their ability to make reference to the literary features of structure, rhyme, imagery and repetition. It should be noted that the focus upon these features in marking responses to this section did not signify an insensitivity to other elements involved in responding to poetry. This section of the instrument was included specifically to gauge respondents' *knowledge* about, in the words of the National Curriculum for English, 'writers' use of sound patterns and some other literary devices', rather than their affective response.

Changes to the post-test instrument

The instrument was administered at the beginning of the academic year. Students were given unlimited time to complete it and many took over one and a half hours to do this. Largely because of this time consideration and the desire not to overload them at the end of their course, it was decided to shorten the instrument for post-test administration. By means of the changes the time required for completion of the instrument was reduced by about half.

Results

Table 4.1 shows the mean percentage scores at pre-test, for each group of student-teachers and for each section of the instrument. It is difficult, of course, to decide what a desirable level of knowledge on this instrument would be. Nevertheless, the scores achieved do not seem to suggest an extensive knowledge about language. There are, however, some interesting features to these results when group scores are examined. The early

Table 4.1 Scores on pre-test – knowledge about language (per cent)

Section	Maths	Science	Music	Early years	Overall
1	50.0	41.6	44.3	67.2	47.8
2	26.0	17.5	22.4	20.8	21.6
3	65.5	65.5	62.8	59.5	63.3
4	54.2	43.7	42.8	42.9	45.9
5	23.7	38	41	47.7	37.7
Total	44.5	38.4	39.8	46.1	42.3

years group, for example, achieved a comparatively very high score on section 1, parts of speech. This group also did better than the others, although less markedly, on section 5, literature. This might have been expected from the fact that the student-teachers in this group had academic backgrounds with a much stronger emphasis upon English language. They did not, however, score higher than the other groups on sections 2, 3 and 4, which focused upon aspects of knowledge about language not traditionally included in advanced study of the English language.

The maths group, on the other hand, scored comparatively well on all sections apart from section 5, literature, where their mean percentage score was 15 per cent below that of the next lowest group. They did much the best of all the groups on section 4, language variation. Table 4.1, however, vastly oversimplifies the full picture and it is necessary to put more flesh on these bones by looking in more detail at the responses to individual sections and questions.

Section 1: parts of speech

It appears from the overall results that the level of grammatical knowledge of these student-teachers was not particularly high. There was, for example, only a 30 per cent success rate in the identification of adverbs and 23 per cent in the case of pronouns. There are two important observations to be made. The first is that the marking scheme used for this section was quite rigorous in that it specified the deduction of marks for incorrect answers as well as the addition of marks for correct answers. This form of marking heavily penalizes guessing. This feature is particularly evident when examining responses to the request to underline verbs in the given sentence. Only one student-teacher failed to underline all the verbs in the sentence. However, fifteen wrongly underlined one word as a verb. (This word, incidentally, was the same in all cases. They underlined 'whingeing' as a verb, which role it clearly does usually serve. In this particular sentence, however, it is used as an adjective.) Similarly, in the responses to the invitation to underline nouns, only five failed to identify all the nouns but four of them wrongly underlined other words.

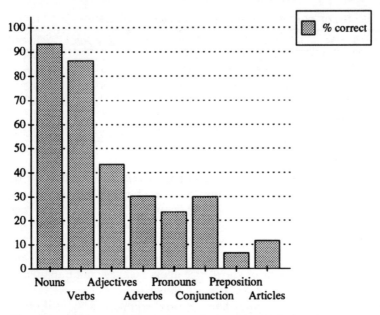

Figure 4.1 Mean percentage scores for each part of speech

While bearing in mind the severity of the marking system, the results still bear further analysis. Of particular interest, although not unexpected, is the differential knowledge shown of the various parts of speech. Figure 4.1 shows this clearly. The results suggest a three-fold grouping in terms of ability to identify parts of speech in sentences. Over an 85 per cent success rate was achieved with nouns and verbs. There is then a large drop in success to between 23 and 43 per cent for adjectives, adverbs, pronouns and conjunctions. Finally there was very little success (from 6 to 11 per cent) in the identification of prepositions and articles. In the case of articles there was a notable tendency for respondents to confuse the grammatical usage of the word with its everyday usage and to underline nouns in the sentence.

The fact of these student-teachers' lack of extensive knowledge about parts of speech is not, of course, terribly surprising and an explanation for it not very controversial. Many of them will have attended primary and secondary school during an era in which explicit teaching of grammar in these terms was unfashionable.

What is more controversial is whether this lack of knowledge is significant. On the one hand it is possible to argue that, in order adequately to discuss linguistic forms with their pupils (e.g. for National Curriculum English, writing attainment target, level 5 'show in discussion the ability to recognize variations in vocabulary according to purpose, topic and audience and whether language is spoken or written, and use them appropriately in their writing') teachers will need an explicit set of terms such as those referring to 'parts of speech'. It is also possible to argue that, while linguistic terminology will be needed for purposes such as this, it does not have to be 'parts of speech' terminology. The National Curriculum itself appears to adopt this line, using a quite different terminology. In the LINC training materials, for example, grammar is explicitly dealt with at the level of text and discourse rather than at the level of the sentence and the terminology of cohesion, text organization and clause structure is preferred to that of sentence structure. The lack of security of the student-teachers in this study with terms such as 'adverb' and 'preposition' is of interest, therefore, but may not be a crucial element in their knowledge about language.

Section 2: statements about language

This section of the instrument consisted of four statements, and respondents' reactions to each of these is shown in Table 4.2. It can be seen from this table that there was considerable variation in response to each of the statements with the maths group scoring comparatively well overall but the science group scoring comparatively badly. The most uneven set of scores was obtained by the music group, whose mean scores ranged from 7.7 to 34.5. A closer look at the responses to each statement in turn reveals some interesting features.

Table 4.2 Mean scores on each statement about language (per cent)

Statement	Maths	Science	Music	Early years	Overall
1	19.0	14.3	7.7	16.7	14.7
2	26.8	10.8	34.5	25.0	24.0
3	35.5	25.0	27.0	39.5	32.0
4	25.0	28.5	15.5	28.5	24.5
Total	26.0	17.5	22.4	20.9	21.6

Statement 1. *A verb is a doing word.*

This statement was included as an example of a commonly used definition which, however, is only partially correct. Many verbs do denote action, as for example, *run, jump, argue.* Many others, however, signify no action but rather denote a state of being, for example, *have, can, own.* Even in traditional grammar, this distinction is made (Newby, 1987) and it might have been expected that respondents with a developed knowledge of grammar would have commented upon this. Marks were awarded to responses to this statement on the following grounds: a response which said that the statement was only partially correct gained one mark, a response which gave examples of when it was not correct a further mark, and a response which attempted a more complete definition a further mark. Marks given thus represent a grading in terms of the level of detail in responses, a grading which, while not necessarily reflecting what respondents actually *know* about verbs, reflects the extent to which they were able, or saw fit, to express the detail of their knowledge.

In the event none of the respondents gained full marks on this question. Only one gained 2 marks – for the following answer:

> All 'doing words' are verbs but not all verbs are doing words. Transitive and reflexive verbs for example are likely to not involve 'doing'.

A further twenty-two respondents were given one mark. This left over 58 per cent of the group unable to score at all on this question. In the light of this group's unfamiliarity with traditional grammar, as suggested from the responses in section 1 of the instrument, this is perhaps not surprising, and again begs the question of whether this lack of knowledge is significant.

> Statement 2. *I will always insist that the pupils who I teach follow the rules of English so that they learn to always speak and write correctly. I will make sure they always use 'shall' with 'I', that they use 'whom' when the accusative form is required, that they never split an infinitive and that they never use a preposition to end a sentence with.*

This was rather a trick statement. A response to it could be made simply at the level of emotion, that is, reacting against the obvious pedantry which it expresses. Almost all the respondents did just this (all, incidentally, disagreeing with the sentiments expressed). It was hoped, however, that they would be able to go further and make a response based upon their knowledge about the workings of the English language and that this knowledge would permit them to notice that the statement itself breaks all of the grammatical rules it defends. Responses were given one mark for each of these breaches that they mentioned: i.e. one mark for noticing the incorrect use of *who*, one for noticing that *to always speak* contains a split infinitive, one for noticing that *with*, a preposition, ends a sentence, and one for noticing the use of *will* for *shall*. In the event, over 63 per cent of respondents made no mention of any of these problems; 12.7 per cent of them mentioned all four, suggesting perhaps that the extent of knowledge of this kind is polarized among this group of student-teachers: they either knew very little, or a lot. The success rate is shown in Figure 4.2.

The curious thing about this pattern is that the statement problem most likely to be mentioned by respondents was the ending of a sentence with a preposition. From the responses to section 1 it seemed that only 10 per cent of student-teachers could recognize a preposition when they saw one, yet in this statement 31 per cent identified the 'incorrect' use of the preposition *with*.

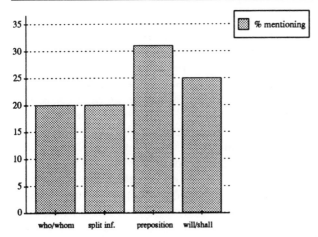

Figure 4.2 Percentage of respondents mentioning problem features in statement 2

Statement 3. *I'm proud of our great and ancient English language. We should resist these modern colloquialisms and the corruption of our language by Americanisms. Let's keep our language pure.*

This statement was included in an attempt to gauge respondents' aware-ness of the dynamic nature of language. All languages evolve and develop, largely as a result of increasing use of 'modern colloquialisms' and, because of this, it is very difficult to describe any language as 'pure'. Indeed, a language which might be described as 'pure' would, by that token, be a dead, or moribund, language. Statements such as this are the direct result of a tradition, criticized in the Kingman Report (DES, 1988b, p. 3), of considering contemporary languages in the same way as one might consider Latin or classical Greek. Respondents were given one mark if they mentioned in their answers the fact that language is continually evolving, and one further mark if they questioned the idea of the English language being 'pure'. Forty-five per cent of them gained the first mark but only 18 per cent the second. These scores do not suggest an extensive awareness that language is dynamic. There were, however, some who did well on this statement, as, for example, the following response which scored the maximum two marks for the question:

This is an impossible thing to achieve. Languages have always been growing and developing since the beginning of time. A 'pure' language tends to be a dead one.

Statement 4. *It's important that children speak with the same correctness as we would expect when they're writing.*

It was expected that this statement would allow respondents to demon-strate their awareness of the crucial effect of context upon judgements

about language correctness. Most commentators upon language in education agree that 'correctness' is actually a much less useful concept than
'appropriateness', and that one of the aims of language work with children
should be to develop their abilities to use language appropriately in
particular contexts and for particular purposes. The differing demands of
speech and writing are a key aspect of this awareness, clearly recognized
in all the National Curriculum documents relating to English. In their
reactions to this statement respondents were given one mark for attempting to define and/or query what might be meant by 'correctness' when
talking about language, and one further mark for mentioning the fact that
speech and writing are different. In the event, less than half of them (45
per cent) gained the first mark and only two gained the second. As with
the results of the previous statement, it does not appear that the awareness
of this aspect of language was very extensive among these student-
teachers.

Section 3: language functions

This section was divided into two sub-sections, one testing respondents'
linguistic knowledge (i.e. their ability to rewrite a piece of spoken language
in a written form appropriate to a particular audience) and one their meta-
linguistic knowledge (i.e. their ability to explain their rewriting). The
actual task began with a piece of speech from someone involved in a car
accident.

> *Well, it's like this . . . I was driving down here, see, and he came out of
> there and I didn't see him and, er, he must've been doing 50 at least and
> I didn't have no time to stop so he hit me, he did, and he broke this right
> off so here I am with no blooming bumper. Still he said it was his fault
> so I suppose I'll have no trouble.*

Students were asked to rewrite this in the form of a letter to an insurance
company. To do this successfully involved, firstly, ensuring that the
information was contextualized by defining all pronouns used (e.g. rewriting 'down here' as 'down the high street'), secondly, adopting standard
English grammar and, thirdly, matching the tone of the letter to that
appropriate for a particular audience. One mark was awarded for each of
these aspects.

After writing the letter, they were asked to explain the changes they had
made and one mark was awarded for their mentioning each of the three
aspects above. This marking scheme permits a direct comparison to be
made between linguistic and meta-linguistic knowledge, and Figure 4.3
shows this comparison. In each case the percentage of respondents gaining
the mark for their meta-linguistic knowledge was much lower than that
gaining the equivalent mark for their linguistic knowledge. Indeed, the

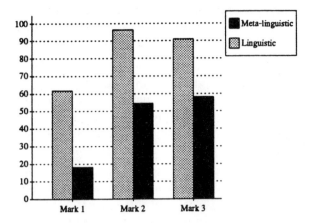

Figure 4.3 Comparison between percentage correct scores on linguistic and meta-linguistic elements of each mark for knowledge of language functions

linguistic ability of these student-teachers was, as one would expect, quite high. Very few of them produced a piece of writing which was inappropriate to the purpose set. But many of them seemed to have real problems in explaining the processes through which they had gone in order to produce this writing. In posing the question of whether this relative lack of ability to explain linguistic decisions is important, a crucial point to make is that probably all of these student-teachers will, at some stage in their future experience as primary teachers, have to attempt to explain exactly this kind of process to the children they teach.

Section 4: language variation

In the first question in this section respondents were asked to explain the difference between an accent and a dialect. Marks were given for mentioning that accent differences are concerned with pronunciation (1) and that dialect differences are concerned with vocabulary choice (1) and grammatical structure (1). A clear difference emerged between the success rates for each of these marks. Whereas 60 per cent scored the first and 69.1 per cent the second, only 16.4 per cent mentioned the fact that dialects vary according to grammatical structure. As an example of this tendency, the following answer was given maximum marks:

> *An accent is the way in which diphthongs are pronounced: a dialect is the syntax and vocabulary used.*

The following answer was, however, much more representative of the overall picture:

> *A dialect is actually a different language in many ways with different words for many things. People of different dialects may not understand each other at all. An accent, however, is just another way of pronouncing the same word.*

This lack of awareness of grammatical elements in dialect speech may partially explain the results on the second part of this section.

Here they were asked to read a transcript of part of the Red Riding Hood story as told by a London girl with parents of Jamaican origin, and to pick out some ways in which her use of grammar differed from standard English.

> *All of a sudden she see a wolf. The wolf say, 'Where you going little Red Riding Hood?' She say, 'I going to my grandmother house.' 'And where you grandmother house?' 'Up on the other side of the wood.' So he say, 'OK then, little Red Riding Hood, I go see you.' And off he run.*

Marks were available for mentioning the use of standard English present-tense forms for the past tense, the omission of subsidiary verbs (e.g. 'are'), and the omission of possessive apostrophes. The student-teachers who mentioned these aspects were 61.8 per cent, 56.4 per cent and 65.5 per cent, respectively. From a maximum possible score of 3 marks, the mean score achieved was 1.84. It seems unlikely that those who did not do well on this question (and only 21.8 per cent of the group scored maximum marks) did not actually notice the variations from standard English in this transcript. From section 3 it appears that the command of standard English among the group was very high. What seems, again, to have caused some problems was finding a suitable language with which to explain language variation: in other words, a meta-linguistic difficulty. Again, there must be a concern about how these student-teachers might go about explaining to children the grammatical demands of standard English.

Section 5: literary language

In this section respondents were asked to write a comparison of two children's poems and were given marks for their mention of particular literary devices, that is, structure, rhyme, imagery and repetition.[1] The percentages of student-teachers mentioning each of these aspects is given in Figure 4.4. Neither of these literary devices was mentioned by a majority in their comparisons of the poems, although it is perhaps not surprising that rhyme was mentioned by the largest number of them (34.5 per cent).

The question of whether this apparent lack of technical language with which to discuss literature is important is a difficult one, and perhaps even more controversial than the equivalent question about language to discuss grammar. It is quite rare for text-books and professional materials which

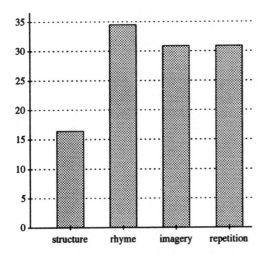

Figure 4.4 Percentage of respondents mentioning particular literary devices

deal with the teaching of 'creative' aspects of language use to discuss texts (poetry, stories, etc.) using explicit language of the kind anticipated by this question (cf. Dunn, Styles and Warburton, 1987). Much more attention is almost always given to affective aspects of language use and appeals made to feelings rather than to the use of literacy devices, although at least one popular series of teachers' guides to poetry teaching does take a more 'structural' line (Brownjohn, 1980; 1982). One of the responses to the two poems shows this difficulty well:

> *These two poems give opposing views of death. The first is a pessimistic and gloomy view – the fact that after death there is nothing. This is contrasted with the writer's obvious love of life with all its rich colour and experience. The second poem is a more positive view of death. The writer remembers Grandad in a contented, nostalgic tone, but seems happy with the memories. The first poem makes death seem very dramatic, as life had been, but the second is more down to earth and peaceful in tone.*

This response is clearly sensitive and based upon an affective appreciation of literature. It does not, however, attempt to discuss the poems in terms of their use of language or literary devices (in the terms used in the National Curriculum for English) and, therefore, was given no marks in this section.

CHANGE IN KNOWLEDGE ABOUT LANGUAGE

A direct comparison of pre- and post-test scores is provided in Table 4.3. It can be seen from this that overall there was a significant improvement

Table 4.3 Mean percentage scores of student-teachers taking both pre- and post-tests on questions common to both tests

Section	Maths		Science		Music		Early years		Overall	
	Pre-test	Post-test	Pre-test	Post-test	Pre-test	Post-test	Pre-test	Post-test	Pre-test	Post-test
1	41.2	60.3	40.7	51.9	43.6	39.7	52.5	56.4	47.4	52.1
2	23.6	27.8	15.3	18.1	22.2	29.2	33.3	36.1	23.6	27.8
3	41.7	55.6	44.4	44.4	52.8	47.2	38.9	52.8	44.4	50.0
4	63.9	80.6	55.6	63.9	38.9	61.1	47.2	55.6	51.4	65.3**
5	18.8	39.6	31.3	37.5	29.2	52.1	37.5	39.6	29.2	42.2**
Total	37.4	53.3	36.7	44.4	38.4	41.9	45.5	50.3	39.5	47.5**

** $p < 0.01$.

in scores during the span of the training course, although this improvement was largely accounted for by large changes in scores in sections 4 (language variation) and 5 (literature).

Subject-group variations are apparent from this table. Easily the greatest gain overall, for example, was made by the maths group who increased their scores substantially on all sections except section 2, statements about language. Both they and the science group made their largest improvement in section 1, parts of speech, whereas the music group's performance actually declined here. The music group's scores show a particularly interesting pattern. They made large gains in two sections (4, language variation and 5, literature), where their improvements largely account for the significant overall changes in these sections, but their scores declined in two other sections (1, parts of speech and 3, language functions). The early years group made their largest gains in section 3, language functions. More detail can be obtained by looking at each section of the test in turn.

Section 1: parts of speech

A comparison of the scores for each part of speech on pre- and post-tests suggests that the student-teachers' ability to recognize adjectives and adverbs had apparently increased, whereas their ability to recognize pronouns and prepositions had apparently decreased. For other parts of speech scores showed little change. The three-fold pattern of recognition identified from the pre-test scores appeared to have remained in the post-test. Nouns and verbs were generally recognized by all respondents, prepositions and articles by only a few with other parts of speech recognized by some and not by others.

From these results it seems sensible to conclude that there had been little overall significant change in awareness of parts of speech, although, as mentioned earlier, the maths group did seem to have increased their knowledge in this area.

Section 2: statements about language

The results for this section, which seem to show a negligible improvement only, are confused because of a clear difference between the two parts of the section. The first part, in which respondents were asked to comment upon statement 2 from the pre-test, showed a substantial decline in scores. Out of the four marks which were available for responses to this statement, a mean score of 0.89 was achieved on the pre-test compared to a mean of 0.54 on the post-test. In the second part, on the other hand, where two marks were available for comments upon statement 4, a pre-test mean score of 0.52 became a post-test mean score of 1.13. This distinction is clearly shown graphically in Figure 4.5, which compares pre- and post-test mean scores as percentages of the maximum scores for both statements.

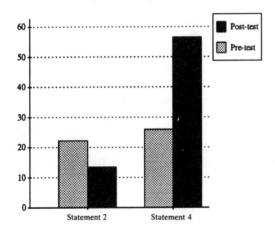

Figure 4.5 Pre- and post-test mean scores as a percentage of maximum scores for statements 2 and 4

A possible explanation for this apparent discrepancy may lie in the distinct nature of what each statement appears to be testing. The marks for statement 2 were largely given for identifying the grammatical problems in the statement itself. From the results of section 1 of this test, both at the beginning and at the end of the training course, it seems quite clear that these student-teachers were not terribly familiar with the technical features of traditional grammar. Their low success rate for statement 2 may, therefore, be explained by this lack of familiarity, although quite why their scores should have been *lower* at the end of their course than at the beginning is more difficult to account for. Although the course they had taken did not set out to increase their knowledge of traditional grammar, it certainly did not try to *decrease* it.

The marks for statement 4, on the other hand, were given for a recognition of more functional features of language and some attention to these aspects was certainly given during the course when these student-teachers had been asked to look specifically at the differences between speech and writing (only one mentioned this on the pre-test as opposed to twenty-three, almost half of the group, on the post-test), and the concepts of language 'correctness' and appropriateness had been discussed (50 per cent mentioned this on the pre-test and 64 per cent on the post-test). The varying results in this section might, therefore, be taken simply as indicators of the content of the course these student-teachers had experienced.

Section 3: language functions

In the earlier discussion of the pre-test results for this statement, attention was drawn to the gap there appeared to be between the student-teachers' linguistic and meta-linguistic knowledge. On the post-test only their meta-linguistic knowledge was tested, that is they were asked to explain the changes they would make to a piece of speech when writing it for a particular audience. It appeared that modest improvements had been made in this, although these are largely accounted for by the 85.4 per cent of the group who now mentioned the need for writing to adhere to the grammatical conventions of standard English (56.3 per cent had mentioned this on the pre-test). Again this change might be thought to have occurred as a result of the course these student-teachers had taken, during which opportunities had certainly arisen for the discussion of the demands of particular language contexts, purposes and audiences.

Section 4: language variation

On this section of the post-test they were asked only to describe the differences between an accent and a dialect. As this question had been explicitly considered during the training course, it was unsurprising to note the substantial increase in scores. The pattern remained the same, however, with significantly fewer mentioning the fact that dialects can be distinguished by their grammatical structures as well as by their vocabulary choice. Although the proportion mentioning this had risen from 18.8 per cent to 31.3 per cent, the majority still did not refer to it. It is difficult to explain this persistent under-referral, especially as the issue had certainly been discussed during the course, and examples of it given. Perhaps, as was suggested earlier, it is symptomatic of the general lack of awareness of matters grammatical which these student-teachers seemed to have.

Section 5: literature

This section was identical in both pre- and post-tests and it was here that the greatest improvement in scores was noted. This improvement can be largely accounted for by the increases in the number of respondents mentioning the structure of the two poems they commented upon (16.7 per cent pre-test, 43.8 per cent post-test) and the number who mentioned imagery (29.2 per cent, 60.4 per cent).

Considerable time had been spent during the course discussing not only children's literature, but also the writing, including poetry, which children had composed themselves. During the course of these discussions, a technical language had inevitably been used on occasions and it appears from these results that this may have rubbed off on these student-teachers.

Summary of changes

The data obtained on the student-teachers' knowledge about language seem to suggest a pattern in the changes which occurred over the period of their training course. While little improvement could be seen in their knowledge of grammar, i.e. language structure, there seem to have been improvements in their awareness of functional aspects of language. While not increasing their explicit knowledge about how language is constructed, they did seem to be more aware of how it is used and the constraints on this usage.

This pattern may be related to the content of the course they had undertaken. The major ostensible aim of this course was to introduce student-teachers to the study of language in use in primary classrooms and the influences upon this, and the majority of the work on the course had been concerned with this. Language structure had been studied explicitly only as a means to this end. It is not therefore surprising that these student-teachers demonstrated an enhanced knowledge of functional aspects of language. Neither is it surprising that their knowledge of language structure should have advanced little. Their course had rarely drawn this to their attention.

This does leave the question, of course, of whether the emphasis of the course was an appropriate one. Should more attention have been given to structural aspects of language? In other words, do student-teachers training to become teachers of primary children need an extensive knowledge of the grammatical structure of English? The question is an open one.

BELIEFS ABOUT LANGUAGE AND LITERACY

In order to find out student-teachers' general opinions about language and literacy in education, a Likert scale was designed containing seven statements. The statements, although placed in random order in the questionnaire, were grouped in four categories. Statements A and E related to the importance of enjoyment as an aim for literacy and language teaching. Statements B and D concerned the importance of 'basic' skills such as spelling and handwriting. Statements C and F focused upon language as a process rather than a product, that is, they stressed the idea of learning *through* language rather than simply the learning *of* language. Statement G concerned standards of literacy and was included because, at a time of intense mass-media interest in 'standards', it was felt to be of interest to get a picture, however limited, of student-teachers' relative response to the simplistic, but pervasive, analysis of the media and to the more sophisticated analysis they would encounter during their training course.

The questionnaire was administered at the beginning and end of the course to forty-six student-teachers. The results in the four sections of the questionnaire will be analysed separately.

1. The importance of enjoyment

Statement A: *The most important thing about learning to read is learning to enjoy books.*
Statement E: *If schools produce children who can read, write and use language fluently but do not get much enjoyment from doing so, they have failed badly.*

The pre- and post-test results for this section of the questionnaire are shown in Table 4.4. The results show a slight strengthening of feelings in favour of children's enjoyment as an important aim for literacy and language teaching. The majority of the respondents clearly agreed with this idea before their course of training, with 85 per cent giving statement A either strongly agree or agree, and 82 per cent statement E. While the overall agreement figures changed little on the post-test (94 per cent statement A; 81 per cent statement E), the increase in the proportion of strongly agree responses suggests a firming-up of this agreement. On each of the statements 50 per cent of respondents made no change to their responses.

Table 4.4 Mean pre- and post-test responses to statements A and E

Mean responses	Maths	Science	Music	Early years	Overall
Pre-test	1.8	1.8	1.9	1.7	1.8
Post-test	1.5	1.8	1.8	1.4	1.6

1 = strongly agree; 5 = strongly disagree.

2. The importance of basic skills

Statement B: *The first task in teaching children to write is to teach them to form their letters. This will make sure they do not pick up bad habits.*
Statement D: *Teachers do not place enough emphasis on basic skills such as spelling and grammar.*

The pre- and post-test results for this section of the questionnaire are shown in Table 4.5. The pre-test responses to these statements were fairly evenly spread around the mid-point response, with very few expressing strong feelings one way or the other. Feelings were much more positive towards statement B which can perhaps be explained by the 'common-sense' nature of what it claims. On the post-test, however, feelings had clearly swung towards disagreement and this change was significant, although there were still few signs of strong feelings. This swing was more pronounced in the science and early years groups and in the case of statement D, with which a majority of respondents now disagreed. For statement B, there were still a sizeable number of agree responses, albeit none of these were strongly agree, which perhaps indicates the in-built attractiveness of the idea behind this statement.

Table 4.5 Mean pre- and post-test responses to statements B and D

Mean responses	Maths	Science	Music	Early years	Overall
Pre-test	3.2	2.9	2.6	3.5	3.0
Post-test	3.5	3.5	3.1	4.1	3.5**

1 = strongly agree; 5 = strongly disagree. ** $p < 0.01$.

3. Language as process

Statement C: *Children can learn as much through talking about things as they can through reading about them.*
Statement F: *Because all education is conducted through language, all teachers should think of themselves as teachers of language.*

The pre- and post-test results for this section of the questionnaire are shown in Table 4.6. The results for these statements, as for A and E, suggest a strengthening of positive feelings towards the idea that language is a process through which learning takes place as much as a product of learning, especially among the science group. While respondents were very positive towards these statements at the beginning of their course, with 80 per cent agreeing with statement C and 60 per cent with statement F, by the end of the course these proportions had increased to 85 per cent for each statement. Moreover, the number of strongly agree responses had also increased, suggesting that opinions had strengthened considerably. On

Table 4.6 Mean pre- and post-test responses to statements C and F

Mean responses	Maths	Science	Music	Early years	Overall
Pre-test	2.2	2.3	2.3	2.1	2.2
Post-test	2.0	1.8	2.2	1.8	2.0*

1 = strongly agree; 5 = strongly disagree.
* $p<0.05$.

statement F the significant number of not-sure responses at pre-test had largely disappeared at post-test.

Taken overall, therefore, the responses to these six statements suggest a fairly uniform movement of opinion about language and literacy among this group of student-teachers. This can be expressed broadly as a movement against seeing language and literacy in terms of basic skills and towards a more sympathetic and broader view of them as media for learning and for enjoyment. It should be noted, however, that this movement was more a confirmation of views already tentatively held rather than a radical change of opinions. Some respondents did swing widely in their opinions but these were very few.

4. Standards of literacy

Statement G: *Standards of basic literacy in this country have declined in recent years.*

The pattern apparent in the results of the first six statements of the questionnaire is not repeated in those for statement G, which concerned standards of literacy. The pre- and post-test results for this statement are shown in Table 4.7. The pre-test responses to this statement suggest that feelings about standards of literacy were more or less normally distributed with the largest number of responses (by a very small margin) being in the not-sure category, and a substantial number of respondents (46 per cent) disagreeing with the statement. On the post-test, however, this distribution had completely altered with now a full 60 per cent of respondents choosing not sure. These contrasting distributions of responses are clearly shown in Figure 4.6.

Speculations as to what might account for this change are interesting.

Table 4.7 Mean pre- and post-test responses to statement G

Mean responses	Maths	Science	Music	Early years	Overall
Pre-test	3.5	3.7	3.2	3.2	3.4
Post-test	3.0	3.1	3.1	3.6	3.2

1 = strongly agree; 5 = strongly disagree.

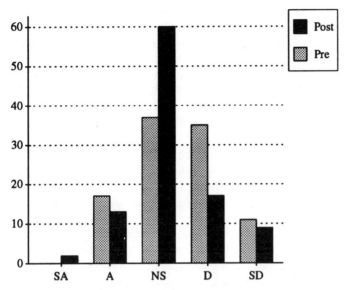

Figure 4.6 Frequency percentage distribution of responses to questionnaire statement G (standards of literacy) pre- and post-test

One thing which cannot account for it is an increase in feelings among the respondents that 'basic skills' are the most important consideration in language and literacy development. As can be seen from responses to the other six statements in this questionnaire, respondents' opinions had, on the whole, moved in the opposite direction. That is, they seemed to have come increasingly to feel that there were other, more important, considerations in language and literacy teaching. An explanation might, perhaps, lie instead in the national context in which these student-teachers responded to the post-test questionnaire. This was completed in July 1990, in the same month as concerns about national standards of reading claimed major mass-media attention. This was sparked off by the 'leaking' to the press of claims that reading standards of 7-year-old children in nine local education authorities had been consistently falling over the past five years. This initial report led to national surveys, research and polemic which still occupied headlines in the national and educational press almost two full years afterwards. It is not really conceivable that such headline news did not affect answers to the questionnaire but these same student-teachers, as seen above, had been moving towards a much more sophisticated view of literacy and reading in particular than that underlying simplistic media concerns about 'basic' standards. In the circumstances it would not have been surprising if they had simply been confused by apparently conflicting messages and the preponderance of not-sure responses may reflect this confusion.

Also of note is the fact that the responses of the early years group to this statement had moved in the opposite direction to those of the other three groups. More in this group disagreed with the statement on the post-test than on the pre-test. It might be that debates about standards in basic skills are more sharply in conflict with the 'early years' philosophy of education that this group had encountered during their course.

CONCLUSION

In general terms it seems likely that the course these students had undergone had had some impact upon both their knowledge and beliefs about language and literacy and this impact is discussed in greater depth elsewhere in this volume. Changes in knowledge and beliefs were certainly in evidence.

In terms of knowledge about language more was known after the course about functional aspects such as the use of language in a variety of contexts and social/cultural backgrounds. More was also known about literary uses of language. Little improvement could be discerned, however, in knowledge about the structure of language, especially the grammatical structure.

In terms of beliefs students had moved towards a view that language is a process through which learning takes place rather than a set of skills to be learnt and practised and towards an understanding of the holistic nature of literacy learning. This philosophy of language and literacy learning naturally stresses the uses rather than the structure of language. Consequently it can be seen that developments in their knowledge and beliefs had been consonant with one another.

Note

1 *The shadow of death*

I stood under the rainbow
And my shadow became the seven colours.
I stood by the boiling furnace
And my shadow turned red.
I stood in the greenhouse
And my shadow became green.
I stood under the noon sun
And it was short.
I stood under the moon
And my shadow became grey.
I died and there was no shadow,
Only death's.

Grandad

A quiet man,
A thinking man,
Always down in his shed
Working on a broken clock
Or fixing a car instead.
A quiet man,
A thinking man,
But now he's dead.

Chapter 5

General beliefs about teaching and learning

Elisabeth Dunne

INTRODUCTION

It has been argued that teachers have implicit beliefs about teaching and learning which guide both their planning and their decision-making in the classroom. It has also been suggested that teachers possess a 'rich store of knowledge' yielding theories, beliefs and values about their role and about the dynamics of teaching and learning (Clarke and Peterson, 1986). Yet despite the likelihood that teachers' beliefs provide a framework of reference for all interpretations and actions in the classroom, they are also likely to remain only partially articulated – if articulated at all. If belief systems are as important as suggested above, if they retain a 'presence, persistence and power' (Grossman, Wilson and Shulman, 1989), and if they really do have an impact on classroom behaviours, then arguably, student-teachers should be made aware of this relationship. However, research on implicit beliefs is a relatively new and undeveloped field; it is also difficult to achieve since beliefs themselves are unobservable until translated into practice, and yet practice does not, in itself, necessarily indicate the beliefs, or 'theoretical orientations' (Harste and Burke, 1977) which underpin it. In addition, argues Deford (1985), 'the extent to which teachers' behaviours are influenced by their theoretical orientations has been difficult to demonstrate'.

Some beliefs that impinge on teaching may belong to a belief system that is part of the everyday philosophy of a teacher and which may have an impact on their lives outside the classroom. For example, a belief in sexual equality could be important to an individual and could influence their lifestyle as well as their classroom behaviour. However, many beliefs about teaching relate specifically to classroom practice and may develop only in the context of classroom teaching. Such beliefs relate to Shulman's category of general pedagogical knowledge, or 'those broad principles and strategies of classroom management and organization that appear to transcend subject matter' (Shulman, 1987a). Both of these kinds of belief were classified as 'general beliefs' about teaching and learning. The purpose of this chapter is to highlight student-teachers' general beliefs and the extent of change in these between the beginning and end of the course.

ELICITING BELIEFS

It has been found that student-teachers have definite ideas about both teaching and learning when they enter a training course, but that they cannot necessarily articulate these (Lortie, 1975; Zeichner and Liston, 1987). In order to elicit general beliefs from student-teachers, two methods were used: firstly, a pair of Likert scales in order to provide information on beliefs about current educational aims and issues; and secondly, a series of vignettes reflecting classroom practices in order to promote discussion about such aims and issues.

The rating scales allowed for investigation of both aspects of belief illustrated below – that is, everyday philosophy and pedagogic knowledge. A five-point scale was used, ranging from strongly agree to strongly disagree. The statements used for each scale were selected directly from those used by Bennett (1976) when assessing experienced teachers' aims and opinions about education; these had in turn been adapted from a survey by Ashton *et al.* (1975). There were, however, two additional issues that were included – those of gender and racial equality – since both have taken on a greater significance in the intervening years.

The vignettes tackled two basic pedagogic issues: the kind of classroom environment which is most conducive to learning, and the teacher behaviours which best promote learning.

The term 'vignette' needs definition. Elbaz (1983) suggested that teachers use 'images' or 'mental pictures' of teaching activities and of 'good' teaching. These mental images of good teaching reflect the teachers' values, beliefs, conceptions and principles of practice. It was these kinds of image that were drawn to the attention of student-teachers in a series of 'scenarios', either of specific incidents in the classroom or of general approaches to teaching and learning. An example of a vignette is given in Figure 5.1.

As in this example, each vignette provided two scenarios which reflect different attitudes to an educational issue. The student-teacher was asked to make a choice between statement A and statement B. Although the dichotomy provided a rather stark choice, each one characterized specific attitudes with which it was possible to identify as a teacher, or which it was possible to reject as being alien to one's thinking. In each vignette, additional information was sought by asking *why* one approach was preferable to the other, or by requesting an extension of the scenario.

Although the situations presented by the vignettes were imaginary, they had validity in that they tackled current issues in education and portrayed aspects of classroom life over which teachers themselves have some control

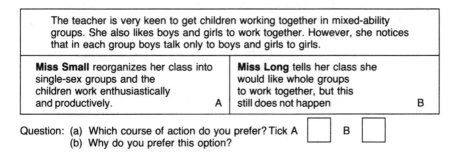

Figure 5.1 Example of a vignette – gender in the classroom

and about which they inevitably have to make decisions. Some also encompassed a dilemma which made the decision-making process more complex; thus, for example, the choice was not merely between single- or mixed-sex groups, but was confounded by the question of quality of work. This kind of complexity was included in the belief that it best reflects the reality of classroom dynamics. Educational beliefs and values are inevitably dependent on the general politico-social environment of the time and the place in which they are set, this background providing a 'current wisdom' or a selection of 'current wisdoms' about what constitutes good practice. However, these are constantly under review, subject to change and open to conflict and debate. It is this kind of conflict and debate which is brought to the forefront by the vignettes.

It would have been possible to design vignettes portraying scenarios about a great many educational issues; the following rationale offers some explanation about the choices made. In all, seven vignettes were used both pre- and post-course so that change in beliefs could be monitored; an additional one was used pre-course only, but is of interest when considered in the light of data taken from diary reports at the end of the year. They fell into three major categories, as outlined below.

Category (i) Ways that teachers talk to children; individual discipline; settling a whole class; managing a class discussion.
Category (ii) Different kinds of learning environment; classroom contexts; groupwork; the gender issue.
Category (iii) The wider context of education; the curriculum; postgraduate courses.

(i) Ways that teachers talk to children

The ways in which teachers talk to children have been under scrutiny for some years (e.g. Furlong and Edwards, 1978; Edwards and Mercer, 1987). Although there is evidence of some change over time in the way that teachers manage their lessons, and at present many schools in Britain would characterize themselves as having a 'child-centred' rather than a traditional approach to education, the notion of 'child-centredness' has a wide range of interpretations. However, elements of this approach find expression in the extent to which teachers respond to children as individuals, both in terms of learning and social development. Thus children are treated with individual care and understanding; their school work must start from 'where they are'; creativity must be nurtured.

At the same time, individual teachers may have continued to adhere to more traditional ways, and there is currently concern from the government itself about child-centred policies. Student-teachers will therefore enter schools in which they find a range of emphases (dependent on both whole-school policy and beliefs of individual teachers). Such issues were tackled by the first three vignettes in order; firstly, to tease out beliefs about the kind of interaction thought to be most appropriate for the management of learning; and secondly, to consider the kinds of interaction thought most suitable for discipline and control, both of individuals and the whole class.

(ii) Different kinds of learning environment

Recently in Britain there has been a focus on individualization of tasks as a consequence of 'child centredness'. This feature has led to a plethora of programmes of individualized work, especially for maths and language. Although there is now a growing body of writing which suggests that individualized work is an inadequate means for managing effective learning (e.g. Alexander, 1984a; Bennett and Dunne, 1992), it often prevails in schools. This is despite the fact that the majority of children in British classrooms are seated in groups (see Galton, Simon and Croll, 1980; Bennett *et al.*, 1984). The National Curriculum has made it clear that some kind of cooperative groupwork should be undertaken in school. Thus the issues surrounding individualized and cooperative work need to be addressed.

In addition, it seems important that student-teachers should consider the kinds of overall classroom context that best suit their preferences. In very generalized terms, the child-centred approach to learning tends to be characterized by certain classroom features – an emphasis on interactive work, problem-solving, and so on. In comparison, more traditional classrooms tend to be seen as quiet and orderly, with, for example, a concentration on written work and grades for parents. Such features will clearly have an impact on the classroom atmosphere and the learning that takes place. The second group of three vignettes therefore encourages comment on groupwork, gender and classroom context, each of which impinges on the learning environment.

(iii) The wider context of education

At the time of this study, the National Curriculum – stating what children should learn by certain ages within specific curriculum areas – had been met with some concern from practising teachers. One of the vignettes therefore addressed issues central to this. As well as conflict over pedagogical practices in schools, the content of teacher education courses has been debated for many years. The 'incessant tension and disagreement' was highlighted by Lanier and Little (1986); that is, whether courses should provide specific practical solutions to specific practical problems or the knowledge teachers could use to solve problems on their own. This was the issue presented by the final vignette.

BELIEFS ABOUT EDUCATIONAL AIMS AND ISSUES

Since there is a focus on change, each of the statements in the two Likert scales has been ordered in terms of the amount of change between the beginning and end of the course. For each rating scale, the statements are grouped together to show those for which student-teachers became more sure in their agreement and those for which they become less sure. The original five-point scale is reduced to three points for the purpose of clarity. Also, since there was little clear difference between specialist strands, these are not considered separately.

The first scale allowed investigation of beliefs about the aims of

Table 5.1 Teaching aims, showing change in response from pre- to post-course (per cent)

Primary education is about	Course	1–2 Agree	3 Neutral	4–5 Disagree	Average score
The encouragement of sexual	Pre-	58	34	8	2.3
equality	Post-	79	14	6	2.1
The promotion of the view that all	Pre-	88	12	-	1.6
people are equal irrespective of race	Post-	94	6	-	1.5
or creed					
Preparation for academic	Pre-	62	22	16	2.1
work in secondary school	Post-	41	28	30	3.0
The promotion of a high level	Pre-	42	33	24	2.7
of academic attainment	Post-	41	35	24	2.8
The acquisition of basic skills	Pre-	100	-	-	1.2
in reading and number work	Post-	93	6	-	1.5
The enjoyment of school	Pre-	93	6	-	1.4
	Post-	93	6	-	1.5
The encouragement of self-	Pre-	96	4	-	1.3
expression	Post-	100	-	-	1.35

teaching. In general, very little change was apparent, as illustrated by Table 5.1, which shows the proportion of student-teachers that agreed, disagreed or felt neutral about any statement. It also gives the average score for the whole group.

The average for all statements (pre-course 1.7; post-course 2.0), shows considerable agreement that all the given aims are important. Slight positive change was seen for two statements only – those touching upon the issue of equality, both racial and sexual, both of which were discussed during the taught course. For all other statements, the student-teachers became slightly less sure in their agreement over the year although self-expression and enjoyment in school continued to be rated highly, as did the necessity for the acquisition of basic skills. The belief that school is about a high level of academic attainment remained similarly positive, whereas the belief that children should be prepared for work in secondary school was less well supported at the end of the year.

The second scale illustrates beliefs about educational issues. The average for all statements (3.3 pre-course and 3.4 post-course) demonstrates more neutral feelings about these statements than for the 'teaching aims' scale. Greater change can be seen than for the previous scale, at least for two of the statements (see Table 5.2).

They moved from tending to disagree that there is too little emphasis on keeping order, to agreement that this *is* the case. The most change was seen in response to the statement about needing to know the home background of pupils. Clear agreement on this before the course changed to disagreement at the end. What is not clear is why either of these marked

Table 5.2 Educational issues, showing change in response from pre- to post-course

Issues	Course	1–2 Agree	3 Neutral	4–5 Disagree	Mean
Too little emphasis is placed on keeping order in the classroom nowadays	Pre-	10	34	56	3.5
	Post-	82	12	6	2.0
Children working together in groups waste a lot of time arguing and 'messing about'	Pre-	8	16	76	3.7
	Post-	8	27	65	3.5
Most pupils in primary school have sufficient maturity to choose a topic to study, and carry it out	Pre-	28	28	44	3.2
	Post-	35	25	40	3.1
Teachers need to know the home background and personal circumstances of their pupils	Pre-	88	10	2	1.8
	Post-	6	19	75	3.9
'Creativity' is an educational fad, which could soon die out	Pre-	2	6	92	4.4
	Post-	-	2	98	4.5

changes should occur. Most strongly supported, both pre- and post-test, was the belief that 'creativity' is *not* an educational fad.

THE VIGNETTES

The difference between the rating scales and the vignettes is that the latter encouraged them to consider 'reasons' for their choices, and hence it was possible to monitor reasons for change in beliefs. For each vignette, a brief summary is given, so that the kinds of option (A or B) faced by the student-teachers can be understood. The accompanying figures show the proportion selecting an option as well as the proportion involved in change between the beginning and end of the course.

(i) Ways that teachers talk to children

(1) Individual discipline: 'How should a teacher deal with a difficult child?'
    A. A gentle approach; kindness and understanding is all important.
    B. Direct disapproval of inappropriate behaviour; threat to involve child's mother.

All students selected option A – that is, the gentle, kind approach to discipline. This is the only vignette for which there was a unanimous vote both pre- and post-course – hence there was no change. Approach A was thought to be particularly important in terms of the kinds of relationship that develop in classrooms – based on mutual respect and understanding. Negotiation between teacher and child become central to discipline; barriers between them must be broken down and this can only be achieved if the teacher is kind, encouraging and positive. 'Telling off' and threats were thought likely to cause resentment.

Although approach A was chosen by all, by the end of the course 10 per cent discussed occasions on which statement B might be more appropriate, whereas only 2 per cent considered this pre-course. It was suggested that the child 'might well just need a good telling off' or that, although she must be given an opportunity to explain herself, 'she must be made to realize that she is in the wrong and that things must change'. Practicalities of classroom life and the issue of compromise also emerged: approach B 'may be the only option in a class of thirty children'. In addition, despite an overriding belief that understanding and kindness is the best means of approaching discipline, some felt that a 'sharp shock' may sometimes be more appropriate – 'it depends so much on the type of child and her usual standards of work'.

(2) Settling a whole class: 'How should a teacher quieten a noisy music lesson?'

A. A threat to abandon a popular and enjoyable lesson – a punitive attitude.
B. A calm and positive statement that the lesson should begin.

Ninety per cent selected approach B as their preferred way of acting at the beginning of the year, and this increased very slightly to 92 per cent by the end of the course. The clear trend was thus to prefer a positive beginning to the lesson. Altogether 18 per cent changed their opinion over the year. Of particular interest is that the 8 per cent who moved to the firmer, more authoritarian statement of teacher A, comprised musicians, who were most likely to have learned from practical experience of taking music lessons.

Selection of approach B was often promoted by firm rejection of teacher A whose threat was considered likely to defeat the purpose of the lesson; by the end of the course, this became more important (a rise from 4 per cent to 14 per cent). A sense of 'partnership' in the classroom between teacher and children emerged strongly from the post-course answers, with pupils responsible for their own behaviour and showing interest in the activity offered, so that there was no need for the teacher to dictate and punish, but rather to build on enthusiasm.

There was a general opinion that music lessons with instruments will inevitably be noisy; indeed one of them was indignant: 'to call it noise does not value what the children are doing.' The view that children should be allowed to experiment and should not be sanctioned for enthusiastic exploration of sound gained support over the year. However, alongside this, there was evidence of a growing realization that underlying discipline has an essential part to play in the effective management of practical lessons (a rise from 4 per cent to 28 per cent). There was criticism of the vignette itself, since it was thought that no teacher should have been in that particular situation in the first place: 'If I hadn't set out rules of procedure at the start of the session then it would be my fault for the rising noise level.'

Post-course replies demonstrated that experience of working with children had enabled them to make practical decisions; they knew how to draw pupils into an activity by carefully thought-out strategies – either predicting difficulties before they arose and avoiding them, or dealing clearly with pre-planned disciplinary actions when they did occur. From many there seemed to be a recognition that only when children understand what is required of them in terms of behaviour can the teacher take action with those who step out of line; thus it is essential that the teacher's expectations are made clear through the establishment of 'ground rules'.

(3) Managing a class discussion: 'To what extent should the teacher follow children's interests?'
    A. A child's deviation from the teacher's lesson plan is pursued.
    B. An immediate return to the pre-planned subject matter.

Although the majority vote for A (picking up on the child's interest) remained constant at 72 per cent, this figure hides a 28 per cent change between pre- and post-course votes. The music and early years groups gave the most support to the majority vote, with a third of the early years group moving towards this during the year so that their final vote for A amounted to 90 per cent. This high figure is not surprising when seen in conjunction with responses to other vignettes, when the early years group in particular showed a determination to respond to the individual needs and interests of very young children. In counterbalance, the science group demonstrated a majority move in the opposite direction.

A high proportion (46 per cent), believed that children's talk should not be dismissed; 54 per cent pre-course suggested that talk is one of the most important aspects of learning and should be valued highly; however, post-course only 16 per cent specifically stated this to be so. This marked drop is not significant in terms of believing in the value of talk *in general*, but may demonstrate the feeling that the planned content of the lesson must also remain important. Only the early years group considered that children's talk must always be encouraged.

On the whole, there was a greater awareness of the difficulties of handling any kind of discussion with children, of keeping it under control and not losing the thread of the lesson. The problems are highlighted by the following post-course response from one of them who believed that a child's contribution must be accepted and valued:

> It's a bit of a risk, but hopefully the teacher will be able to pull the conversation back on course. However, I try and remember that a class discussion is shared by the class, so really the teacher should act as a chairperson rather than director. It depends on the situation as to the degree of freedom you allow.

Thus the complex and problematic nature of learning to teach is illustrated, as well as the feeling that there is still a good deal more to learn about managing discussion; also that beliefs about the best ways of enabling children to learn may be hard to implement in the classroom.

(ii) Different kinds of learning environment

(4) Classroom contexts: 'What kind of classroom context promotes the best ethos for learning?'
   A. A quiet classroom; emphasis on neat written work, homework and grades sent to parents.
   B. A busy, 'chaotic' classroom; emphasis on conversational work, problem-solving, teacher always available to parents.

At the beginning of the course, the majority (88 per cent) preferred statement B, and over the year, there was a 10 per cent rise in this preference. Thus, the change was unidirectional; no reasons for choices were asked for (due to pressure of time). The older student-teachers might have been expected to choose statement A pre-course, this pattern of working being more familiar to them. However, this proved not to be the case, the range of ages of those selecting A being spread from 21 to 40 years.

(5) Groupwork: 'Cooperation or individualization?'
  A. Joint activities, cooperation and discussion are an essential preparation for adult working life.
  B. Individual learning is the essence of education.

The majority (84 per cent pre-course and 100 per cent post-course) opted for approach A. The change was again in one direction only, that is, towards a belief in the value of cooperation in the classroom. The most change occurred within the music and early years groups, with a 23 per cent rise for both towards favouring teamwork by the end of the course. The maths group showed no change, all within it having opted for teamwork both pre- and post-course. Yet again, however, the overall figures hide complexities – for example, 24 per cent stated that, although they have a preference for teamwork, it is important to use both kinds of activity in the classroom.

Although many responses were similar both pre- and post-course, there was some uncertainty shown at the beginning of the year. 'I think probably it is easier to introduce individual work and attention in a group situation than groupwork in an individual situation'. By the end of the course, as well as 100 per cent opting for teamwork, there was far greater conviction about its benefits, and this was often demonstrated by those who at first preferred individualization. One of them stated prior to the course that children *must* work at their *own* level to avoid dominance by others, but wrote later:

I think it is vital children learn to work together. If there is a way to make them take joint responsibility, all the better. I have found this aspect difficult to attain.

The issue of how to put beliefs into practice emerges again.

At the end of the year, there was also a greater understanding of the difficulties involved in monitoring individuals in groups, and a recognition that effective teamwork has to be worked at, but the overall feeling was clear:

It's vital that we think about preparing children for later experiences in life. I want to be helping children to become sensitive, caring members of the society who know how to relate to those around them in every aspect of their lives. I do not want children to become isolated cells of existence working at the expense of everyone else.

(6) Gender: 'How important is it to encourage mixed-sex groups?'
 A. Satisfaction with single-sex groups which work well.
 B. Continued encouragement of mixed-sex groups despite a failure to work well.

Although there was a preference for mixed-sex groups both pre- and post-course, it became a less popular choice by the end of the year (62 and 53 per cent respectively). Although there was a trend (24 per cent overall) to move towards single-sex grouping, the music group changed in the opposite direction, moving from being the least disposed to mixed-sex groups to being their greatest advocate. Overall, there were four kinds of preference:

 (i) Those who prefer single-sex groups, who want to promote happy, enthusiastic and productive lessons, and who are not concerned with the gender issue, or do not think they can have any impact on it (18 per cent pre-course; 6 per cent post-course).
 (ii) Those who prefer mixed-sex groups at all costs – that is, gender is a central issue and mixed groups are therefore always important (14 per cent pre-course, 4 per cent post-course).
 (iii) Those who prefer single-sex groups, but who would hope to move to mixed-sex groups in some contexts or at some point in the future – for example, single-sex groups may be a starting point to be used only in the short term (20 per cent pre-course; 38 per cent post-course.
 (iv) Those who prefer mixed-sex groups, but see it as problematic; they would tackle the issue slowly, persisting over a period of time or by means of specific strategies (48 per cent both pre- and post-course).

The decrease in responses favouring groups (i) and (ii), which represent the simple categories – A or B, – may demonstrate that a greater number recognized the complexities involved in achieving mixed-gender groups. The rise in response to (iii), tolerating single-sex groups, if used as a stepping-stone for mixed groups at a later stage, shows a recognition of the use of short-term strategies to achieve long-term aims. Both pre- and post-course the largest proportion were those 48 per cent who believed that mixed-sex groups are important, but that it may take a good deal of hard work on the part of the teacher to achieve effective groupwork. Their approach was more hesitant, pragmatic rather than idealistic. Considerably more attention was paid in the post-course responses to the detail of strategies to promote mixed-sex working, to the fact that it takes a long time to overcome prejudice, and to the reality that simply 'telling' children what is required is not sufficient.

   Those opting for single-sex groups also demonstrated a complex pattern of beliefs; as a *long-term* aim, the majority felt that children should work together, that gender issues must be seriously addressed and that teachers have a social responsibility to do so.

(iii) The wider context of education

(7) The curriculum: 'Should the National Curriculum dictate what children learn?'

    A. It is appropriate for a national body to dictate what children learn.

    B. Teachers 'know best' about learning appropriate to the pupils they teach.

There was a marked preference for a clear statement on what children should learn, with an overall increase of 20 per cent by the end of the course (from 62 to 82 per cent). The greatest movement towards this can be seen amongst the maths and the early years groups, both of which groups were least disposed to the National Curriculum at the beginning of the year. There was a wide range in the kinds of response to this vignette; 10 per cent of them admitted before the course that they knew little about the National Curriculum; many of the replies were tentative or dependent only on what was picked up from teachers during the two weeks' school experience prior to the course, and there was a lack of clear opinion.

The main reasons for selecting option A were that frameworks, structures, or guidelines were thought to be important (34 per cent pre-course; 50 per cent post-course) and that it gives equal opportunities to children to study subjects previously neglected – such as science (6 per cent pre-course; 30 per cent post-course). The notion of a 'broad and balanced' curriculum was also repeated in post-course responses, jargon perhaps picked up during the course. As well as there being a clear framework, there were considered to be specific advantages in the way it operates. A growing body believed by the end of the year that it is perhaps not as restrictive as they thought it would be, that it is flexible since it does not restrict teaching methods, it does not restrict what is taught and it can be adapted to the needs of both class and individuals (22 per cent pre-course; 56 per cent post-course). Many of the expressed fears were allayed by the end of the year.

These kinds of change in opinion in the light of experience explain the 20 per cent increase in preferences for the National Curriculum. Further to this, it became important since, as student-teachers, they felt they needed 'a guide to curriculum planning'. As one of them questioned: 'How can one teacher be sure she knows what each child's whole year of learning "should" contain?' Without the National Curriculum they would have to look for other guidelines and a less communal set of targets. Although it was never stated *per se*, it seems that many course members were beginning to think that the National Curriculum, rather than setting up a series of obstacles, would actually ease the difficulties of their professional lives as beginning teachers.

(8) Postgraduate courses: 'What should be the qualities of a postgraduate course in education?'

A. Structured, skills-based and dependent on feedback.
B. Designed to promote reflection and self-evaluation.

The majority (72 per cent) demonstrated a preference for reflection and evaluation with a further 14 per cent hoping that a course would incorporate elements of both approaches. The 14 per cent who selected A were concerned about their ability to reflect on their own progress; they set value on guidance from more experienced others; they believed feedback is essential. The three main reasons for the choice of the reflective course were that: teaching is essentially about thinking (50 per cent), a course must be for the development of oneself (42 per cent), and that teachers must be flexible/adaptable in a modern world (30 per cent). They were concerned that they should not become stereotyped 'into the mould', that they should be able to find solutions to their problems by themselves; and that, since in the future they will have to evaluate themselves, they should start to do so from the beginning. They wanted to be 'made to think – even though it may be painful at times' and stated that as a student-teacher you must 'find out what suits you instead of being handed something on a plate'. They wanted to be involved in the 'broader ideas and philosophies behind teaching', not the tackling of 'particular circumstances' covered by a skills-based course.

It is interesting, in the context of this vignette, to consider evidence provided in the diaries of those members of the year group who were followed in greater detail. None selected the more structured option when responding to the vignette. However, by the end of their course there was some evidence that this is what they might have preferred. Twelve of them wrote in detail about the content of the course. Of these, ten made it clear that the aspects of the course they found most useful were those which pertained most readily to their perceptions of statement A of the vignette. They wanted to be shown how their knowledge could be translated into ideas for teaching, and told about pedagogic skills. There was constant demand for 'more input', and 'more depth'. Those tutors who provided a dynamic role model, insight from their own experience and knowledge and specific guidance were praised; those who made statements such as 'we don't want to turn you into clones' were considered annoying since 'cloning' can provide a useful starting point. There was frustration, above all, at the lack of feedback, both for written assignments and on their progress in the classroom. Further details of reactions to the course as a whole are given in the following chapters.

It appears from the diary statements at the end of the year that what they required from the course was somewhat different from what they suggested before their course, in response to the vignette, was their preferred mode of learning. One of them interpreted the situation in a way that seemed to reflect the views of many: that course B is 'a more idealistic approach and would be more suitable as a follow-on course to A, once the basic problems of teaching have been overcome'.

SUMMARY

Across the seven vignettes both pre- and post-course, there was not a great deal of change, the average per student-teacher being 1.5 out of a possible seven changes. There was a range from 'no change' to a maximum of four changes, and the majority of the sample (52 per cent) made one change only. The maths group were the most stable with a maximum of two changes.

Change was fairly well balanced across all age-groups, though the 25- to 29-year-olds showed most stability. Of interest is that the 40+ age group were as open to change as any others, which belies the common wisdom that people become more fixed in their ways as they become older and shows that this age-group were prepared to adapt to current trends in education.

Overall, the following were supported: a kind approach to individual discipline, a positive approach to managing lessons and a (qualified) need to follow children's interests. In these areas, there was very little change. More change occurred in category (ii) – different kinds of learning environment – with a movement towards favouring a conversational approach to learning, and cooperative teamwork. This fits well with the present-day emphasis in education as a whole and of the course itself. The declining preference for mixed-sex groups might appear to be an anomaly in the findings, but it must be remembered that single-sex groups were considered to be an interim strategy in the quest for effective learning in mixed groups. The greatest movement was seen in category (iii), with more support given to the National Curriculum. During the taught course it became clear that the National Curriculum provided them with a foundation on which to build and a clear outline for curriculum knowledge.

CONCLUSION

In so far as change was apparent in both rating scales and vignettes, it represented a move towards current trends in education. In addition to this, student-teachers demonstrated in their 'reasons' a move from the ideal to the pragmatic, with the notion of constraints and practicalities moving to the forefront of their thinking. They realized, too, that clarity about classroom rules and procedures is central to the effective management of learning. If there was little change in beliefs themselves, there was a great deal of change in the understanding of how these beliefs relate to practice.

Until this point, the discussion has been in terms of there being 'very little change'. There are two issues of interest here. Firstly, many of these student-teachers held beliefs on entry which were not alien to the prevailing wisdom of the course. Secondly, it is important to note the implications of change in general beliefs. It is possible that change in response to any one aspect could mean a change in orientation that has an influence on performance as a teacher. As many as three or four changes could mean a radical change in underlying philosophy which could have a marked impact on practice. However, change is not necessarily a prerequisite for improving practice, whereas understanding of the role of beliefs may be crucial.

Although the purpose of these vignettes and rating scales was simply to elicit beliefs and to monitor change promoted by the course, it became clear that this exercise was in itself valuable in promoting self-awareness. It gave student-teachers the opportunity to clarify for themselves how they felt about aspects of education. When reporting on their first reactions to the vignettes, they made statements such as, 'I didn't know I felt so strongly . . . ', and said they had been asked to think about things they had never thought about before; for this reason, some of them found it particularly difficult to frame a response. For some, there was the sense that they had been confronted by their own beliefs for the first time.

This kind of awareness, according to Ross (1979), is essential if beliefs are to be transferred into classroom practice. He states that there are four factors of importance in terms of the implementation of beliefs:

(a) clarity of beliefs;
(b) the ability to perceive a connection between beliefs and practice identified previously as being important;
(c) an awareness and thorough understanding of possible alternative practices;
(d) the teacher's perceptions of the beliefs of school system officials.

The vignettes enabled them to make a start on addressing these issues. The alternative practices built into the framework of the vignettes (as options to select) demanded that differences were carefully considered and that the consequences of a particular choice were understood. This activity could be important in the process of clarification and in developing awareness of the relationship between beliefs and practice. If growth and change are to be a part of the educational process, and if it is true that examination of beliefs is crucial to this, then it may be that the use of vignettes could become a valuable part of training courses.

Chapter 6

Learning to teach – the impact of curriculum courses

Elisabeth Dunne

INTRODUCTION

The purpose of this chapter is to investigate the kinds of learning which were available from taught curriculum courses during the postgraduate year. Although there is a growing body of research on learning over training courses, this focuses on such areas as the nature of knowledge reflected in classroom practice (e.g. Wilson, Shulman and Richert, 1987) or stages in the growth of knowledge (Calderhead and Robson, 1991). There is little research on the content or impact of courses other than surveys conducted by Her Majesty's Inspectorate (HMI) and outlined in the first chapter. The 1991 survey concentrated in particular on the content of twenty taught courses, taking into consideration the need in British primary schools for a broad knowledge of a wide range of subjects as well as a deep knowledge of any one specialized area. It was shown that the quality of courses in academic subjects ranged from satisfactory to weak. In addition, small-scale studies (e.g. Calderhead and Robson, 1991; Wubbels, Korthagen and Broekman, 1991) have indicated that student-teachers' knowledge of what curriculum entails can be fairly crude – for example, mathematics is seen simply as calculation, science as the doing and writing up of experiments; alongside this, classroom teaching may be envisaged as no more than telling and showing. It is suggested by Calderhead (1991) that such factors may work against attempts in teacher education to develop sophisticated notions of teaching and learning processes.

The major difference between this study and others is that the following descriptions are based on self-reported learning. The few previous examples of self-reported learning do not provide optimistic evidence about taught courses; for example, teachers in their first year of practice stated that their coursework was not useful to them (HMI, 1988), and in a detailed case-study of one student-teacher (Shulman, 1987b), Debbie said at the end of the year that her education course was 'a waste', she had not 'learned anything' from her English methods course and that, 'I really don't think what I've learned in college has helped me'. If this were really the case, then teacher education must indeed be in a sorry state. However, there was no documentation of the kinds of learning offered in these instances and it was not possible to test the veracity of the statements.

ANALYSIS OF THE CURRICULUM COURSES

Student-teachers in this study participated in one specialist curriculum course and a range of general curriculum courses, as outlined in Chapter 1. This chapter highlights features of the English, mathematics, science and music courses. Data came from two main sources: tutor descriptions of aims and outlines of their courses, taken from interviews and from the course handbook; and student-teacher diaries describing the input to all sessions, the kinds of learning in which they had been involved and evaluation of their personal learning experiences. To guide their thinking, they were given a list of categories to write to, but it was stressed that these were to provide a sense of direction rather than impose a set structure; they were asked to write about what knowledge they gained and what was of importance to them in the process of learning.

Analysis of diaries allowed a detailed picture to be built up of every session on each of the specialist and general curriculum courses. Altogether, there were over 1,300 descriptions and associated critiques of sessions on the taught courses. The main focus of analysis was based on categories similar to those given for the diary guidelines. The seven categories linked clearly to aspects of Shulman's categories of knowledge growth, as well as highlighting areas of interest in HMI reports. Each is defined and exemplified below; many further examples are given in the descriptions to follow, serving both to illustrate the categories and the term 'knowledge gain'.

Subject-matter knowledge   This category was used to cover any knowledge or understanding of subjects at their own level rather than at the level of children. For example, 'Found it difficult to differentiate between weight and mass (shame on me!); all became clear by the end of the lecture.'

Curriculum knowledge   Covering knowledge of ideas, activities, ways of working, demands of the National Curriculum, packages, resources, etc., i.e. all content knowledge at the level of children or for the specific purpose of teaching children, including reasons and purposes; characterized by, 'what shall we teach, and why?' For example, 'Looked at the uses of number patterns and the many different ways they can be helpful in maths . . . so many simple concepts can be reinforced and discovered there is much more potential than I realized.' (This is a much wider definition than that of Shulman (1987a) who conceived curriculum knowledge in terms of programmes and materials.)

Knowledge of children's learning   Covering theoretical aspects of how children learn, and why; developmental sequences; expectations for different age groups, learning difficulties, etc. For example, 'Important for children to believe they have discovered something for themselves.'

Teaching skills   Characterized by 'how shall we teach? How do we present the curriculum?' Covering all kinds of management of learning, planning, developing work, matching of tasks, forms of interaction with children, and so on. For example, 'How an activity can be adapted to fit particular age group/level – alerted us to the skills involved.'

Teaching styles   The manner of presentation, of interaction, features of personality, etc. For example, 'The great thing about these sessions is that they operate on two levels: at one level he is putting over the content as tutor to students; on another level he is a teacher presenting material to a class of children.'

Classroom organization   Including aspects such as classroom layout, the use of whole-class and small-group teaching, and the creation of an ethos conducive to learning. For example, 'Should try and create favourable conditions for good talking and listening in schools. I will need to be aware of this. Too often schools do not provide the right environment for talk and discussions.'

Assessment   Methods of formal recording, planned diagnosis of errors, etc. For example, 'I feel that I would have always carried out some form of personal assessment of children and felt that the guidelines we examined gave me a useful structure to use.'

All diary entries were categorized, each statement, or series of statements on a single theme, being allocated to a category according to its content.

KNOWLEDGE GAINS FOR CURRICULUM COURSES

The description of categories is the central focus of this chapter. Approaches to the curriculum were closely linked with beliefs about children's learning, both of which impinged directly on the need for certain kinds of skill, or organization, and so on. The split into knowledge categories might therefore be considered artificial (cf. Leinhardt and Feinberg, 1990). However, they highlight the variety of knowledge available from these courses. In the descriptions below, it is only possible to present a flavour of the learning. It is not possible to represent every viewpoint, though there were clear trends and patterns. Further, all comment is based on student-teachers' perceptions, views and analyses and may not fully represent the tutors' aims or intentions.

Trends across all subject areas, and similarities between specialist and general courses can be seen in Tables 6.1 and 6.2. The figures for self-reported learning in each category give a picture of the proportion of diary writing devoted to each area. They may not reflect all that was learned, but it could be assumed that they reflect both what was available to be learned and what was most memorable or of most significance. Distinct patterns emerged.

For all specialist courses, the majority of learning occurred in relation to curriculum knowledge, followed by knowledge of teaching skills. Overall, there were greater gains in relation to children's learning than subject content, though in science this was outweighed by subject-matter knowledge. Comparatively less attention was given to assessment. In addition, they wrote at greater length about their chosen subject specialism, perhaps indicating their real interest in it.

The figures for general curriculum courses are similar (see Table 6.2). Overall there was somewhat less emphasis on curriculum knowledge, though this remained central; there was a boost to subject knowledge for maths and music, but not science which was oriented towards processes; and there was generally a greater gain in knowledge of children's learning.

Table 6.1 Student-teachers' self-reported knowledge gains from specialist curriculum courses (per cent)

Knowledge of	Maths	Science	Music	Average
Subject matter	10	18	10	13
Curriculum	37	36	40	38
Children's learning	15	13	13	14
Teaching skills	23	22	23	23
Teaching styles	9	4	8	7
Classroom organization	5	5	2	4
Assessment	2	1	3	2

Table 6.2 Student-teachers' self-reported knowledge gains from general curriculum courses (per cent)

Knowledge of	Maths	Science	Music	English	Average
Subject matter	18	8	15	9	13
Curriculum	34	33	26	29	31
Children's learning	12	21	25	19	19
Teaching skills	22	23	22	28	24
Teaching styles	8	3	4	5	6
Classroom organization	4	7	4	3	4
Assessment	3	5	0.7	7	4

DESCRIPTIONS OF COURSES

Descriptions of courses are provided through the analysis of categories. Where the content of categories was specifically different for each subject area, then each one is considered separately; for other categories, the content was similar across all subject areas and the descriptions are therefore combined. Illustration of the categories is prefaced by a brief summary of tutors' aims for each course, and concluded by the student-teachers' evaluation of their own learning experiences and of themselves as learners in each subject area. This kind of evaluation was a major part of the diary writing for many, often being over half the total.

AIMS

English The central aim of this curriculum course was for student-teachers to develop an understanding of the nature of language and its acquisition in all modes – talking, reading and writing – and to explore how language contributes to learning in the classroom. It was anticipated that the course would: 'explore the nature of the processes through reflection on ourselves as readers, writers and learners as well as through looking at children. From an understanding of the processes, the implications for teaching children can be explored, methods can be examined and criteria for the assessment of materials (textbooks, schemes, workpacks, etc.) can be derived.'

Mathematics The aims of the specialist course were to broaden and deepen mathematical background, to explore ways of working with children, to review resources and materials, to look at the implications of the National Curriculum, to consider assessment and to look at the place of mathematics in relation to other subjects. It was expected that they should become aware of current areas of research and development and of the role of a mathematics consultant in school.

The general curriculum course stressed the contribution of mathematics to children's development as 'creative and confident problem solvers' and the role of processes and strategies within this.

Science Those in the specialist group were expected to become conversant with the National Curriculum and its implications, develop an informal awareness of the role of science in the primary curriculum and in the context of how children learn, gain significant background and experience to feel confident in teaching a balanced range of topics, and be aware of the role of a science consultant in a primary school.

Since all teachers are now required to teach science, no matter their previous experience, the emphasis of the general curriculum course was somewhat different, concentrating on 'the nature of primary science, the relevant skills, attitudes and concepts', and on seeing science as an enjoyable and productive activity for both teacher and pupils. This difference in emphasis was apparent in the analysis of categories.

Music   As well as learning to apply expertise in the classroom, the main aim of the specialist course was to prepare for music consultancy. Thus they considered approaches to music-making which were not dependent on high-level skills, so that they could fulfil their role of helping non-specialist teachers.

The general curriculum course did not rely on any formal skills in music. There was an emphasis on music being active and enjoyable, with any kind of musical experience being useful to lead children and facilitate music-making. Some knowledge of the role of music in the curriculum and its relationship with other curricular areas was expected, as well as an awareness of resources for primary music.

CURRICULUM KNOWLEDGE

English   Debate was a constant feature of the course. For example, discussion of reading raised passions by tackling issues surrounding the role and value of phonics; debate on writing raised a central dilemma for teachers – to what extent children should adhere to the form of language. Pressures from outside school were related to their own developing beliefs about enacting the curriculum, for example, with regard to 'emergent writing'; or to issues such as: 'Why does spelling matter?' They were given information on approaches to teaching all aspects of reading and writing and on the purposes of different kinds of classroom activity.

At the level of children, they played poetry games and practised poetry writing, they worked on Cloze procedure exercises and re-arranging of texts, and tried out a range of computer programs. The whole was related to gaining an increasingly better understanding of the National Curriculum. They worked at the analysis of children's writing development; they learned how to work out reading ages, to appraise children's books, to extract information from texts. They considered the role of the home in developing language and reading, the use of dialect and accents, and non-English speakers in the classroom. Many sessions were backed up with booklists and handouts as well as video and audio tapes for closer examination of the curriculum in action.

Mathematics   Sessions for the specialist course were devoted to reviewing activities and prerequisite resources for an activity-based curriculum with the central purpose of providing understanding. The National Curriculum and problems of mathematics teaching were central. The first sessions dealt with simple number activities at the level of young children. Later, they dealt with more complex ideas (e.g. fractions and algebraic functions). Topics covered included: learning to count, number lines, place value, probability, Fibonacci sequences, arithmetic operations, commutative and associative laws, graphs, estimation, shape. There was a constant linking between these topics and activities for the classroom and an emphasis on 'the kind of mathematics which is used and applied in everyday life', as well as on learning and playing mathematical games.

The general curriculum course had many similarities. A wide knowledge base was covered and understanding was constantly reinforced while meticulously working through activities. There was a demand for active involvement at the level of children and for themselves, breaking down preconceptions, clarifying content, providing terminology and exploring relationships. They investigated different ways of teaching concepts and became aware of what kind of content constituted a 'teachable unit'.

Science The specialist course concentrated on covering as much curriculum knowledge as possible, while providing a closer understanding of classroom science, how it feels to undertake problem solving or investigative activities, and the kinds of process that are available to children. Topics covered included flight, electricity and electrostatics, structure and forces, properties of materials, designing and constructing vehicles, designing and carrying out experiments, urban trails, or the production of sound. They were expected to review and assess curriculum packages. Many sessions were reinforced and extended with practical handouts. There was evidence of a constant extension of knowledge for teaching with regard to the National Curriculum and relationships between different attainment targets.

For both courses, there was an emphasis on 'learning from experience', 'hands-on' activities, and resources and materials. The content of general curriculum sessions was similar to the specialist course, though the focus was specifically on scientific processes in the classroom, for example: 'Science is a subject about discovery, communication and sharing experience. It also involves a lot of observation and cooperation between individuals.' They gained clarification of knowledge rather than new knowledge, as well as many ideas for activities. To reinforce these, they were presented with science texts, computer programs, television and video packages.

Music Most of the activities covered at the level of the children were the same for both courses, but the emphases were different, the specialist approach being more academic, covering more ground and focusing in detail on resources. The general curriculum course was simpler and more practical at the level of children's learning. They all focused on 'composing', considering different methods and materials and performing their own compositions to the rest of the group, making use of either conventional or graphic notation, or a combination. They discussed aims for primary music and the proposed place of music in the National Curriculum. They watched videos of children composing in the classroom and the methods available to a non-specialist teacher working with them.

They then tackled 'performance', discussing how this could be undertaken with children. They tried out a range of ideas appropriate for classroom use. Specialists tried activities dependent on their musical expertise, playing pieces composed by each other as well as a published work, and taking part in jazz improvization. Both groups listened to recorded music as a rehearsal for listening in the classroom. All sessions were interspersed with games and simple musical activities to be taken directly into school. None of these demanded any real expertise but enabled them to envisage a curriculum in which music is available to all children and in which all teachers can play some part.

SUBJECT-MATTER KNOWLEDGE

English   A voluntary session for those who lacked a basic knowledge of English grammar was the only one which directly addressed subject knowledge. General discussion raised a few fundamental questions about, for example, the reasons for 'story' in our culture, its role and its nature.

Mathematics   Half of those on the specialist course commented on a wider understanding of number and the nature of mathematics: 'Am getting to see maths much more as a whole subject now rather than compartments of numbers, shapes, algebra, etc.' The general curriculum group referred constantly to revision of knowledge and sharpening of understanding. For both groups, there was interest in new vocabulary, as well as a series of individual learnings and understandings.

Science   For the specialist course, input on subject-matter knowledge was negotiated with the tutor. However, the needs of someone with a degree in mechanical engineering were different from those of a psychologist/ biologist. Comments from the general curriculum group were somewhat vague: 'it was good for my subject knowledge'; one suggested that their attention had been specifically drawn to knowing about the stages of scientific enquiry.

Music   Those on the specialist course commented on learning a new instrument. They also touched on profound questions such as 'what, exactly, music is'. In the general curriculum group, some were enabled to read music for the first time. They learned basic musical terms, how to accompany songs using pentatonic scales, and how sound is produced on a variety of instruments. Some felt that the doors of music had been opened for them.

CHILDREN'S LEARNING

The great thing about these sessions is that they operate on two levels: at one level it is putting over the content as tutor to students; on another level it is a teacher presenting material to a class of children.

Many sessions, by providing typical classroom activities appropriate for pupils, but to be tackled at their own level, allowed them in some sense to experience learning as would a child, to know about 'how it feels', and how practical activity provides involvement and hence motivation. It enabled them to understand how children might approach their tasks, and to consider the kinds of learning that were available from the experience. The link between their own learning and that of children was referred to constantly: 'We recognized the way *our* thought developed and so could see how the same principles applied to children in the classroom.'

They discussed insights into the complexity of learning, understanding that there was much room for confusion in all subject areas; they began to recognize the complexity of skills and processes, that learning is not necessarily straightforward, and that children may make retrograde steps before progressing; that learning may be a gradual process and that there is a difference between children experiencing, say, electrical phenomena, and understanding them. They discussed how activity-based learning, as promoted by the course, is purposeful: 'Abstract concepts are always harder than concrete units to understand . . . [they] must be taught using practical devices so the children *can* conceptualize.' They saw how important concepts had to be built up clearly and slowly and how 'fun activities' could 'become a foundation of knowledge for harder concepts'.

Many began to see that the teacher's role in promoting purposes and quality in learning links closely to the nature of any child's learning; also, that learning is dependent on clear aims by the teacher, which may mean having a structure to activities which belies the 'apparent freedom'. Further, they recognized the way that a teacher interacts with children can have a significant impact on learning. Overall, the comment 'I am building up a deeper understanding of children and their capabilities' reflected the feelings of many, and there was growing awareness of the intricate interrelationships between their developing beliefs and practice, as well as between learning and teaching.

TEACHING SKILLS

Emphases were different in each subject area, though there was much overlap and reinforcement across courses. There were also strong links with 'children's learning', particularly because beliefs about how children learn have an impact on how teachers teach. Since, for example, in English, it was accepted as essential that reading should be highly valued, it became important for the teacher to learn about providing a 'reading environment' and strategies to promote reading that are both meaningful and pleasurable.

For music, the majority of comments were on the management of order and picking up 'useful tips on how to handle lessons in such a way as to end with 'music'. They considered the management of instruments to be a skill that needs a good deal of attention, with the teacher 'very much in charge to harness and direct the energy of the children.'

In maths, it was suggested that 'there can be no learning unless there is good teaching'. Thus it is 'important to work out what concepts really lie behind what we are trying to teach/convey and think of simple, meaningful and motivating tasks'. In order to pitch tasks at an appropriate level some kind of background knowledge of pupils was considered necessary, as well as constant diagnosis through talking to children and questioning them.

Science sessions developed awareness that teachers' management of learning has an impact on what is actually achieved. For example, although there is 'no one right way' to present a task to children, there are particular ways that are better for achieving certain ends; and so, too, for promoting understanding: 'The trick is to learn how to ask the questions "why" and "how" in a productive way.' Tutors modelled this kind of approach – 'drawing out ideas', 'asking the sorts of questions we should ask in a classroom to get us thinking about different ways of experimenting', constantly drawing attention to different aspects of the task. The skill of teaching 'thus lies in the ability of the teacher to focus on what is important', at the same time as being 'careful to avoid imposing too many of our own ideas on the children'.

In general, they discussed how concepts could be built up by skilful teaching, how all aspects of the curriculum could be made exciting or challenging. They considered how variety of experience and teaching pupils by different approaches is important to reinforce the development of concepts. There was also recognition that their new-found knowledge of learning difficulties and likely misconceptions would enable them to plan more effectively, especially in conjunction with better ideas of activities and resources appropriate to certain age ranges.

Role play of teaching alerted them to many difficulties – for example, in explaining:

> The basics I felt very confident with, yet when I tried to 'teach' them to my neighbour I realized how it can come across in such a muddle.

This was a very valuable lesson in opening my eyes to problems. It made me realize that unless I've got this sorted out, how can I expect a child to understand?

TEACHING STYLES

Many comments were on the enthusiastic and detailed presentation of the sessions which served as a good example for classroom practice: 'We learn not just what to present, but also a way of presenting it.' Video of teachers was also greeted with interest since different kinds of role model could be provided in this way.

A first session of the year prompted the statement: 'It is hard as we are going to have to develop our own styles of teaching . . . but I feel quite excited about the challenge.' In general, they clearly felt that their beliefs about the best ways of teaching and enabling learning would have an impact on their style, and that personal style is something that develops over time and as they learn more. There was some feeling that style develops not only naturally as a result of gradually coming to know how one stands in relation to different kinds of approach, but that it is something that can be consciously adopted. They observed that teaching styles were extremely important since style and approach have a major impact on how learners feel. This point was discussed in relation to their own experiences with tutors and the recognition that different styles could be appropriate.

CLASSROOM ORGANIZATION

Similarly, they were aware that the organizational strategies used with them were appropriate for the classroom – for example, tutors set up small groups and maintained interest by circulating from one to the other, or groups were deliberately left to their own devices to solve problems by themselves; or a tutor coordinated and demonstrated an investigation. Sometimes several different activities were organized at the same time with a reporting-back session to share findings, or they worked as a class with the tutor taking on a highly didactic role.

The kinds of preparation and organization that went into providing their sessions were taken as a model to work towards. Comments also addressed ways in which decisions about classroom layout and management may, or may not, provide a stimulating environment. They appreciated the 'solid, practical ideas' on how to organize, for example, an attractive reading area, or a 'listening corner'. A few also discussed how their deeper knowledge of curriculum and materials helped focus decisions on the best way to organize a class.

ASSESSMENT

Comments on assessment often related to the diagnosis of difficulties through working closely alongside children, and to generally learning about children by talking to them and observing them. There was an emphasis on teachers assessing for understanding and remedying lack of understanding. Assessment was also considered in terms of looking for development in learning. For example, in music sessions, a video about children composing over a period of weeks highlighted 'how they became increasingly able to distinguish between, and create, a range of different sounds and to modify and develop what they had already done'.

During their taught sessions, the need to evaluate one's own and each other's work was stressed; this feature was considered to be directly transferable to classrooms.

In terms of formal assessment, they learned about the use of developmental checklists and, in particular, the recording of reading strategies and difficulties by means of miscue analysis.

EVALUATION OF LEARNING

English Overall, they felt they had learned about a wide range of essential background features, 'gained a good basic idea of what language teaching is about and enthusiasm for it' and were provided with an understanding of current issues. They learned a great deal about children, about how they tackle the English language and the nature of their difficulties; they liked the positive message, 'concerned with enabling children as readers and writers'. The nature of the course meant that discussion played a focal role; many appreciated how they were asked to develop their own values and beliefs (which tied in well with their lectures on children's learning). The majority were quite clear that they must come to their own decisions and that this is not something that could be done lightly or even, necessarily, during the course.

Both expectations and personality seemed to play a role in terms of perceptions of learning. For some, discussion was not considered to be 'input' or 'content', they felt they were given few activities to take directly into the classroom, and were not specifically recommended ways of managing and organizing, and this is what some of them had hoped for. Most, however, enjoyed the expectation that they would have to form their own opinions, develop their own styles and work at what they, themselves, wanted from the teaching of English:

> It's made me think why I do what I do rather than just taking on board new ideas, without questioning their validity. It means that I've some theoretical structure and framework to refer back to, to see where I can go now.

Mathematics   An interesting pattern was apparent in specialist sessions. Firstly, there was excitement at the kinds of learning available. However, the demand to question their knowledge and to re-approach mathematics seemed to lead to growing concern and lack of confidence. Yet, this soon changed with the general realization that the tutor had been working purposefully: 'skilfully . . . widening our conceptual boundaries' so that a 'clearer and more extensive picture of the realities of mathematics began to emerge'. For some there was a sudden burst of understanding and continued excitement: 'Maths is beginning to make sense to me . . . suddenly I can see where we are going. I understand things I never did before.' Another stated:

> Today I fully appreciated the need to understand mathematical processes rather than just applying formulae learnt by rote, which is how I was taught. If you have a full understanding, then you can apply that to any suitable method or situation. If you have no understanding but merely a rote-learned method, you have no flexibility and have to re-learn methods each time the situation requires it.

The general curriculum course also led to some marked changes in attitude, especially for those who had 'hated maths at school'. It achieved this through 'providing knowledge on how to bring maths alive and make it fun'. The constant relationship with practice and the numerous ideas and activities held their interest, alongside the perception that they were definitely being taught *how* to teach children. The only disappointment was lack of time to do more than 'scratch the surface'.

Science   Appreciated by both groups was the number of ideas and activities which could be taken directly into school, and the sense of progress and security provided by working through the National Curriculum. They appreciated the range of experiences provided and the management of sessions, as well as valuing the variety of ideas from their peers. Having to present work or to 'teach' their group was considered important – obliging them to 'think through and clarify our thoughts'. Although the 'hands-on' activities were enjoyed by everyone, about a third of them considered that continuing with investigative work did not provide enough curriculum input or ideas on 'how to teach the subject', and 'more opportunity to look at developing skills' was wanted.

Many in the general curriculum group showed particular excitement that the 'fear' and 'mystique' of both science and technology were removed through their involvement in practical work at the level of children. However, whereas some needed the confidence-boosting, fun approach, concentrating on involvement in processes, others, with greater experience and no fear, might have coped with a more demanding course.

Music   Specialists suggested they learned about a 'simple side' to music which they had not experienced for many years. Those who felt they were previously 'musically illiterate' gained confidence and were enthusiastic about trying activities in the classroom: 'once the mystique is removed, everyone is finding how many activities there are which they can do'. They all felt they learned about 'practical ideas for the classroom'; above all, they really enjoyed themselves: 'Great . . . I like the idea that both the children and I can make music together.' They recognized that music is 'enjoyable and fruitful' for children, and watching each other's sense of satisfaction boosted them still further. As well as being excited by musical activities, both groups appreciated the heated debate surrounding the role of music teaching. The overall opinion was that they had 'gained a lot of valuable experience and understanding of music in school'.

For the general curriculum group, the requirement to learn to play the recorder had a mixed reaction. There was a varied intake ranging from those who found learning an instrument extremely difficult and became despondent, to those who were excited by their new-found talents, to those few who were already qualified in music (e.g. grade 8 violin) but were expected to spend long periods on beginners' recorder exercises. The majority did, however, appreciate that they must broaden their own musical experiences to be more effective as teachers.

SUMMARY

There was evidence of a wide range of learning in each of the categories. Although most individual aspects of curriculum knowledge were not new to them, they clearly lacked real understanding, particularly in maths. Thus, what tutors provided by giving 'hands-on' tasks and problems to solve at the level of children was the much needed opportunity to come to terms with previously barely understood ideas. They were able to fill gaps, make links, consolidate and rehearse their knowledge and skills: they often restructured their knowledge and came to new understandings. Thus, the learning was at their own level; this was probably crucial to the process of becoming a better teacher of that subject.

Teaching skills and children's learning were well represented in the categories: this is not surprising, being consistent with the stated aims of tutors and the fact that the design of the course was to draw together content knowledge, 'methods' and knowledge of children and to demon-strate links. HMI (1991) were especially critical in their survey at the lack of learning about assessment; although the 4 per cent devoted to assess-ment here is a comparatively low figure, it must be viewed in the context of being one particular activity from a wide repertoire of teaching skills. This was a period when there was a great deal of talk about assessment in primary education but few clear statements about how it should be achieved. Some courses, especially English, did focus in detail on assessment procedures; also, much comment on the need to question children and check for understanding – that is, to constantly monitor tasks in hand and informally assess – was included in the 'teaching skills' category.

In terms of evaluative comment on their learning from these sessions, 76 per cent overall was positive and, as has been shown, criticism was often subject to revision as understanding of the tutors' aims and their impact developed. The majority of course members made it clear that they felt excited, motivated, enthusiastic to try out ideas in the classroom. They constantly reported on their own learning especially when their tutors presented a variety of input and activities. They respected their tutors for the ability to teach them as student-teachers at the same time as providing them with the skills needed for teaching children. On occasion, the learning experiences they provided were so positive and so powerful that certain individuals felt that they had grown in stature as a consequence of their learning. There was appreciation of the 'vision' of teaching presented to them, what was possible, even if it was not at present observable in schools.

There was a clear difference in the diaries between comments on specialist and general curriculum courses. Whereas specialist courses provoked comment on their developing beliefs about the nature of teaching appropriate for their subject, general curriculum courses were often characterized by excitement, created by a perception of success in an area in which they had previously failed.

IN RETROSPECT

Student-teachers were asked to include in their diaries a brief review of the training course on two different occasions – firstly, at the end of the main taught course (the end of term 2 and after one teaching practice) and, secondly, at the end of the year. Of particular interest is that, of those who did this on both occasions, 85 per cent suggested on the first occasion that, in general, the taught course had been useful, that they had gained either a great deal of knowledge or, at least, some knowledge, that it had been enjoyable, that it had made them think about classroom practice; one of them stated: 'setting out to plan my (second) teaching practice, I am amazed at what I have learned'. However, after this teaching practice, at the end of the year, perspectives had changed. Only 37 per cent stated at this point that the taught courses had been significant in their development as teachers. Some were highly critical of the input or complained at the lack of it. Others, having previously documented their learning from coursework, spoke as if the source of that learning was completely forgotten. Many said they definitely learned more from practical experience in school. From classroom practice they could say: 'I've realized that I *can* do it', that is, take full control of a class of children, and this may have been the high point of their training. However, some of them, and nearly always mature student-teachers, were more aware of the nature of knowledge growth and that it was perhaps the interaction between the two kinds of learning that was important: 'knowledge has come to me bit by bit, it's not always easy to see where I got what and when I got what, to what stage'.

CONCLUSION

An issue which became apparent – that student-teachers have a wide range of different background knowledge and experience – was also identified as problematic in the 1991 HMI survey. Whereas this often contributed to the richness of relationships and learning on the course, it also meant that those who already had higher level subject-matter knowledge of a discipline were still obliged to follow the whole course. They felt their time, which was so precious to them, was wasted. Yet, despite having certain kinds of subject-matter knowledge, they still needed access to the related curriculum and pedagogic knowledge.

It is also clear that perceptions of the course linked with different kinds of personality, or perhaps with a range of conceptualizations of what the process of learning to teach entails, which may have had an impact on interpretations of coursework experiences. Calderhead (1991) summarizes research which suggests four student-teacher approaches to training: (i) those who expect to be told how to teach; (ii) those who believe that teaching skills 'grow out of oneself'; (iii) those for whom hands-on experience is central since learning is from experience; and (iv) those who see teaching as unproblematical with nothing particular to learn. An obvious dichotomy in the data reported here is the one between, in simple terms, 'thinkers' and 'doers'. Both enjoyed hands-on experience, but this was not considered enough; beyond that, there were those who thrived on the development of their personalities, their beliefs, the way the courses demanded that they make their own choices; a similar number constantly requested more 'telling', more 'ideas on a plate' from tutors, more clear-cut ways of operating, and it is of interest that these were usually the ones most lacking in confidence or least secure in their subject knowledge, or with least previous experience of children or experiences related to teaching.

Suggestions of the inadequacy of curriculum courses in the retrospective analyses may have indicated that, on reflection and in the light of 'real experience', they were found to be weak, or inappropriate in preparing them for the realities of classroom life. They may have highlighted that curriculum courses had failed to supply professional learning that could be used for teaching, that the efforts to provide individual understanding of knowledge as well as teaching skills were inadequate (although the fact that 72 per cent of activities observed in school were taken either fully or in part from the curriculum courses would seem to deny this). It may have suggested that, at a time when many felt insecure at not having gained employment, or were feeling unprepared for the responsibilities of the following year, it was only too easy to turn round and blame the course for its failures. It may have been any combination of factors. As suggested by these data, it may have been that, as they became more removed from it, they actually forgot the sources of their knowledge and were unaware of the developmental aspects of their own learning.

Chapter 7

Theory into practice

Elisabeth Dunne

INTRODUCTION

There is currently an emphasis on practical competence in teaching, an assumption that it is achieved best through school-based training, and a questioning of the need for any kind of theoretical input into this (e.g. Lawlor, 1990). McIntyre (1992) is adamant that this is a 'remarkably primitive view of teacher education' and 'frightening for serious educators', but he also argues that it is time to reconsider the nature and the place of theory in training courses. Alexander (1984b) suggested that theory should 'incorporate (i) speculative theory, (ii) the findings of empirical research, (iii) the craft knowledge of practising teachers'. He also stated that 'none should be presented as having prescriptive implications for practice'. McIntyre (1992) argues that this kind of notion of 'theory as intellectual process', which he states has informed an increasing number of British teacher education courses, is inadequate; what should be offered is theoretical knowledge which may be tentative and to be questioned, but which is also specifically believed 'to be of practical value' and usefully assimilated into the professional development of student-teachers.

It is against this background that the specifically theoretical aspects of the course are described: a series of lectures on children's learning. This is followed by a description of student-teachers' first attempts at teaching during a one-day-a-week school experience, and the kinds of link made between practical and theoretical aspects of the course. The 'children's learning' lectures were expected to link closely to school experience.

CHILDREN'S LEARNING

The course on 'children's learning' was stated in the handbook to be 'about the theoretical principles in teaching and learning'. A detailed statement of its philosophical perspective was given in order to 'provide theoretical coherence to the whole course', and it was hoped this statement would be returned to throughout the year. Briefly, it was suggested that assumptions about good teaching differ, that not everyone will agree with what course-tutors propose, but that, above all, being a teacher 'involves being reflective about one's practice, understanding the principles that underlie practice and recognizing the value-laden nature of educational activity'.

A further statement highlighted current constructivist thinking in the institution about the nature of learning, a background which had implications, in its emphasis on learning as a social process, for approaches to teaching.

The children's learning course consisted of a series of eight hour-long lectures over the first term, each followed by small-group seminars lasting about an hour. Diary writing about these sessions was categorized in the same way as the taught courses and this analysis is outlined later in the chapter. The following descriptions of sessions make use of the diaries to build up a picture of content, responses and understandings. Again, they provide only a flavour of what was available and may not summarize the lecturer's intended coverage.

SUMMARY OF LECTURES

Learning to be a teacher   An introduction to the idea that all class-teachers and all student-teachers will have their own 'schemas' for teaching; by considering the styles of two very different teachers, they were drawn into recognition of their own personal schemas and 'whether they need changing or adapting'. The notion of examining their own values and judgements was new to some. So, too, was the idea that teaching is not simply a straightforward transmission of knowledge: 'it is difficult and complex and for every teacher it is different.'

Many instantly linked first experiences of, or early beliefs about, teaching to the lecture: 'I started to question some of my own values.' There was also discussion about how these ideas could be related to future practice. As well as accepting that schemas are derived from previous personal experience, there was a recognition that they can be consciously shaped and developed. In the follow-up seminar, tutors 'explicitly linked' the themes covered with experience in school. This was described as 'valuable, enabling us all to make that practical link' and useful to 'put things into a more realistic perspective'. It also provided 'an explanation for some of the things that have happened in school'.

The nature of children's learning   A theory of complex learning was proposed. The lecturer also 'asked us what we thought was the difference between good and bad learners. Various theories were proposed, all of which were objected to by others – illustrated nicely that it depends on each person's schema.' Discussion prompted a variety of questions such as: 'Are there any differences in people's learning abilities or is it just the way they are approached? Is there any such thing as intelligence?' The suggestion that one child 'may attain more than another, but this has nothing to do with any innate intelligence' was challenged, as were many other statements. They proposed further questions: 'You still have to ask why some children appear to learn more easily and swiftly than others; are the suggestions feasible and practicable, and if so, how can they be achieved?' For some, the lecture gave the impression that challenging schemas is easy, and adapting one's teaching approach something that could be instantly achieved. For others, the theoretical content seemed 'thought-provoking but ultimately irrelevant'; it got 'everybody all worked up and it certainly made people think – but I really didn't learn anything at all'. Presumably expectations of learning about, for example, teaching skills and practical activities meant that 'thinking' was not in itself enough. The difficulty of reconciling theoretical stances with current experience was also apparent.

Match/mismatch: diagnostic interviews   Again based on a model of learning, and leading into the practical aspect of 'matching' of tasks, and the degree of mismatching in classrooms highlighted by research. The lecture was constantly related to their own needs. They felt obliged to 'think about classroom planning, management and allocation of time'. They appreciated that management has to be handled carefully; that diagnosis should inform planning and 'matching'; that it is possible to emphasize process rather than end product.

Several were realistically sympathetic about the difficulties of matching in the classroom, felt that teachers 'are fighting a losing battle trying to accurately match tasks to the children's attainments', and understood why lessons tend to be pitched at the average-ability child. The need to devote time to assessment was accepted. Discussion of a teaching cycle led to the statement: 'the strength of it will become apparent much later in the course and throughout our careers'; this kind of consideration of long-term learning was fairly unusual at any point of the taught course. Although appreciating that their 'schema' were developing, they were also critical: 'No ideas for dealing with the problems. . . . I don't want fixed answers – there aren't any!' However, some seminar tutors again helped to provide links with the classroom.

Groupwork   A research-based lecture on cooperative groupwork and the implications for classroom management, appreciated for being 'full of practical ideas'. It highlighted 'the complexities of teaching' and that it is 'a deep and involved question to decide how to group children, but one which must be at the core of any effective classroom management'. Individuals related the input to their own perceptions of teaching: 'One of the keystones for being a happy and successful teacher is to really get to grips with classroom management and thus create time for other tasks.' Others were interested by the specific groupwork techniques proposed, but remained unsure of practicalities. Comment highlighted the importance of being provided with a 'detached' vision of schooling. These lectures were also beginning to provide new ways of 'seeing': 'I am observing the children in the classroom through different eyes and understand a lot more about what I see.'

Some felt that lectures such as this led to unrealistic expectations; one sounded almost depressed: 'All this makes the goal of being the perfect, or simply a good teacher so incredibly remote'; but most were keen to 'try out' some of the ideas. At this point, many came to some kind of understanding about the role of their personal beliefs in teaching: that classroom organization is dependent on subjective judgements, and that value systems are not 'divorced from the kind of teaching that we will do'. One of them stated: 'The most important thought that I came away with was of the values that I possess and how I apply those in the classroom.'

Primary school knowledge and the structure of academic work   What does school learning look like? What should it look like? What kind of knowledge should be taught in the classroom? The lecture suggested that it was their 'professional responsibility' to emphasize processes rather than products, and learning rather than management features. The way in which they were asked to 'think very hard' about the role of schooling was welcomed, especially in terms of awareness-building and bringing to their attention aspects of teaching which had previously seemed straightforward. Means for making learning more 'meaningful and lasting' were addressed.

The suggestion that the National Curriculum and ensuing pressure to achieve levels might work against change was seriously discussed in terms of ideal versus reality. Several summarized aspects of the lecture that they found most relevant to their developing views of good teaching, for example: 'Essential that we let children learn as much as they can on their own, but we should also draw the threads together and make sure children have grasped the aim.' They also discussed their difficulty in translating beliefs about learning into practice.

Values   It was suggested that teachers constantly communicate their personal values in the classroom, and mostly unintentionally, and that children will 'pick these up'; also that 'Religious education has always been a major vehicle for the transmission of values.' The lecture addressed a series of questions, such as:

> What is our role as a classroom teacher? To prepare children for adult life? To prepare them for the real world – including moral prejudices, societies, ideas, etc.? To be happy and content within themselves? To be fraught with worry, because they are not good enough . . .?

Overriding questions seemed to be, 'What is the teacher's role in moral education? What values *should* the teacher be transmitting to the children, and is it the teacher's responsibility to do this?'

The lecture was considered to provide food for thought. It was not considered practical enough, but certainly reinforced understanding of the role of values and their impact in the classroom. The statement: 'Everyone has them and for the most part, everyone's are different. That is crucial for teaching!' was a serious recognition of the place of values in education. The demand to reflect on personal values was heeded: 'We are in the business of shaping whole people, not just facts machines.' It was also suggested that clashes in values can be problematic in schools.

Classroom organization A lecture from a local headteacher addressing the basics of classroom management. The fact that it was personal, about 'how *he* manages', was significant and led to comments such as: 'Magic!!! Useful, down to earth, first-hand suggestions.' These were found of practical and instant use. Themes, such as developing independent learning and creating time for teaching, which occurred throughout the lectures, seemed to take on greater value when revisited by this 'real live' teacher.

It was stressed that each one would have to make their own decisions about organization. The message was well received in this instance because it was surrounded by practical activities and suggestions of how links between overall aims and day-to-day practice could be achieved. This, in turn, reinforced understanding of the issues. There were also messages which boosted morale and comforted them: 'being a teacher is about surviving first, teaching second', and that 'it was worthwhile in the end, and this is surely why we continue to try to be good teachers'. An important point was raised about the timing of the lecture: 'coming at this stage when we have had a fair bit of experience in classrooms, it was very useful', the implication being that if it had been too soon in the term, the significance would have been lost.

Understanding the classroom Based on observational research in classrooms, this lecture focused on routines and expectations that were suggested as dominating and stifling learning rather than encouraging independence in children. It helped to develop the 'deeper understanding necessary to become a fully functioning teacher', and promoted awareness of the 'complex social interactions' of classrooms. They related this to their own observation and practice. 'It does alert us to traps we could easily fall into – too much dull routine work – and so make us much more reflective about how we set about teaching in general.'

Interpretation of the lecture seemed in part dependent on the personal confidence of each student-teacher at this point of the course. Some were concerned at the number of negative points raised with 'no answers as to how we might change this'. Others took the message that the importance of understanding classroom life is to improve it. Some recognized that they would soon be in a position of authority and that the forces of change lay within their own hands.

For several of them, awareness of being in control of their own learning, as well as that of children, had been developing over the course, and this particular lecture provoked some interesting personal statements:

> I became extremely frustrated with the course as I felt that I was not being directed enough. I then decided to take from my learning environment what I felt to be of value, and what I felt would personally benefit me, rather than trying to think how I might please my tutors. This has been a valuable experience for me, and I feel that at thirty-one I have taken another step along the road of 'growing up'.

Such experiences are likely to have an impact on them as teachers, and this point was emphasized: 'I am finally becoming an autonomous learner myself and thus more able to help my pupils to achieve this.'

KNOWLEDGE GAINS FOR THE 'CHILDREN'S LEARNING' COURSE

Although these lectures have been individually described in order to retain the content and pattern of their development, an analysis of categories was undertaken – as for the curriculum courses in the last chapter. Table 7.1 gives the results of this analysis, showing both the percentage of each category in relation to the total, and the proportion of student-teachers who wrote about each aspect.

It is of interest that, in direct contrast to curriculum courses, there was almost no reported gain in curriculum knowledge; as might be expected, there was a good gain for knowledge of children's learning, but the highest figures were in relation to teaching skills, suggesting that, in their eyes, the lecture course had a strong practical element.

Table 7.1 Reported knowledge gains from 'children's learning' lectures (per cent)

Knowledge of	Proportion of all categories	Proportion of sample
Subject matter	16	59
Curriculum	2	14
Children's learning	24	82
Teaching skills	34	91
Teaching styles	5	32
Classroom organization	13	73
Assessment	6	41

DISCUSSION

Overall it was clear that a critical approach to classroom life was valued and perceived in the spirit it was given – asking 'How can we improve educational practices?' In relation to this, it is of interest that a class-teacher involved in curriculum sessions aggravated them by always 'sticking up for schools'. They wanted a questioning outlook, rather than a defence of existing practices; they wanted to know about ideals as well as realities. From the very first session, there was evidence of challenging what they heard, and this challenging gradually became deeper, more knowledgeable, better related to the realities of teaching, and showed more determination for change. However, as for curriculum courses, there were differences in reception. Some continued to regret the lack of practical application. Some enjoyed the input but complained at the lack of direct relevance to their needs. Others were excited: 'So many unanswerable questions! I love it though; it encourages us to think more, question ourselves and our beliefs.' It was generally this group who were more aware of the need for long-term development and were prepared to 'store away' knowledge and ideas to use as they came to understand them better. One described these sessions as a 'tool kit' to equip them for their teaching career.

In diary-reviews at the end of the year many of them felt that they would have liked more input into children's learning: 'to get *inside* children's minds'. Others stated that the 'children's learning' lectures remained important: 'they made me think really hard about how to teach' and 'enabled me to develop a philosophy of teaching'. One concluded:

> For me, the most valuable aspects have been in the 'children's learning' course not because I think it's taught me any specific points that I can think of to help me in a classroom but because it's opened my eyes to some of the pitfalls and problems of teaching and the school system itself.

SCHOOL EXPERIENCE

School experience consisted of one day a week in school over eight weeks of the first term, and two days a week for the early years group. Student-teachers were sent out in teams of from two to four per school. They were expected to fit in with what the class-teacher was doing, to prepare two or three teaching activities for the day, to start with small groups and gradually move to larger, to cover core curriculum areas, and music for the musicians, and to take some responsibility for pacing their own progress. There was little school-based supervision from the institution except for the early years group, for whom the additional day in school was equivalent to curriculum input and was thus given time by tutors.

KNOWLEDGE GAINS FOR SCHOOL EXPERIENCE

Diary writing for school experience was characterized by two kinds of
commentary. Firstly, there was evidence of a good deal of general learning
about teaching from observation of the classroom without involvement,
and from class-teachers and their fellow student-teachers. Secondly, and
providing the major part of the diary writing, there was constant evidence
of learning *by* teaching, by being involved with children, by trying out
activities, and by evaluating their own efforts. Each of these aspects is
described below. The analysis of knowledge gains was repeated for school
experience and is shown in Table 7.2.

Table 7.2 Reported knowledge gains from school experience (per cent)

Knowledge of	Proportion of all categories	Proportion of sample
Subject matter	–	–
Curriculum	8	21
Children's learning	31	79
Teaching skills	29	73
Teaching styles	16	35
Classroom organization	12	30
Assessment	5	17

There was little reported gain in curriculum knowledge, and none at all
for subject matter. This suggests that learning about subject knowledge
from school-based activity could be a very slow process. Most comments
on the curriculum came from the early years group who spent longer in
school and were given more tutor time, but despite this only a small
proportion wrote about developing knowledge in this area. Except for the
early years group, most of the activities undertaken were directly from
their general curriculum courses. Knowledge of children's learning and of
teaching skills again figured well.

The following descriptions include aspects of the analysis of categories,
chosen particularly because they highlight features which relate to the
'children's learning' lectures. Of particular interest is the attention paid to
the development of personal beliefs about effective teaching; these beliefs
underpinned interpretations of learning *about* teaching, and were discussed in relation to learning *by* teaching when they consciously put beliefs
into practice and analysed the consequences of so doing. Both curriculum
courses and the 'children learning' lectures were used to promote the need
for this kind of reflection and self-analysis.

LEARNING FROM CLASS-TEACHERS

There was very little extended conversation with class-teachers, and even
less individual interaction when there were several student-teachers in one

classroom. Most communications were felt to further learning about teaching. Observation of the class-teacher before taking on any teaching was not often found useful, especially when there was no clear guidance to focus attention. Class-teachers mainly helped with planning outlines for lessons, appreciated because this provided familiarization with National Curriculum demands.

About a quarter mentioned 'feedback' from class-teachers. Although almost all were considered encouraging and keen to help them learn, especially with the very first attempts at teaching, only 14 per cent commented on the significance of the class-teacher in their learning at this stage. Almost 70 per cent of diary comments were concerned with thoughts and opinions about their own teaching activities and developments and their learning from and about children.

LEARNING BY TEACHING

Although they seemed happiest with their chosen specialism, efforts were made to teach in other areas. There was some description of the content of these lessons but most diary writing was concerned with children's responses to tasks and with the quality and general effectiveness of pedagogic skills – the maintaining of discipline, organization and management, presentation of the task, and so on. It was working with a whole class that was seen as the 'high point' of the experience in school, and when successful significantly boosted confidence. This led to statements from a small proportion of them to the effect that 'learning by teaching is the only way to learn', but this was not a view shared by all.

Particularly noticeable was the lack of confidence discussed by the majority at the beginning of school experience. For most, this was quickly overcome. Confidence in subject content was most apparent in the musicians, especially at the beginning of the year, presumably since they were all true specialists in their field. Some of the science group quickly realized that they too had a lot to offer.

Apparent throughout was a feeling of involvement with children, a deep regard for them and a determination to do the best for every individual. When children responded well to tasks, they reported pleasure and growing confidence. There was at times almost a sense of euphoria: 'Today I really found out what it was like to work with children, to teach them, and I really love it.' Alongside this, at least a quarter of them felt moments of depression: 'a tiring and demoralizing day – but I'm sure you have to have one'. There was also a resilience and willingness to keep trying. A few suggested they learned a great deal from mistakes, as examples 'to look back on critically when preparing and taking future lessons'.

The analysis of knowledge gains shows that the major areas of learning were for 'teaching skills' and 'children's learning' in particular, as well as for 'teaching styles'. Descriptions in these three areas illustrate the ways in which knowledge was reported as developing in the practical context of the classroom.

CHILDREN'S LEARNING

By teaching and working alongside pupils, they began to form new understandings about the nature of children's learning. 'I realize now that you must only attempt to introduce one new idea at a time', or: 'I have learned that to teach a topic once does *not* ensure all children have assimilated that knowledge.' They discussed strategies taken directly from the taught course that could be used to enhance learning: 'I think it is important to make links with other lessons and relate information to things that children already know.'

Most comment focused on their developing knowledge of how children respond, which gave them insight into how children learn. Statements touched on the many ways in which they reacted and behaved. Descriptions were interspersed with beliefs about learning, management issues, ideas for extending learning, etc., all building up a picture of student-teachers who were really interested in what they were doing with children, and in the children's responses to the tasks. There was evidence of a developing sensitivity to the nature of these responses.

Beliefs about teaching reflected beliefs about learning, and vice versa, and it was not always easy to distinguish between them in the diary writing. The main thrust of beliefs centred around pupils learning through being involved in action, through 'discovering for themselves' and through being responsible for their own learning. Linked to these features were the importance of interest and enjoyment to stimulate and motivate children.

TEACHING SKILLS

They were often highly critical of their own efforts at teaching but the diaries suggested rapid learning about the interrelationship of pedagogic skills and their impact on children's learning. The descriptions below highlight a few of the areas found problematic – the development of discipline, planning, the organization of time and matching of tasks.

Development of relationships and discipline

During the first days in school, several reported it difficult to establish a 'teacher' rapport with the pupils. It was suggested that children saw them 'more as friends', thereby losing the teacher/pupil relationship; but being 'liked' was considered important.

Comments illustrated the complexity of developing a teacher-like relationship with children. There were suggestions that this needed a certain distancing from pupils, which apparently conflicted with an ideal of a kind and caring, child-centred teacher who remains 'close' to the children. Several discussed the need to be 'assertive'. It seems that the act of disciplining pupils was one of the factors which had an impact on the process of distancing them from the children, and yet, perhaps because of this, many of them found their very first attempts at discipline difficult.

A quarter of them stated that discipline and control was an aspect of teaching which was particularly worrying, yet also reported 'less difficulty than they anticipated'. There was almost a sense of surprise that they could exercise the control they wanted. By watching the class-teacher in action and by working with groups of children, they had become aware of specific features of discipline and techniques for control. They also recognized that their own attempts at discipline were very much set within a context predefined by the class-teacher. They noted that it *is* possible to be authoritative whilst retaining a friendly relationship with children, that a class which appears to be noisy and inattentive will be quiet and listen when so requested. It was recognized that certain words and signals meant more to children than instantly apparent.

They came to recognize the role of clear instructions and the impact of individual appeals to children to follow these instructions. Small-group teaching allowed them to experiment with discipline and test the effectiveness of their own approaches. There was a growing awareness that pupils should be told about standards expected of them.

At the end of school experience, they commented on their own improvements: 'I am acquiring the eyes in the back of the head necessary to all teachers, and also the ability to overhear many conversations at once!' Overall, it is likely that these early experiences in school laid the foundations for approaches to discipline during the later teaching practices. At this stage they obviously still lacked experience in disciplining children, but the kinds of observations and the development of beliefs about how discipline should be managed were fundamental in their progress as teachers.

Planning

Recognition of poor planning most often occurred during the presentation of a task. Many commented on their failure to present a task adequately because they were not clear in their own minds about what they were attempting: 'I don't believe that I had the aims of the experiment firmly in my mind, and as a consequence I don't believe any one thing sunk into the children's minds.' They came to recognize that planning and preparation do not simply mean 'knowing what you are going to do' or 'having the appropriate materials available', but also 'knowing how you will interact with the children', especially when introducing a task. 'I'll have to make sure I have really thought everything out clearly in my own mind before I start explaining to the class.' A similar relationship between lack of clarity in instructions, due to poor thinking through, and lack of understanding by pupils, was also noted. One also reported a major breakthrough in the understanding of lesson plans: 'They are less important than I thought they would be in that they act as a basis, not an exact line-by-line document.'

Organization of time

One-third of them commented on the difficulties associated with managing time. They saw how class-teachers kept a 'close check on the division of time' and how they were constantly 'juggling with so many things', but translating awareness of time into good management of time was difficult. This problem continued throughout teaching experience. Poor planning of time led to particular disappointment when it was felt that lessons were not well concluded. One of them wondered if she would ever be able to cope with this aspect of teaching.

Matching of tasks to pupils' abilities

There were occasions during school experience when they felt totally inadequate, since tasks had failed through poor preparation, poor organization or an inappropriate level of work. Failure of an activity was recognized through the unexpected, inappropriate or lack of response from pupils: 'I realized how unprepared and inexperienced I was – all my questions seemed wrong and they didn't answer them the way I was expecting.'

At first, they mostly tended to overestimate what children could do. As they became more aware of children's varying abilities and of the impact of different kinds of task, half mentioned either matching or catering for different attainment levels, and a desire to provide a learning experience for all children was evident. One of the consequences of being over-ambitious was that they attempted to 'engineer' situations so that the task was not a total failure. Thus they were willing to compromise their beliefs about how they should manage child-centred learning in order to rectify a problematic situation.

An advantage of working with small groups of children was that it was possible to use the same prepared lesson with different groups in order to assess differential impacts. This gave valuable feedback. It also allowed them time to observe closely and devise strategies to overcome pupil difficulties.

TEACHING STYLES

At first, comments focused on the class-teacher: 'Her manner with the children is wonderful!' One of them observed: 'Styles develop – mine hasn't yet. I am different to the student-teacher and my fellow student but I couldn't say how.'

The topic most written about in terms of styles was the extent to which teachers or children should direct learning – an issue constantly discussed during coursework. Three different kinds of comment emerged in the diaries, as they gradually recognized their own beliefs in this area. At first there were comments prompted by observation. They became aware of certain management strategies which related to the class-teacher's style as a director of learning: 'Children are being guided but also being encouraged to explore and find out things for themselves.' Gradually, a slightly different kind of comment appeared as they began to make personal statements on what they themselves believed to be appropriate practice. One of them, when thinking through her own approach to teaching, stated there is a need to: 'Find a balance between child-centred activities and teacher structuring. Sometimes necessary to impose a structure or make a rule to prevent activity becoming chaotic or frustrating.'

Finally, there was a stage when they reported on their own experiences, having translated their beliefs and understandings about an appropriate role into practice. Responses were varied as regards the ease with which they fulfilled their chosen role. For example, one stated: 'I felt relaxed and happy with the children and allowed them to lead in their learning. I very much played the role of the provider of the learning environment and the helper and adviser when required.' Another found her experience more problematic: 'I felt the group went really well, [but] I do find it difficult to stand back (leave direction to the children).'

Some felt that their actions were constrained by school ideologies but, in general, their teaching experiences supported and strengthened their beliefs in the benefits of child-centred approaches; they discussed how children's first-hand experience of discovering for themselves provided motivation; how 'hands-on experience' provided interest; how giving children responsibility for their own learning allowed them to develop. This, in turn, reinforced their beliefs that their chosen teaching style was the one they wanted to adopt.

LINKS BETWEEN TAUGHT COURSES AND SCHOOL

Many of them made specific links between learning from coursework and practical classroom experience, though what seemed like good ideas on the taught course were not always easy to establish in school. For example, when pupils were asked to try spelling words for themselves, unaided, they responded by going to the class-teacher for help.

Although some diary commentary related to features which could only be learned about or observed in the context of school, much was reflective, drawing their own links between aspects of the course and practical experience in a constant development of theoretical understanding. However, a problem in asking student-teachers about the links they made between theory and practice was that many of them treated everything from taught courses as theory, and everything from classrooms as practice. Only the most sophisticated were able to distinguish more complex relationships, especially at the beginning of the year. Whatever their personal definition of theory, there was a range of opinion about its relevance. Whereas one stated: 'Theory provides the foundations of a new teacher's development, upon which is built experience', another said: 'in practice, in the heat of the moment, the theory would go out of the window and my commonsense would take over', thereby suggesting that theory and practice were separate.

By the end of the year, there was evidence that most had a better idea of what theory meant to them, although a few were still not able to make the connection with practice: 'It just seemed like the classroom and theory were two different things.' Others felt that theory was something with which they would come to terms in the future, believing, for example, it related to 'ultimate goals', which were at present too distant to focus on. All believed that theory is, or should be, useful.

CONCLUSIONS

It is clear that, even if not fully understanding the role of theory, they put many of the more theoretical aspects of the taught course to the test in the classroom. The opportunity to try out a small range of activities allowed them to put into practice both ideas for tasks and ways of managing them, these often being taken directly from the taught courses. Their first chances to interact with children were seen as invaluable since many needed the opportunity simply to find out what young children were like. Being given small groups to work with, by themselves, allowed them to test their capability in relation to children, without interference from teachers or tutors. The kinds of language they used in their diaries reflected the learning they described at both practical and theoretical levels: 'I have learnt . . .', 'I realize . . .', 'I can see . . .', 'I understand why . . .' and there was optimism as well as realism about the task of learning to teach. Tutors suggested that these student-teachers had 'completely changed and broadened their view of what the primary teacher's job was all about'. It was clear they had taken on board many of the child-centred principles of practice emanating from a constructivist philosophy of teaching and had the chance to test out beliefs and actions in the classroom context.

Feiman-Nemser (1983) warned that student-teaching can 'foster bad habits and narrow vision' and that a 'deceptive sense of success, equated with keeping order and discipline, is liable to close off avenues for further learning'. Tabachnik and Zeichner (1984) summarized similar research findings and emphasize that a quiet and orderly lesson 'becomes the major criterion for evaluating the teaching activity'. Taking small groups, in the context of the class-teacher's overall framework for discipline, meant that these student-teachers could concentrate on teaching and learning, and especially on children's responses.

Researchers also suggest (e.g. Goodman, 1986) that unless encouraged to be reflective about their practice, student-teachers are likely to adopt practices they remember from their own experiences as pupils. For this group, it is apparent that the combination of taught courses and school experience promoted self-evaluation, self-knowledge and the development of personal beliefs, and the opportunity for 'deliberating about the nature of the expertise that he or she *wants* to develop' (McIntyre, 1992). They recognized that schools did not always reflect the kinds of learning suggested as appropriate in taught courses, but did not show any evidence, at least at this stage, of being dragged into existing systems without being aware. Some of them did compromise their ideals, but these were not destroyed by the school context; there was a feeling that compromise was probably an essential part of being a student-teacher, but something they could cope with in anticipation of taking responsibility for their own class in the future.

Chapter 8

The purpose and impact of school-based work: the supervisor's role

Richard Dunne and Elisabeth Dunne

INTRODUCTION

The role of school-based work in learning to teach is most often taken as self-evident. Recent pronouncements and consultation documents emphasize the need for student-teachers to spend more time in the classroom with the assumption that learning takes place through working alongside experienced teachers. This movement is accompanied by an interest in expressing teaching as competence statements (DES, 1990; Dunne and Harvard, 1992a, 1992b; Dunne, 1992; Harvard, 1992; Whitty, 1991); in the role of a mentor (Harvard and Dunne, 1992); and in the relationship between schools and training institutions. As a normal part of course development, all of these points were being addressed by the institution before and at the time of this study. There had been successive attempts to create a set of criteria for teaching practice which adequately summarized the expectations for primary students' development in initial training which on the one hand was faithful to a view of teaching as a complex and constructive process, and on the other hand was acceptable to schools on a daily basis. One initiative had been widely criticized by practising teachers for not providing usable criteria. A further attempt is outlined below in the context of an experimental study. The role of the supervisor is discussed against this background.

ORGANIZATION OF SCHOOL-BASED WORK

School-based work was organized in the following way:

Term 1 – School Experience: a day a week in school for ten weeks.
Term 2 – Teaching Practice: four days a week in school for five weeks, one day in training institution.
Term 3 – Teaching Practice: five days a week in school for seven and a half weeks.

School experience has been discussed in Chapter 7; the focus of this chapter is on the two teaching practices. The first block teaching practice was in some ways continuous with the earlier serial practice of school experience. The same supervisors worked with their own group of student-teachers in schools known to them, and shared the supervision with other course tutors. In general, student-teachers worked in pairs. Second teaching practice was differently organized: student-teachers were placed in schools by the institution; the supervisor was selected, as far as possible, to be one who had not previously worked with that student in school-based work.

THE ROLE OF THE SUPERVISOR

For both teaching practices, there was an expectation by the institution that supervisors should liaise with teachers; ensure that student-teachers carry out a suitable pattern of experience; monitor progress by checking students' personal files, observing and using feedback from the class-teachers; and submit an evaluative report. However, in the second teaching practice, a small experimental group of student-teachers experienced a different pattern of supervision which needs placing in context.

The pressure of increasing student-teacher numbers on local schools meant that additional schools were sought which were some considerable distance from the institution: thus, for each teaching practice, a group of students had to live away from the 'home' site. The design for working with these new schools anticipated many currently-favoured recommendations, in particular the training of a school-based mentor who was to take on some aspects of supervision.

Three aspects of the mentoring role were identified: one concerned with meta-cognition; one with analysis; one with experiential learning. These were assigned respectively to the supervisor, a school-based teacher-tutor and the class-teacher. The supervisor was expected to see the student-teacher in the classroom on relatively few occasions but to make substantial use of specially-prepared accounts. The class-teacher's account, based on focused observation of classroom work, comprised as nearly as possible a factual record of individual lessons taught by the student-teacher; the teacher-tutor's work, in detailed discussion with the student-teacher, involved analysing classroom events in relation to a set of criterial statements and agreeing a report of this discussion. The supervisor used this evidence to address with the student-teacher questions of how learning was taking place; what was valuable; and what represented an appropriate goal for further development. The roles of the supervisor, the teacher-tutor and the class-teacher were coordinated by the centrality to the scheme of a set of criteria for teaching practice written specifically for this purpose. In order to prepare for this process, a course was provided for teacher-tutors which established them as the link between the school and the institution.

Eight student-teachers comprised the 'experimental' group working in this new context, distinguished from the 'home' group who received the established method of supervision.

PERSPECTIVES ON THE SUPERVISOR'S ROLE

Eleven supervisors for the home group, and two involved in the experimental study, were interviewed in order to elicit views on supervision. The forty-one class-teachers involved over both teaching practices were also interviewed. The interviews took place at the beginning and end of each practice so that changes in responses and behaviours could be monitored. The student-teachers were interviewed and their diaries analysed. There are, then, three perspectives on school-based work: that of the supervisor, the class-teacher and the student-teacher. Their perceptions of the role of the supervisor are discussed in this chapter. In a similar way the three perspectives on the role of the class-teacher are considered in Chapter 9.

THE SUPERVISOR'S PERSPECTIVE

Some of the home supervisors had a strong interest in supervision, a detailed knowledge of different kinds of supervisory practice and a well-thought-out personal vision. Others, being subject tutors for the post-graduate year-group, tended to be motivated more by an interest in and knowledge of particular individuals and their progress, rather than by an intrinsic interest in supervision *per se*.

There was considerable variation in the extent to which they were informed about issues and problems relating to supervision – either at a theoretical or at a practical level. One quarter of them did not articulate a coherent role for themselves as supervisors and tended to see it as unproblematic. It was evident that there was no overall coherence to supervision and that roles were perceived in different ways.

Since the two supervisors for the experimental group had devised the new programme, they shared a commitment and a clear view of the purposes and procedures of supervision, emphasizing that a view of progression in learning to teach was built into the hierarchically organized criteria central to their approach. They were positive about the reasons for the separation of the mentoring role and confident that school-based staff were adequately informed.

For both home and experimental groups, three distinct kinds of role were identified: an ambassadorial role, a cognitive role and a judgemental role. Four of the home supervisors talked about aspects of all three roles; two discussed two roles and the rest considered one only. For the experimental group, each of the three aspects was intrinsic to the organization of the scheme.

The ambassadorial role

The ambassadorial role was mentioned by eight of the thirteen supervisors. Described by one as an initial 'clearing of the ground', it entailed negotiating organizational details, for example, first contacts with schools, student-teacher involvement, hours of teaching, areas of the curriculum to be taught, etc. One tutor's comments summarized the need for an ambassadorial approach, particularly in the role of:

> troubleshooter – to try to facilitate communication between us and the schools, and the student-teachers and the schools. You've got to pick up problems quickly. I think that's part of the skill of the job – to try and nip things in the bud.

The ambassadorial role also included ensuring that relationships continued to flourish and that communications between all parties involved remained easy.

The tutors for the experimental group put considerable emphasis on the established and continuing contact with the schools, via the teacher-tutors, and the formalized close association of the class-teachers with student-teachers' development. It was hoped that this would remove the need for the typical investment of time from supervisors in smoothing out difficulties.

Although a majority suggested that the ambassadorial role was central to ensuring that the teaching practices proceeded smoothly, evidence from diary-writing by the student-teachers suggested that ambassadorial skills were, on occasion, lacking.

The cognitive role

Four supervisors for the home group who discussed their ambassadorial role also talked about the cognitive one, and about the relationship between the two. Overall, nine out of the eleven supervisors discussed a wide range of aspects of the cognitive role, though two made no mention of it. Discussion of cognitive development was not often very precise, largely because of the contention that the specific school context was an important determinant of learning.

The tutors for the experimental group saw cognitive development as the central purpose of the work of all those involved in helping the student-teacher: the class-teacher, the teacher-tutor and the supervisor were all expected continually to address the student-teacher's work in relation to the criteria in order increasingly to promote self-evaluation. The supervisor's role was specifically 'to challenge the student-teacher to see their performance in a wider context . . . the criteria should be used to provoke consideration of other possibilities'.

In the home group there was some vagueness with regard to the use of criteria for development in teaching. Only five of these tutors mentioned any kind of framework. Two others, who had been involved in earlier pilot work with the new teaching practice criteria, continued to work at and make use of some of the ideas. Two supervisors expected student-teachers to provide their own developmental programme based on self-evaluation of personal weaknesses. This latter activity seemed to be premissed on a widespread belief that teachers must be reflective and self-critical: 'In the end, as teachers, if they aren't critical of themselves, well who is going to be?' Yet without an agreed framework for progress or skills, reflection and self-evaluation were difficult, the more so when supervisors, for example, responded to 'whatever seems to come from the lesson. I don't think I have a schedule in my head of things I'm looking for.'

For the experimental group, the situation was quite different. The handbook available to all involved laid out nine foci for observation, each of them subdivided, and established a requirement for each of these to be observed at some time. The student-teacher was expected to take responsibility for ensuring that this happened.

Seven aspects of teaching were identified on which supervisors for the home group stated that they focused with student-teachers. About half mentioned relationships with children and planning and preparation; about one-third referred to self-evaluation, children's responses, and classroom management; task management and relationships with staff each received attention from two. One supervisor mentioned five of these features; the majority talked about two or three, and two made no mention of any.

Most of the categories are illustrated in the following statement, which makes clear the ways in which one supervisor expected to operate:

> My role will be to observe their forms of instruction, their direction as they deal with children, their relationship with children, the manner in which they respond to the children's comments or questions. Within this observational period I would hope that I could see some indication of their management of materials, and the way in which they structure their conversation – based upon the children's responses. So that's what I'll be looking for during the presentation. Afterwards then I intend to possibly have an opportunity to talk about the way they see that item – or that isolated lesson – in the entirety of the theme they're dealing with.

Several others talked in a similar manner about how they would approach their contacts with student-teachers, although it was not always clear in interviews whether observation should be for the purpose of evaluation only or for feedback to student-teachers. There was evidence of some sensitivity towards the ways in which feedback should be given, with a general feeling that it should be positive and supportive. This was considered especially important during first teaching practice, when confidence building was thought to be all-important.

Confidence and competence were generally believed to be linked. One stated:

> I used to rather play that down I think, rather like teachers in classrooms, and not give a lot of positive feedback and encouragement. I am now convinced that the anxiety of the situation is such that you actually must use a lot of positive reinforcement, a lot of encouragement.

A few also stated that they always tried to respond to the stage of development of individuals:

> I ask them to give an account of what's been happening, and then I use that to tune my thinking in to what I might be able to say to them.

In this sense, responding to the individual context is clearly essential, but it leaves uncertain how progress or skills could be developed or monitored. One supervisor suggested how this aspect of supervision might be achieved:

> I try and help students to define a particular area on which they can focus and make further progress. So they set themselves a target and a goal, and I help them then to try and achieve that goal.

Four of them emphasized the need for coherence over the whole course, each experience building up to provide a 'continuum'. It was suggested that class-teachers should perhaps be told more about 'this flow and continuity so that they see how it all fits'.

Three suggested that a priority in school must be to establish a relationship with the cooperating class-teachers and encourage a partnership since the need for shared understandings is so important if supervision is to be effective: 'If I haven't got what I think is some kind of trusting relationship between the teacher, a lot of what goes on can be a charade.' It was felt that class-teachers should be seen to be valued:

> I must talk with the class-teachers because I'm relying on them. It very much depends on them.

One stressed in particular the need to work through practical problem areas with the class-teacher, those areas often overlooked, but often crucial to providing good supervision: 'Should she be there most of the time? Should she intervene at a point when she disagreed with what the student was doing? At what sort of level do you intervene?'

Four tutors mentioned the need to gain feedback on progress from the class-teacher, one of them stating: 'I see my role as being one of reflecting back to the student-teacher the responses from the school, via constructive comment.' They felt that generally 'teachers do want to talk about the student-teacher – they are interested in them becoming better teachers'. However, the problem of time emerged again: class-teachers are usually teaching and often busy during breaks and after school. Repeatedly, it was lack of time which militated against any serious kind of development between teacher and supervisor. As one of them said:

> I think they're pleased to be involved in the partnership. I think the sustained role between supervisor and teachers in a school is very important. I feel that we need to make more time for discussing their role, the school's role.

It was also clear that the number of visits allocated for the first teaching practice was a cause for concern to supervisors: 'What one can actually do as a supervisor is then tremendously constrained and shaped by what you are allowed to do within the institutional framework.' Thus,

> You are reduced in a way to more of a superficial checking up, troubleshooting, keeping-the-communication-channels-going sort of a role.

The judgemental role

There was very little discussion of the judgemental aspect of supervision and no consistent view. One supervisor suggested that the nature of the role was contradictory:

> We should be constructive helpers. We should be helping students to develop as teachers. So we see ourselves as having the same sort of facilitating role as a teacher has with a pupil in the classroom. But on the other hand – the other side of it is that we have an assessment, judgemental role. In a sense we are gatekeepers to the teaching profession, and those two major dimensions are always in conflict with one another.

The lack of discussion of this role may be due to its being taken for granted as essential, but not as being a focus of the practice – unless real problems emerge.

For the experimental group, supervisors intended that judgement should be inherent to the scheme. The criterial statements were organized hierarchically in order to indicate what represents progress and student-teachers were involved in making judgements about their level of competence.

THE CLASS-TEACHER'S PERSPECTIVE

Information about each teaching practice had been made available in a letter to all participating schools. Some supervisors made arrangements with schools by telephone, and student-teachers themselves were made aware of the requirements of the practice. However, written details sent to schools often were not received by the appropriate class-teachers. Visits to schools early in the practice allowed supervisors to remedy such situations without there being any ill-feeling at lack of information. Despite this, about 20 per cent of the participating class-teachers felt they would have liked more information about the general organization and development of the practices.

The majority of class-teachers had clear ideas about the supervisors' role. About half of them felt that it was, primarily, as observer and evaluator or assessor, that is, it was judgemental: 'He is very supportive, but ought to be assessing whether this person is going to be a good teacher.' There was a strong feeling throughout that the roles of class-teacher and supervisor should be complementary, and especially with regard to assessment. Many class-teachers felt that their everyday contact with student-teachers allowed them a detailed view of performance and progress, whereas a supervisor could be involved in but a small part of this. For this reason, they felt that supervisors should involve them in any evaluation, preferably by talking to them before observing a lesson so that they could offer their own perceptions and opinions. Additionally, they expected feedback from supervisors; they wanted a view from someone who was 'divorced from the classroom situation' and who could be objective in ways different from their own. There was also approving reference to the supervisors' knowledge of up-to-date methods and trends, and the importance of this in bringing a wider view to evaluation than their more context-based view: 'I'm just using my gut reactions and what *I* would do.' In order to interpret student-teacher performance and to evaluate fairly, class-teachers also felt that supervisors should be aware of the contexts and constraints of individual schools and how these might interfere with the implementation of strategies learned on courses.

Over half the class-teachers felt that the role of a supervisor was to be 'generally supportive'. This included ambassadorial features – helping, sorting out organizational problems and being available, if necessary, to ease the relationship between class- and student-teachers or to allow them to 'get things off their chest'. In addition, it was considered that supervisors should impress on student-teachers their responsibilities and need for professionalism when entering a school. Being supportive 'also related to cognitive aspects, giving feedback in terms of constructive criticism, advice, guidance and ideas, suggesting something to try out or a different way of working, and by encouraging progress rather than being the 'big brother' who engenders fear. Forty-five per cent of them felt that supervisors should act as a mediator or coordinator between the institution and its courses and expectations and the school and its ways of working. From their point of view, this meant that some background knowledge of the student-teacher was necessary and some idea of where the course was leading so that, for example, it was possible to know if the cognitive aims of the course were being fulfilled.

Although 89 per cent of them had clear views about the role of supervisors at the beginning of teaching practices, a few were less sure at the end of each practice. A feeling of uncertainty pervaded some responses. Many felt that they barely had time to observe any aspect of the anticipated role for supervisors. There was little of the expected involvement in evaluation, or in any aspect of the practice, and many visits were reported as fleeting: 'supervisors just come in, get an impression and leave'; 'they've kept themselves very remote'. On occasion, they were so busy with children that they did not even know that a supervisor had been in the school.

The discrepancy between the expected kinds of coordination between school and the institution and the lack of attention to overall development was commented on by 30 per cent of the class-teachers. One summarized: 'As far as I'm concerned he's come in, seen the lesson, discussed with the student-teacher how she thought the lesson was going, looked at her plans and gone away again. She [the student-teacher] didn't discuss the work at all with me.' There was concern at this: although perceived to be efficient, it gave class-teachers the feeling that their role in the development of a student-teacher, and their knowledge of the progress of that person, was given no real value.

When discussion between supervisor and class-teacher did take place it was not always considered optimal: 'Yes, they're doing wonderfully well' was not considered adequate feedback to class-teachers anxious about their own contribution. One of them stated that the supervisor was 'very positive and very forthcoming', but despite this did not give any help over 'actual practical teaching skills'. The lack of input about how to improve performance consigned the class-teacher to acting instinctively and caused some anxiety. One of them said: 'I assume that everything is running as it should be, but I don't have that knowledge. I just assume.' There was a desire to know from supervisors 'if there was anything we should particularly help the student with, so that we could focus our mind on some aspect', and one plea summarized the voice of many: 'How can I help her become better if I'm not given guidelines?' At the same time, there was a continuing faith in the supervisor: 'I think their ideas are clearly defined in their own minds, but they're not coming across.'

In the experimental group, class-teachers also felt a need to have 'more to do with the supervisor'. Even when the methods of the scheme were clearly enabling them to help the student-teachers, they still felt they needed more support. Although the techniques associated with classroom observation were 'the best thing about it' and 'we knew what we were looking for', it was clearly not enough that supervisors had provided useful ways of working. The relatively strong contact of the institution with the school in the form of the teacher-tutor also proved insufficient to meet the needs of the class-teacher. This is important because, in recognition of there being a succession of class-teachers involved on future teaching practices, the policy for these remote schools was to establish a single, stable contact in the teacher-tutor. However, it seems that the demands of this role could not be met without a specific staffing allocation in schools for this purpose.

THE STUDENT-TEACHER'S PERSPECTIVE

A major difference between the two practices was in the number and length of supervisory visits. For the home group, the intention was that twice as many be made during the second practice. This was reflected in the diary comments which show that two-thirds felt that there had not been enough visits in the first practice, whereas this concern was expressed by only one-third on the second. During the second practice, two-thirds of these visits included the observation of a whole lesson (rather than only a part, or none, of the lesson); this represents a reversal of the proportion during the first practice.

Again for the home group, there were more expressions of satisfaction about supervision during the second teaching practice; this was due to the greater amount of contact or input from supervisors afforded by the increase in both the number of supervisory visits and the number of whole lessons observed. Overall 81 per cent of the student-teachers felt they received satisfactory ambassadorial support on one practice or the other; 86 per cent reported satisfactory cognitive support; only one person felt that at no time did she receive any kind of support at a level to satisfy her.

Table 8.1 shows that, from the experimental group, half expressed dissatisfaction about both the ambassadorial and cognitive aspects of the supervisors' work. However, the major purpose of this study was to play down the role of supervisor so that the responsibility of supervision was handed over to schools. Of more concern was the disappointment that school-based supervisory parties did not give enough attention to their particular roles, particularly the focused, close observation of nominated lessons. Dissatisfaction in the experimental group also arose because their perception of the supervisors' role was very different from that intended. Although the formal observation by the class-teacher was productive, the teacher-tutor provided additional support, and clear progress was reported, there was nonetheless a continuing faith that regular visits by the supervisor would have been helpful.

Overall 45 per cent of them felt that their expectations for the cognitive aspect had not been fulfilled for the first teaching practice, yet they remained optimistic that there would be an even greater emphasis on cognitive development for the second teaching practice, perhaps since this

Table 8.1 Student-teachers' levels of satisfaction with supervisors in the two categories of ambassadorial and cognitive (per cent)

		Ambassadorial			Cognitive		
		TP 1	TP 2		TP 1	TP 2	
			Home	Exp.		Home	Exp.
Level	Good	20	54	25	40	62	25
of	Average	40	15	25	15	15	25
Satisfaction	Poor	40	31	50	45	23	50

(Number of student-teachers reporting given level of satisfaction: total number of student-teachers reporting in this category) × 100 per cent.

feature was stressed in the course handbook: 'Constructive feedback and support using the teaching practice assessment criteria will be given during each visit by the supervisors'; there was also a developing expectation of the need for a distinct ambassadorial role (20 per cent for the first practice; 40 per cent for the second).

Expectations about the judgemental role did not increase, suggesting that there was more concern about how supervisors could be used to their benefit during the practice rather than focusing only on the final evaluation. This was again expressed in the course handbook: 'It is essential to remember that the teaching practice is a learning situation. Certainly there is a need for assessment, but it is not the prime purpose.' Only a few stated that they felt constrained by the judgemental aspect, and many were prepared to try new methods and ideas during visits so that they could gain feedback on these. The question of assessment was discussed mostly in relation to the lack of visits and observation:

> He went through my file and made comments on it and said I had improved, etc. But he actually saw so little of my teaching and being involved with the children, that I find it quite hard to believe that he could have summed me up and written me the good report that he did.

The student-teachers experienced various types of ambassadorial support; the frequency of reference is shown in Table 8.2 in which the five most frequent types (for the student-teachers) are listed. These criteria were important in that they reflected trends about what was wanted and valued, although they may not fully represent all the supervisory activities undertaken.

Over both teaching practices, supervisors were regarded as being generally supportive. This included having a good relationship with them as a central feature, and it was this which had a major impact on cognitive aspects of development. When it was lacking, there was a feeling of unease or even of real depression. A good relationship also allowed for the development of confidence, substantially increased in the experimental

Table 8.2 Student-teachers' experience of ambassadorial support by supervisors (per cent)

Type of ambassadorial support	TP 1	TP 2 Home	Exp.
Generally supportive	53	69	53
Good relationship with student-teacher	59	50	60
Builder of confidence	35	14	64
Took interest, participated in lesson	24	38	22
Good relationship with class-teacher	6	19	7

(Number of student-teachers reporting given type of ambassadorial support: total number of student-teachers in sample) × 100 per cent.

group (64 per cent). A sense of pleasure was apparent when tutors took an interest, or sat down with the children and participated in a lesson, with this being reported by 24 per cent during first practice and by 38 per cent of the home group, later. For the second teaching practice, a higher proportion were aware of the importance of supervisors having a good relationship with the class-teachers. A few were critical of the lack of politeness or lack of communication between them. Poor relationships with class-teachers meant that there was constant tension:

> The teacher seemed quite disgruntled with the supervisor, because work she was expected to do actually left supervisors with very little to do, and *what* she was expected to do was not made clear until too late.

Good relationships provided more of the feeling of 'partnership' that some supervisors valued so highly. In addition to these above criteria, occasional mention was also made of an ability to sort out problems or to make a good impression in school; on the negative side, there was criticism of a lack of consistency in approach between visits – a feature which, although rare, caused a great deal of upset.

The types of cognitive support provided by supervisors, as reported by the student-teachers, are shown in Table 8.3. Giving feedback on an observed lesson, especially for the second teaching practice, was considered the most important aspect of the supervisor's role; only half felt that they got this for both teaching practices. The impact of feedback was to make student-teachers more thoughtful and analytic about their own practice. This is reflected by the 80 per cent of student-teachers in the experimental group who recorded this, with one writing:

> it made me more aware of issues that are already in my mind and my planning, such as developing children's skills. The supervisor helped me to bring these issues to an explicit level of consideration in my mind from a previously slightly low level of thought.

Feedback was also used to encourage linking between theoretical and practical aspects of teaching:

Table 8.3 Student-teachers' experience of cognitive support by supervisors (per cent)

Type of cognitive support	TP 1	TP 2	
		Home	Exp.
Gave feedback on the lesson, constructive criticism	47	58	80
Gave something to aim for; stimulus for progress	29	45	81
Gave ideas, practical suggestions for improvement	41	45	55

(Number of student-teachers reporting given type of ambassadorial support: total number of student-teachers in sample) × 100 per cent.

> We talked for almost an hour about aims and objectives, evaluations of lessons, task matching, evaluating the children's learning and my theme of gender equality. It was a very wide-ranging, but productive discussion.

This kind of feedback emphasized the ways in which supervisors were able to encourage an academic approach to learning set within the context of the school, and was slightly different from the usually practical feedback from class-teachers. An example of how supervisors sometimes involved class-teachers in feedback is shown in the following diary extract:

> What I find most interesting is how he discusses the lesson, how the teaching is going in general, with *both* me and my class-teacher. He really makes use of the relations between all three of us.

In some cases, there was no feedback from class-teachers and student-teachers became totally dependent on their supervisor. Equally, some supervisors depended entirely on class-teachers for feedback: 'I do not think much time was spent observing me at work, but rather talking with the teacher who quite naturally knew most about, and could best assess, my teaching.' Feedback in the form of written reports, or comments on files, was valued so long as it provided a stimulus to thinking.

Ideas and suggestions for improvement were highly valued and were most effective when specifically linked to an aim which could be put into practice: 'I really picked up on the points and concentrated on those.' In the experimental group, the formal criteria provided, in their design, something to work to, which meant there was an overall framework and more organized pattern for progress, rather than a random approach; this was found to be useful particularly in terms of self-awareness about the development of skills.

An example of one student-teacher's experiences of supervision on both practices gave further insight into why criteria should be seriously considered in the improvement of school-based training. This student-teacher had no problems with her practices; in comparison to many others she received good supervision and demonstrated herself to be competent. However, she received few ideas on how to improve. As with others, she felt in need of input to satisfy a desire to make the most of her practice. Even a well-liked, committed and experienced supervisor who sought to promote learning, did not provide any kind of overall vision, coherent plan or strategies for her to develop. In this case supervision lacked a well-defined focus or specific aims for improvement, and this was exacerbated by each of the two class-teachers whose classroom she shared; she stated:

> I do begin to feel a bit stale. I have proved I can run the class efficiently and productively but that is all they seem to want. Surely there is more I can be doing or should be doing. I wish they would say so.

CONCLUSION

Interview data from supervisors, class-teachers and student-teachers, together with diary evidence from the latter, has been analysed for its reference to the role of the supervisor. Three broad categories of the supervisory role were identified: the ambassadorial, the cognitive and the judgemental. There was general agreement about the importance of the ambassadorial role, but its practice provided an interesting picture. Although a majority of student-teachers perceived supervisors to be 'generally supportive' and to have a good relationship with them, the supervisor's relationship with the class-teacher received a low rating in this respect.

All the student-teachers expected the supervisors to contribute to cognitive aspects of their work during the second teaching practice. For the home group, there was a high level of satisfaction that this had been done: their comments suggest that this satisfaction reflected the increased number of visits made by supervisors together with longer periods of observation. The relative dissatisfaction experienced by the experimental group has two interesting features. Firstly, there was no evidence of a differential expectation associated with being in a scheme in which the supervisors made it clear that they intended to play a less prominent role. Secondly, the cognitive support they reported receiving was consistent with the supervisors' intentions, and received high ratings. There is some evidence that these student-teachers received feedback, stimuli and practical suggestions from supervisors which, although infrequent, was highly valued and encouraged them to want more, thereby explaining the lack of satisfaction with the amount of feedback received.

The recognition by student-teachers of the centrality of the cognitive role is in accord with the professed aims for supervision in the course handbook; the relative lack of emphasis on the judgemental role can be interpreted as a consequence of this, and consistent with the desire of all involved to build the student-teachers' confidence. Although a substantially different emphasis was intended for the experimental scheme, where the competence criteria were designed for collaborative goal-setting so that assessment, and eventually self-assessment, drove the learning, this aspect proved to be underdeveloped.

Two important factors were evident in these data. Firstly, in all aspects of the supervisors' work, the lack of time available created problems. To some extent, it was a problem of the shortage of time for supervisors to observe student-teachers; perhaps more significantly, it was the difficulty for the class-teacher to put aside time to discuss matters with both the student-teacher and the supervisor.

The second factor is the need for accessible, usable criteria and an agreed structure for the conduct of teaching practice. In the absence of this, student-teachers and class-teachers are dependent on the supervisor for 'the next step'.

Currently, intending primary school teachers undertake school-based work as one part of a wide course and are attached to schools for relatively short periods of time. Supervisors clearly need to include an ambassadorial role as part of their work in order to smooth out often inevitable difficulties. However, it may be that it is simply not possible to devote sufficient time to this aspect. New approaches to initial training, in which the student-teacher spends much longer periods at the same school, more or less as a permanent member of staff, would sensibly locate ambassadorial aspects in the school's normal management structure. However, if this were successful, it might exacerbate another problem: that of appropriate intervention in terms of the cognitive role of the supervisor. It is clear that the supervisors, in virtue of their being outside the school's system, can bring a different quality of supervision and can contribute to the student-teacher's development in significant ways. If new arrangements persuade the student-teacher to identify with the school and view the supervisor as 'exterior', it may become even more difficult to affect the student-teacher's cognitive development. On the other hand, if clearly stated, universally adopted criteria, or competence statements, became a central part of teacher training, these could serve as the focus for a joint enterprise between schools and training institutions. In the same way as the class-teachers associated with the experimental group were prepared to foster student-teachers' development in relation to the criteria, it may be that in future arrangements all supervisory parties will engage in similar ways. In this case, it would be possible for those same people to undertake the judgemental role jointly.

Chapter 9

The purpose and impact of school-based work: the class-teacher's role

Elisabeth Dunne and Richard Dunne

INTRODUCTION

Training establishments rely heavily on class-teachers and their goodwill, and the periods that student-teachers spend in schools are thought to be vital to their development. Some researchers (e.g. Copeland, 1980; Zeichner, 1980) suggest that the role model provided by classroom-teachers has the greatest influence on student-teacher development, and Teel and Hollingsworth (1988) recognize from evidence provided by their case-studies of pre-service teachers that the support and guidance of both supervising tutor and class-teacher are fundamental to progress. However, little is known about the kinds of roles and relationships that develop in this context.

In this institution little formal attention was given to the role of the class-teacher. That they were asked to contribute to the summative assessment of the student-teachers in their classroom carried an implication of the need to observe. They were expected to be involved in planning and ensuring that the student-teachers had a varied practice and increasing responsibility. The class-teachers for the experimental group were given a specific role which included modelling, advising, joint planning, observing and making written comments about observed lessons, in addition to the general requirement to be involved in assessment.

Perceptions on the role of the class-teacher were gained from interviews and diaries as outlined in Chapter 8. There are again three perspectives on aspects of school-based work: that of the class-teacher, the supervisor and the student-teacher.

THE CLASS-TEACHER'S PERSPECTIVE

Class-teachers talked in most detail about a small range of activities, namely: planning; the various restrictions they were asked to impose on student-teachers to ensure that they did not take on too much respon-sibility too quickly; the ways in which they helped and encouraged development; and observation and feedback. These are discussed in turn.

Planning

Most class-teachers felt that since the introduction of the National Curriculum, a tight control had to be kept over planning; 90 per cent of them made the point that the National Curriculum now *had* to provide the core for planning activities. Over both practices, almost a third of class-teachers were involved in team planning for the year group or whole school, and here the planning schedules were tightest, since deviations might have interfered with parallel groups. However, they tried to make student-teachers feel they had 'become members of the team.'

Many teachers, rather than dictating precise areas for planning, attempted to provide a framework so that student-teacher ideas, interests and abilities would be used. Several class-teachers expressed enjoyment or benefit at having to plan alongside student-teachers. Where they were valued for their expertise in a specific subject, joint planning was considered especially useful; this tended to occur for science in particular, with class-teachers admitting that student-teachers were in this instance able to help *them*. One also stated: 'I get quite a lot from [joint planning] as well, because you actually think about the mechanics of teaching, which [otherwise] you never do.'

Restrictions

The institution also suggested that certain restrictions should be imposed on all student-teachers in the classroom. During the first teaching practice, for instance, they were expected to team-teach with the class-teacher or paired student-teachers; in the second teaching practice, they were to build up to whole-class management, to cover core curriculum areas and their own specialism, and be involved in up to 75 per cent of the teaching load. All class-teachers provided small groups of children for the first teaching practice and then allowed whole-class teaching, but a few handed over a whole class straight away for the second practice. Positive decision-making by the class-teacher about the management of these restrictions was important to the development of student-teacher security and confidence and the building of a good working relationship between them.

On the whole, class-teachers gradually reduced these restrictions constraints during each practice, so that student-teachers assumed the greater responsibilities of, for example, larger groups, a wider range of curriculum areas, or school assemblies, and culminating in long periods of whole-class teaching.

Forms of help

Class-teachers perceived their role mostly in relation to the nature and extent of the help they provided and clearly recognized the complexity of this. They all believed that they should offer guidance and support, but there was considerable variation in the ways they interpreted this. The forms of help which they considered most important are outlined in Table 9.1, which shows the proportion of class-teachers who talked about each category during interviews.

Table 9.1 Class-teachers' reports of which forms of help they provided

| | Student-teachers (per cent) | | | |
| | TP1 | | TP 2 | |
Forms of help given	Beginning	End	Beginning	End
Enabling self-evaluation	72	76	100	89
Developing management and control	69	61	74	39
Acting as a role model	64	19	21	17
Allowing learning from mistakes	23	48	37	39
Boosting confidence	31	5	26	22
Monitoring planning	0	38	79	33

The perceived need to help student-teachers with self-evaluation was consistently high, as was the feeling they needed to work with them to improve all forms of management and control. Class-teachers who believed that there was a need to provide a role model gradually withdrew this over each practice; the boosting of confidence also lessened over the same period. On the other hand, there was an increase in allowing them to learn from mistakes, that is, they allowed a gradually freer rein. With planning, class-teachers became more critical over the practice. Initially they did not want to cause upset. They also saw a need for student-teachers to get feedback on their own efforts before they could make clear the relationships between, say, task-matching and children's interest and performance. For the second teaching practice, they felt the need to set higher expectations for planning, but by the end of the practice student-teachers were left far more to their own devices.

Many teachers suggested that the giving of help was dictated by individual needs. Thus, the drop in figures for management and control, and for planning, may illustrate a decreasing need for help in these areas. Some suggested that most of their help was in response to requests: they saw themselves more as a 'consultant'. In these cases, the decreasing figures may indicate a change in needs of student-teachers as their ability or confidence developed. About half the teachers stated that their efforts were of real importance – and often those who believed that their presence as a role model was a powerful method of developing learning. They were also pleased and flattered at the visible evidence of their ways of operating being adopted, but made it clear that, rather than providing the 'definitive' model, they were providing starting points, until, with more experience, student-teachers found their 'own way'.

Observation and feedback

Most observation was informal, with teachers just 'being around, doing things'. It was said to be more difficult in the first teaching practice, since classes were often divided into three groups, at least in the early days, with the teacher taking one and the paired student-teachers taking the others. Observation was considered less necessary towards the end of each teaching practice, and they received very little if they were thought to be 'particularly competent', since observation was usually thought of in terms of 'picking up problems' rather than in the sense of 'developing learning'. A quarter stated that they observed on a more formal basis for the second teaching practice, often two or three times a week. The experimental cohorts were observed frequently and formally, by design; for two-thirds of them this occurred at least three times weekly.

All class-teachers stated that they gave critical feedback after observing. Throughout the teaching practices, much of this focused on management and control, as well as matching of tasks. There was a particular emphasis on these at the beginning of the second teaching practice, making sure they got off to a good start. One-third gave feedback on self-evaluation.

The difference between the home and experimental groups was that frequent and formal observation and feedback for the experimental group was focused by the use of the teaching practice criteria. These were appreciated because they 'narrow down what you've actually got and yet it also makes you aware of the different things that are happening'. They helped in considering progress and development, providing 'something to build on' and allowing one teacher in particular to examine her own practice. Class-teachers in the experimental group were also quite clear about their role with respect to feedback since, beyond their personal judgements, they could refer to specific points laid out in the book of criteria. The system also encouraged putting features raised during feedback into immediate practice, which was considered beneficial.

THE SUPERVISOR'S PERSPECTIVE

The majority of the eleven supervisors interviewed cited the class-teacher's role as the most important aspect of the teaching practice and the relationship with the student-teacher as the 'focal point', or the major context for 'any extensive professional dialogue'. Two supervisors emphasized the need for 'partnership'. Despite agreement on such features, they had very little to say on what the class-teacher's role entailed. Seven of them stated the obvious fact that since the class-teacher is around most of the time the role centres on daily routine and one linked this to the essential passing on of 'craft knowledge'. Reference was also made to the class-teacher's role as multi-faceted being 'adviser and helper and critic'. One supervisor suggested that in general the role needed to be given more thought than at present. A few suggested that a major difference between the role of the class-teacher and their own role is that the class-teacher deals with day-to-day practicalities whereas supervisors should provide links with the more philosophic or theoretical aspects studied in the institution, and should look to future improvements in education. One supervisor summarized: 'I feel that the class-teacher is supervising the doing and I am trying to supervise the reflecting on the doing.' Despite such comments, there was no shared coherent vision of what class-teachers should be doing.

The supervisors for the experimental group had established a specific role for the class-teachers which emphasized modelling classroom activity, joint planning with the student-teacher, formal observation and annotation, and feedback. Much of this was 'fairly typical' practice for class-teachers, but here it was clarified and formalized. The main difference arose in there being a coherent framework provided by the criterial statements, so that clear patterns of development could be monitored.

THE STUDENT-TEACHERS' PERSPECTIVE

Virtually all diary comments referred to the class-teacher's behaviours, involvement and interaction. Since the student-teachers had been asked to write in their diaries about what was of most interest or importance to them, this suggests that, once in school, the role of the class-teacher was what concerned them above all else. Analysis therefore focuses on the specific kinds of behaviour about which they commented.

Teacher helpfulness

The majority (78 per cent) felt that, in general terms, their co-operating class-teachers were helpful and supportive throughout the teaching practices. This was particularly the case for those in the experimental cohort, and was probably related to a particular interest in their welfare, since they were distant from their home institution. Table 9.2 gives an overview of the specific kinds of helpful behaviours discussed across both teaching practices, and the proportion of diary-writers who mentioned each of them. Thus, for example, 55 per cent reported class-teachers giving encouragement (which was found helpful) on the first

Table 9.2 Proportion of student-teachers mentioning helpful behaviours from class-teachers

	Student-teachers (per cent)		
Helpful behaviour	TP1	TP2	Either or both
Gave encouragement, boosted confidence	55	50	72
Gave feedback and critical appraisal	33	63	72
Involved in planning and preparation	55	30	67
Discussed management and control	39	44	56
Provided a positive role model	39	31	56

(Number of student-teachers reporting given behaviour: total number of student-teachers in sample) × 100 per cent.

teaching practice; 50 per cent reported on the same feature for the second practice. Altogether 72 per cent of them wrote about this aspect. Of the remaining 28 per cent, half were concerned about the lack of encouragement (see below) which means that almost all of them wrote about it at some point or in some context. A similar pattern is seen in each of the other categories.

Since there had been no specific guidance in relation to writing about the class-teacher's role, it is interesting that all these five areas were mentioned by a consistently high proportion over the two practices. The feature given most attention at any time was that of feedback and critical appraisal during the second teaching practice (63 per cent). It is also of interest that these categories are very similar to those discussed by the class-teachers themselves.

For each of the categories represented in Table 9.2 there is another category in Table 9.3 which is the converse of it. There is no relationship between the incidence of comments in each category because, firstly, not all diary-writers mention any particular feature and, secondly, they may have written about both (for example, a teacher may give excellent feedback, but not frequently enough for satisfaction). Half of them reported not always receiving the support and attention they felt they needed, though suggestions were offered to explain the lack of help; for example, lack of experience with student-teachers, and the general pressures and insecurities in a period of change in schools.

In addition to a generalized lack of support, there were specific class-teacher behaviours which were considered unhelpful. Across both teaching practices, a common cause for concern was the demoralizing effect of teachers who undermined confidence, or were negative or disapproving in their attitude. However, whereas this was the major cause for complaint in the first teaching practice, it was superseded by the tension created by interference in lessons during the second teaching practice. Issues and comments tended to be similar for both teaching practices; when there

Table 9.3 Proportion of student-teachers mentioning non-helpful behaviours from class-teachers

	Student-teachers (per cent)		
Non-helpful behaviour	TP1	TP2	Either or both
Demoralizing, not encouraging	44	33	56
Not enough feedback, critical appraisal	39	25	50
Restrictions on planning and preparation	33	22	50
Interfered in management and control	22	44	50
Provided a negative/no role model	22	31	39

(Number of student-teachers reporting given non-helpful behaviour: total number of student-teachers in sample) × 100 per cent.

were distinct differences, these are made clear in the descriptions below. This is the case also for the experimental group since there was no real difference between them and the 'home' group in terms of categories; what was different, however, was the content of statements, in particular for the 'feedback' category.

Encouragement and confidence boosting

Student-teachers felt encouraged when, in the early days of teaching, it was made clear that their presence was not a burden and that the class-teacher took an interest in them, welcomed their ideas and allowed them some kind of responsibility. The freedom to try out ideas for lesson-content and to experiment with different methods of management, especially for the second teaching practice, reinforced the feeling of acceptance and trust between them. They talked about class-teachers being sensitive to their needs, not embarrassing them by watching too closely in the early days and taking care not to 'knock confidence': 'She seemed to get the balance right, of being interested in what I was doing and yet keeping her distance and giving me space.' Being given responsibility for the whole class boosted confidence when successful, but was demoralizing when not so good.

Interestingly, the word 'praise' was used by very few. A sense of being part of the ongoing classroom situation, of being useful and valued was more important than direct praise, as was knowing they were making progress, that they were not failing. For the second teaching practice, class-teachers used encouragement to 'push' student-teachers into those aspects of teaching and the curriculum which gave them the most difficulty, and this was appreciated.

There was a tendency to write about negative behaviours in detail since they often had a deep impact on individuals, but direct criticism by class-teachers was rare, and feelings of disapproval may have been attributable more to student-teacher insecurity or over-sensitivity than reality. Comments also indicated a lack of communication between them: 'There have been times when I have sensed uncertainty or disapproval for what I'm doing. . . . I wasn't sure if there was a problem or not and what the problem might be.' A few class-teachers were considered over-critical: 'My organization skills do leave a lot to be desired but I feel you can only learn by experience and I haven't really got much experience.' Interaction with class-teachers was sometimes extremely difficult. On at least one teaching practice, 22 per cent of the student-teachers experienced this. For example: 'If I pushed [the teacher] he would give me some advice, but as a general rule left me to my own devices. On some occasions he would ask me a week later what I had done with the class the previous week.'

Some class-teachers were considered not to want student-teachers in their classrooms at all. This created tension and sometimes difficulties with the student-teacher feeling 'rather an intrusion', sometimes spending the entire teaching practice feeling unwanted and uninformed. One of them stated: 'If I don't ask I'm often overlooked. Arrangements are changed at short or no notice. I adapt, but wonder if they appreciate my position.'

For the first teaching practice, when they were lacking in confidence and concerned about disrupting the class routines and organization, several of them considered they were imposing on the class-teacher's time: 'I feel rather sorry for her being landed with me, upsetting systems, etc., although I have tried to fit in.' However, by the second teaching practice, there was a clearly expressed feeling that, since this was the last chance to get themselves sorted out before taking on their own classrooms, they had to make the most of the situation, whatever they felt.

Feedback and critical appraisal

The rise in feedback from 33 per cent (first TP) to 62 per cent (second TP) can be attributed to several factors: firstly, more time was available to class-teachers for observation and feedback during this practice, with student-teachers being responsible for the whole class for longer periods; secondly, teachers were less concerned about upsetting them or undermining confidence and were more readily critical. Also, since feedback was considered crucial to the development of teaching skills at this stage, student-teachers were prepared to demand feedback more vociferously. Also for the experimental group, feedback was formalized and intrinsic to the scheme.

The majority perceived critical feedback to be the most important factor in the development of their learning, so long as it did not undermine their confidence.

The impact of feedback was evident: 'It is just what I need. If I don't learn from this experience, then it's my fault, no-one else's.' Positive feedback was always valued: for example, 'giving me a very positive attitude towards teaching – which I love'. However, there was a fine line between what they perceived as 'constructive' and what they felt was negative criticism, and therefore unhelpful. The distinction may have been dependent, in the main, on general attitude and confidence. One of them described a teacher who pointed out 'flaws and problems' early on in the practice. At first this was found 'very disconcerting', but after a few weeks the student-teacher 'came to terms with the observations and began to be positive about any criticism'.

The diaries constantly illustrated that they were concerned with themselves as learners. However only a few detailed specific kinds of feedback, for example:

> Control is getting better. Need to be more alert when dealing with one thing as to what is going on elsewhere. Still need to get explanations more accurate. Suggests stopping class at intervals to discuss the next stage. I know when I have done OK as the work is good, but I should sense it before, not after!

They made it clear that critical feedback enabled them to develop by making them aware of those aspects of teaching they needed to practice. When they were provided with situations which allowed them to act immediately on feedback, they reported being most able to incorporate both teacher criticism and self-appraisal into their ways of working. Team-teaching situations, where the same lesson was taught to different groups, allowed a 'feedback into practice' approach. Some class-teachers provided detailed feedback about a lesson with half of the class, which was then repeated with the rest of the children. Some arranged that a similar lesson to one that had failed could be attempted again, having made decisions as to how it might be improved.

One-third of those who were concerned about feedback in their first teaching practice complained that their class-teachers were not critical enough; for example:

> Everything was brilliant or fantastic. She didn't once make any constructive criticism about the way I approached a particular lesson or the way in which I handled the children . . . she might not have wanted to upset me, but surely she should have realized that I was there to learn.

Some class-teachers remained reluctant to be critical even when specifically asked and there was a widely-shared feeling of their being 'slightly uncomfortable about criticizing'.

During the second teaching practice there was slightly more feedback by supervisors, which took the onus off the class-teachers. Yet for some there remained the feeling that feedback should be undertaken more seriously, and that leaving a student-teacher 'to work on my own, planning lessons and teaching them and evaluating them myself' was not appropriate. One stated:

> I realized that in fact I am not being supervised at all, except when I specifically ask for advice. [The teacher] obviously feels happy about what I am doing but a little more guidance would be appreciated.

Involvement in planning and preparation

Altogether, 69 per cent discussed help with planning and preparation and this was consistently high over both teaching practices. Comments during the first teaching practice were little more than passing references to 'good planning advice', increasing involvement, or the length of time devoted to it. During the second practice, planning was written about at greater length and with greater awareness of the different levels necessary.

Experiences of planning varied enormously. For example, in some cases, it was a collaborative activity on a daily basis. For others, a formal weekly plan was developed through organized discussion sessions, and this tended to lead to a greater sense of security. Some were free to plan by themselves; others felt constantly constrained by long-term schemes of work. Planning was structured: 'Planning is very detailed in advance, so I was really falling in line with plans made last term for core curriculum subjects.' Some teachers were seen as uneasy about abandoning their own plans and allowing student-teachers to take initiatives. In general during the second teaching practice there was greater thought given to why teachers behaved as they did. Although illustrating some understanding of the nature of being a teacher, this did not alleviate frustration: constant control on planning each lesson 'did not allow me to make the mistakes I needed to'.

The overriding feeling from the diaries was one of not being quite sure if the kinds of planning undertaken were adequate. Discussion of planning did not always seem to be specific enough for them to know if what they were doing was appropriate. This may have been a consequence of class-teachers not wanting to stifle planning, or not wanting to be over-critical, but it may have arisen from lack of clarity about how much or what kind of help was appropriate.

Classroom management and control

Discussing day-to-day organization with class-teachers was said to be important in maintaining the smooth running of the classroom. Observation periods, especially at the beginning of teaching practices, allowed the student-teachers to pick up tips on what they considered to be the 'skills and techniques' of organization and were reported as enabling them to manage the classroom more effectively. However, general organization often remained problematic for them, and several commented that they looked forward to having their own classroom and deciding on their own ways of operating in the future.

Considerable attention was paid by class-teachers to the basic rules of good practice, such as the initial control of children. They tended to stress the need to 'keep the class in shape', insisting that routines were adhered to and constantly reinforced. Student-teachers were generally keen to adopt the class-teacher's ways, especially when they were helped to understand the reasons for them. It was halfway through the second teaching practice that one of them learned a vital point about managing children:

> Learnt this week the importance of not making idle threats, as kids soon latch on to this. Started now to stop making them – or as teacher pointed out, children will take me for a ride.

One of them in particular wrote about her developing awareness of the personal problems of children, and how this may have related to behaviour problems in school. After talking to the class-teacher about such issues and the influence of home background, she thought that her dealings with these pupils would be more sensitive. Inevitably, a few pupils were found to be disruptive; they turned to the class-teacher for strategies to deal with this, but they did not necessarily gain the help they wanted: 'I felt I could have dealt with it better, but was not given any suggestions how.'

Over both teaching practices, 44 per cent felt they had constraints imposed on them which limited the possibilities in learning to manage and control. Unwanted constraints were discussed more frequently in the second teaching practice (37 per cent from 17 per cent). They reported frustration at not being able to organize the class as they wanted, at constantly having to negotiate what and when they could teach, and feeling that their work took second place. Even some of the most helpful and supportive teachers did, on occasion, constrain them, perhaps not realizing the extent to which they wanted to be involved in all aspects of the daily routine, however apparently trivial.

They also felt constrained at times by the kinds of management imposed on them by the school system. For example, when children choosing their own seating meant that some groups were less task-oriented than others, a student-teacher stated: 'I don't really approve of this set-up, but felt it would create too much upset if I changed it.' However, in this instance, the recognition that certain kinds of organization have certain consequences, which might be worth avoiding in future, may be an important step in learning to be an effective teacher.

ROLE MODELS

Across both teaching practices, 56 per cent of them discussed ways in which teachers did, or did not, provide a role model. They were convinced that the chance to watch someone teaching enabled them to learn about discipline, about dealing with children and about the general organization of pupils as well as about specific techniques. Watching a 'good teacher' was something they enjoyed, and for some of them it seemed more important than any other activity. This feature is interesting since observation of class-teachers was not valued during school experience, in the first term. It seems that at this stage they had a clearer view of what class-teachers were doing and the ways in which this could inform their own learning. For the second teaching practice, different teachers with different techniques created a renewed interest in observation.

Amongst a small proportion, an interesting development was apparent; they stated that they moved from simply watching, to watching and then deliberately modelling themselves on the class-teacher's behaviours: 'I have copied her style of classroom organization and discipline.' Yet class-teachers perceived this modelling to occur right from the beginning of the first teaching practice; it may be that in the early stages it was more a kind of mimicking, which later became consciously adopted or rejected. One student-teacher's account of modelling herself on the class-teacher (during her second teaching practice) is of particular interest:

> The class-teacher was very much a disciplinarian. She had excellent control of her class and made it look so easy. I was fascinated by this and was keen to see how it was achieved. I didn't like the style to start with but soon found that it was successful. The teacher felt I was far too soft and didn't pick children up enough, so I found myself changing to be more like her and began to feel more at home with the style.

This kind of change – as well as this kind of description of change – was unusual, since generally when there were reports of clashes in ideas and views, their pre-existing beliefs were strengthened rather than relaxed.

Several stated that, although they were able to achieve a good personal relationship with the class-teacher, the teaching approach was so alien to their own thinking that they did not want to use it as a model. Otherwise, the lack of a role model was due in the main to the absence of the teacher from the classroom. Periods when the class-teacher was available for observation often had to be negotiated; this was something they became more determined to do as time went on, and as they felt more resolved to gain what they wanted from teaching practices.

During the second teaching practice, four of them were used as replacement teachers while their class-teachers were ill, or covered for other absent staff, or were out on courses. Thus they had no kind of role model, which they continued to want. They felt that the school was taking advantage of them because they could cope by themselves: 'I felt it was wrong as I still have so much to learn. I was coping OK really, but I wanted to cope better.' Awareness of the kinds of pressures on schools did not provide a justification to them for their being left without supervision, since they felt that the class-teacher's role was not being adequately fulfilled.

It was unwanted intervention from class-teachers during their lessons (mentioned by one-third of them) which caused more upset and tension than any other aspect of teacher behaviour. The circumstances in which it arose were many and various. Some teachers seemed, as suggested previously, to find it difficult to 'let go' of their classes for any period of time. It was not always clear whether this occurred because of lack of discussion, which meant there was no clear plan of action, because teachers tried to make life easier and did not fully appreciate that this was not always wanted, or because they wanted to retain their authority.

Perhaps most frustrating was the following kind of situation:

> I subsequently got very angry by this lesson. It was meant to be my lesson but the teacher intervened at several points in a way which very much usurped my position as 'teacher for that lesson', taking advantage of his own status in the school. Pretty much shattered my confidence.

Others reported: 'I find that when she sees me about to, for example, tell a child off, she comes in and does it, which is frustrating', or 'I had expected to be introducing the lesson. I was about to start, when the teacher walked in and introduced it.' Even when there was an awareness of the need to plan and negotiate it was not always easy to achieve: 'It is sometimes difficult to pin my teachers down as to what they exactly want me to do and whether I should be leading a lesson or not.' It was clear that, for many, developing skills in communication and negotiation became central to their progress in school.

Class-teachers also intervened when there were differences in beliefs about principles of practice and educational values. For example, a difference of opinion about correcting spellings resulted in the student-teacher feeling undermined and angry. Such incidents often reinforced existing values and beliefs, especially on the second teaching practice when they were more confident in their abilities as teachers. However, they sometimes also showed more understanding of the teacher's point of view, possibly because these differences often obliged class-teachers to express the reasons for their own views.

CONCLUSION

A feature which dominated the teaching practice diaries was the way in which student-teachers put time, thought and effort into learning to work alongside class-teachers. It was not something they found easy. Supervisors were aware of the need to work at this, suggesting that 'there is no habit of collaborating' and that they 'still treat the teachers – not like colleagues – but like somebody in charge over them'. By the second teaching practice many of them, though not all, were certainly more confident, not only with teaching, but in terms of being prepared to assert themselves and make demands. From their statements, it seems that the intense pressure of such a short course, and the need to make the most of it, served as an incentive for this change in behaviour.

A good relationship with the class-teacher seemed to be the most important aspect of teaching practices and fundamental to learning. The influence of helpfulness and general support in terms of confidence-building and enjoyment, as well as learning, was also evident. When there was little support, there was a feeling of being abandoned, and resentment at the lack of guidance, features which were not conducive to learning. As well as the class-teacher's role being central to development, overall feelings of being 'wanted and useful' were boosted by inclusion in the life of the school as a whole – opportunities for team-teaching, to take other classes, invitations to staff meetings, and so on. Half of them mentioned this kind of involvement, and for some it was very important, especially when individual teachers added to their general experience through additional interest and support.

From the class-teachers' point of view, despite a few uneasy beginnings, there was a sense of warmth towards student-teachers. They were appreciated for their helpfulness, their enthusiasm and their commitment: 'We feel that when they go it will be a sad loss . . . they've supported us, the values that we have and the policies in the school.' There was excitement at the talents of some and at watching them develop. Many of them opened their class-teachers' eyes to new ideas, new ways of working and also, on occasion, to see particular children in a fresh light, so that it became a reciprocal relationship. Despite the time that had to be given to them, especially for the first teaching practice, there was no report of this being too great a burden. Most class-teachers observed, helped, gave constructive criticism and adjusted their ways of working to suit individuals and the stage of the course. However, not all were sensitive to the needs of the student-teachers in their care. That teachers do not always have the expertise to be teacher educators is a point stressed by Feiman-Nemser and Buchmann (1987) who stated that there is a need for time and commitment to develop the necessary understandings, skills and orientations. Although the institution made clear certain aspects of what was expected, there was little time in schools to pay any great attention to this. If the present emphasis on school-based training continues, then clarification of issues will be crucial, as well as time and funding.

Chapter 10

Knowledge bases and teaching performance

Neville Bennett and Rosemary Turner-Bisset

INTRODUCTION

The professional judgements of the Inspectorate and research on teaching and learning in classrooms reported in Chapter 1, have strongly implicated the role of subject knowledge for teaching in teaching performances. Similarly, case studies of learning to teach have identified relationships between types of teacher knowledge and teaching action. Nevertheless current claims for the impact of knowledge bases are stronger than the empirical evidence, particularly with regard to primary teachers, who most often operate as generalists rather than subject specialists. At a time when National Curriculum implementation is forcing consideration of specialist teaching in the higher age ranges in primary schools it is even more important to have a clearer understanding of the relationship between knowledge bases and teaching performance. As such, one of the research questions addressed in this study was – do student-teachers teach their specialist subject to 7–11-year-olds to higher levels of competence than other students?

METHOD

As was explained in earlier chapters the students entered one of four subject strands and followed a specialist curriculum course in that subject together with general curriculum courses. To answer the research question posed therefore ideally required a sampling of student-teachers from each of the maths, science and music strands who had high, and comparable, levels of subject knowledge for teaching. Their teaching performances could then be contrasted with student-teachers having lower knowledge levels. However, as with all field studies, achieving the conditions for a true experimental design was not possible. For example, high and comparable levels of knowledge could not be attained in, and across, the strands. The music group was much better qualified in music than the mathematics group were in mathematics, and the science group in science, and this was reflected in their pre-test scores (Table 10.1).

Table 10.1 shows that the music group is substantially, and highly significantly, more knowledgeable in music than the other groups, both in the students as a whole, and in the study sample. (See Appendix for changes in music scores from pre- to post-test.) This superiority in knowledge is far greater than either the maths or science groups demonstrated in their subject area (see Chapters 2 and 3). A simple rank-order analysis of the pre-test scores of the six student-teachers in the three subjects shows this effect clearly. The average rank order of the music sample was 52, compared to 17 for the mathematics sample and 6 for the science group. This pattern was not present in the mathematics and science scores, where the average ranks of the maths and science groups were only slightly above average, and not significantly different from the average rank order of the other groups.

Table 10.1 Music knowledge: pre-test scores for each group (per cent)

Curriculum group	All students mean	Sample mean
Mathematics	27.5	27.5
Science	23.9	20.6
Music	45.3	47.0
Early years	27.4	27.0
Total	31.1	30.5

In sum, therefore, the music group had a uniformly high level of subject knowledge for teaching in music which was substantially higher than that of the other groups, whereas students in the science and mathematics groups had an average level of subject knowledge for teaching in their subject, which was not significantly higher than that of other groups.

If, as indicated by previous studies, subject knowledge for teaching is a necessary ingredient in competent teaching performances, then the music students should teach music at higher levels of competence than students from other strands, but science and mathematics students respectively would not be expected to teach science and mathematics any better than students from other strands. It was these expectations that were put to the test in this aspect of the study.

The same random sample of six student-teachers per strand who were completing diaries also participated in this aspect of the study. This data collection sample was then reduced for analysis purposes to four per strand, in order to control teaching quality. These were selected on the basis of final teaching reports in order to ensure the same distribution of quality within each strand.

The sixteen student-teachers were observed on both teaching practices, i.e. in weeks 15–19, and weeks 27–34 of the 36-week course. Each was observed for two days in each practice, and on each of these days data were gathered whilst they taught both their specialist subject, and other subjects. Little control could be exerted over which other subjects were observed since this normally had to fit in with school timetables. In total, each student-teacher was observed for four days on a minimum of ten lessons.

The format for each observation was as follows:

 (i) Prior to each lesson the student-teacher completed, and handed to an observer, a pre-lesson questionnaire (see Appendix A.1) which detailed their planning in the following areas:
content and task chosen;
task purposes;
presentation strategies, including use of materials;
classroom organization;
children's learning and its diagnosis;
task differentiation.

 (ii) An audio-recording of the lesson was acquired by equipping the student-teacher with a radio-microphone. The recording was later transcribed for detailed analysis.

(iii) The observation of a trained observer who noted, in particular, those aspects which would be obscured in the audio-recording, e.g. student-teacher and pupil activity patterns, classroom order, grouping arrangements.

(iv) A post-lesson interview undertaken shortly after the completion of the lesson by the observer (see Appendix A.2). The questions in the interview reflected those in the pre-lesson questionnaire, e.g. to what extent they thought their purposes had been achieved; what the children had learned; what the main points of strength and weakness were. These questions allowed them to reflect on, and evaluate, their performance and planning.

 (v) An independent judgement of the lesson by the observer written prior to the post-task interview, based on a similar set of categories to those in (i) and (iv) above.

ANALYSIS

A crucial question in considering the link between knowledge bases and teaching performance is of course the definition of teaching performance. In order to retain theoretical and ecological validity, the criteria adopted in this study had to reflect both the theoretical perspectives underpinning the study and the criteria/teaching competences towards which the student-teachers were being trained. As indicated in Chapter 8, considerable effort had been expended by the institution concerned to develop a set of criteria closely grounded in contemporary theories of, and research on, teaching and learning. This had resulted in an instrument containing nine dimensions of teaching, each of which were differentiated into eight levels of capability or competence (Dunne and Harvard, 1990). These dimensions are:

1 Planning and preparation
2 Teaching (i)   direct instruction
3 Teaching (ii) guided practice
4 Teaching (iii) structured conversation
5 Ethos
6 Management of materials
7 Management of order
8 Monitoring
9 Reflection

The word 'competence' is another term which has attracted multiple definition, and around which still ring echoes of behavioural objectives. In this study we characterize the act of teaching by the word 'performance', and from the observation of performances identify levels of capability within the teaching dimension by the word 'competence'.

Judgements of teacher actions within performances, and of levels of competence achieved, were made on the basis of the following data:

(a) Preactive: judgements of planning and preparation, and reflection/ evaluation, were based on the pre-lesson schedule and the post-lesson interview.
(b) Interactive: judgements were based on the categorization of student-teacher talk from lesson transcripts, supported where necessary by the observation data.

The starting points for the development of a system for categorizing talk were the institution's dimensions of teaching and Shulman's list of knowledge bases. Attempts to integrate these in the developmental process revealed that:

(i) when analysing the act of teaching the list of knowledge bases are not discrete. For example, the act of planning and preparing tasks incorporating appropriate representations of content requires not only a knowledge of content, but also a knowledge of curriculum and a knowledge of learners. Similarly, the provision of an appropriate classroom context for the tasks planned necessitates general pedagogical knowledge, knowledge of educational contexts, and of educational purposes. In other words there appear to be two underlying dimensions of knowledge – pedagogical content knowledge and general pedagogical knowledge, which operate together. These dimensions are very similar in kind to the distinction between the intellectual and logistical aspects of teacher's work proposed by Kennedy (1991). On her definition the intellectual side of teacher's work entails interpreting classroom events as they occur, making sound pedagogical decisions, and judging the outcomes of those decisions. The logistical side entails managing the work as it progresses, bringing off-task pupils back on task, re-directing pupils who are heading in the wrong direction and responding appropriately to pupil questions. Kennedy argues that these work in tandem, 'for the choice of a question to pose is based on the teacher's understanding of the subject matter and an interpretation of what students (i.e. pupils) know . . ., and the interpretation of classroom events is influenced by the teacher's knowledge of his or her own logistical capabilities'.

(ii) Talk fell into two teaching modes – direct instruction and structured conversation, hereafter called didactic and interactive teaching.

(iii) Additional categories become necessary to account for all talk. For example there was no category to record talk relating to task management which was pedagogical in nature but did not contain subject knowledge.

(iv) It became clear that the eight levels within each dimension in the Dunne and Harvard scheme were an unnecessary refinement. Student-teacher performances could, with validity, be categorized on four levels.

The resultant system for analysing talk is represented in Figure 10.1. The first classification concerns whether the talk is intellectual or logistical (i.e. contains pedagogical content knowledge or general pedagogical knowledge). The second classification concerns whether the talk mode is didactic or interactive (direct instruction or structured conversation). The third concerns the purpose of that talk. Two such categories are contained on the intellectual side – the management of input, and monitoring. On the logistical side of teaching there are three – the management of activities, of order and of materials.

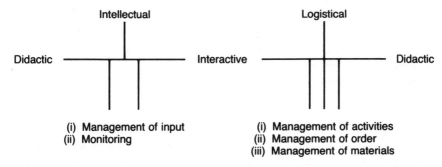

Figure 10.1 Categorization of student-teacher talk

In categorizing the transcripts the procedure was to read through and code each utterance with a category and a level. The number of words in each utterance was then counted.

For example, the following extract contains three utterances:

1 ['They're rhyming words but they're describing words aren't they? They're words which are describing what happens.] 2 [Do you remember the word game that we did last week with the cat in the middle of those hexagons? The word cat and you had to think of lots of different describing words. 3 [Steven put it away please] – lots of different describing words. Do you remember that?]

The first utterance is talk concerned with giving direct instruction input, telling the class something about the rhyming words. The second is direct instruction: monitoring the whole class at level 2 to check recall of previous work. In the middle of this the student-teacher finds it necessary to issue a brief reprimand, a third utterance, which is direct instruction management of order.

When the coding was completed the data were transferred to a summary sheet. The coding was undertaken by two research assistants following extensive training to ensure high inter-judge reliabilities, i.e. better than 90 per cent. Definitions of each category, and of the four levels of competence are presented in Appendix A.3.

Judgements of planning and reflection were based on the responses to the pre-lesson questionnaire and the post-lesson interview. As such there were eight sub-categories in planning, and nine in reflection/evaluation, each relating to the items in the questionnaire and interview. The categories in evaluation are identical to those in planning with the exception of the ninth, which relates to the student-teacher's overall evaluation of the lesson, identifying strengths and weaknesses. The eight common sub-categories relate to tasks, purposes, presentation, materials, class organization, pupil learning, assessment and perceived difficulties.

Judgements were also made of indices of appropriateness. These were more complex. In previous research concerning the quality of teaching actions and of learning experiences analyses have been made of various indices of appropriateness based on the model of the teaching cycle outlined in Chapter 1 (Bennett *et al.*, 1984; Bennett and Kell, 1989). These included:

(a) appropriateness of task to purpose; i.e. the extent to which the task chosen or developed was appropriate to teachers' stated intentions;
(b) appropriateness of presentation; i.e. the extent to which the presentation – be it an explanation, demonstration or instruction – was accurate

and suitable for the purpose, and whether necessary supporting materials were available and provided;

(c) appropriateness of differentiation; called adaptation in Shulman's (1987a) model of pedagogical reasoning, i.e. whether the tasks/input were suitable for the pupils' differing capabilities.

These three indices of appropriateness were utilized in this study to gain an additional perspective on the relationship of knowledge bases to teaching actions. The data allowed a judgement to be made on each index, for each observed lesson by three independent judges – the student-teacher, the observer and a trained independent rater. The student-teachers made these judgements in their post-task interviews when reflecting on their lesson and the extent to which it had met their intentions and expectations. The observer made their judgement after observing the lesson, and the independent rater based judgements on the complete data set including the lesson transcripts.

For each index, judgements were made in three categories – appropriate, partly appropriate or not appropriate. Computations of inter-judge agreements showed that these were high, over 90 per cent between the observer and the independent rater. Agreements between the student-teacher judgements and those of the observer and the independent rater ranged between 79 per cent and 100 per cent. Some students appeared to be hypercritical of themselves. Very few of the judgements were completely opposed, i.e. appropriate versus inappropriate. In the light of the high level of agreement between observer and independent rater, the analyses are based on an average of their combined judgements.

SUBJECT KNOWLEDGE AND TEACHING PERFORMANCE

The findings for music, mathematics and science are presented in turn. In each case the analysis of talk from the transcripts is presented first, followed by the analyses of planning and preparation and reflection/ evaluation from the interviews, and finally the data on appropriateness. These quantitative analyses are extended and elaborated by the presentation of six contrasting case studies in the next chapter.

Music

Twenty-two lessons were observed and analysed, sixteen by musicians and six by non-musicians. Their proportions of talk devoted to the intellectual and logistical aspects of teaching are considerably different, as shown in Tables 10.2 and 10.3.

Musicians spend much more time on intellectual aspects, i.e. talk relating to pedagogical knowledge, whereas non-musicians' talk is much more management oriented.

Table 10.2 Didactic and interactive intellectual talk (per cent)

		Didactic		Interactive	
		Management		Management	
	Intellectual	of input	Monitoring	of input	Monitoring
Musicians	56.8	32.3	16.8	5.4	2.3
Non-musicians	35.4	18.3	13.9	1.8	1.4

Table 10.3 Differences in logistical aspects of talk (per cent)

		Didactic			Interactive		
		Management of			Management of		
	Logistical	Activities	Order	Materials	Activities	Order	Materials
Musicians	43.2	27.4	6.2	6.1	2.9	0.1	0.5
Non-musicians	64.6	26.8	22.9	11.2	2.3	0.8	0.6

The intellectual aspect comprises two basic teaching approaches – didactic and interactive modes – and each of these contains management of input, and monitoring, where pedagogical input is provided and checks made on pupil understandings. Both musicians and non-musicians talk considerably more in the didactic mode, where they provide and control input and steer the class, through various techniques of instruction and representation, to their intended outcome. They vary little in monitoring, but the musicians provide substantially more input to the class in both teaching modes.

In the logistical aspects of teaching there was little talk of either group in the interactive mode. In the didactic mode the non-musicians were much more exercised about management, as Table 10.3 shows.

Much of their talk was at level 1, i.e. basic attempts to operate procedures for orderly activity. The musicians spent little time on the management of order and of materials, and all of the latter was on managing materials directly related to the task.

These differing patterns of talk are of interest, but the critical question concerns the levels of competence with which these were achieved.

Talk was judged to be in one of four levels of competence. In Figure 10.2, levels 3 and 4 have been aggregated since the proportions of talk at these higher levels were small.

Two trends in the intellectual aspects are apparent. The musicians perform at a consistently higher level in both teaching modes. Less of their talk is at level 1, and substantially more at level 2. Occasionally they manage to perform at levels 3 and 4 which the non-musicians never achieve.

It is also clear that even though the non-musicians spent as much talk on monitoring they were rarely able to perform beyond level 1. On the

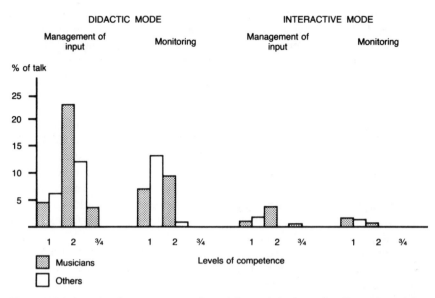

Figure 10.2 Levels of competence of musicians and others (intellectual mode)

Table 10.4 Differences in levels of competence in planning and reflection/evaluation

	Planning		Reflection/evaluation	
	Musicians	*Non-musicians*	*Musicians*	*Non-musicians*
Task	2.4	1.5	2.4	1.3
Purposes	2.5	2.0	2.3	1.8
Presentation	2.3	1.8	2.3	1.5
Materials	1.6	1.0	1.8	1.0
Organization	1.8	1.5	2.1	1.8
Learning	2.4	2.3	2.6	1.5
Assessment	2.0	1.3	2.2	1.5
Difficulties	1.6	1.0	1.8	1.0
Strengths/ weaknesses	–	–	2.6	1.8
Average	2.1	1.6	2.2	1.5

other hand, nearly 60 per cent of the monitoring of musicians was at level 2. As such, the former limited their actions to checking work and instructions, whereas the majority of the musicians' talk indicated competences in appropriate questioning for understanding and simple diagnosis.

Planning and reflection

Table 10.4 presents the judgements of competence levels in the eight sub-areas of planning.

The differences between the musicians and others and non-specialists is substantial. The musicians demonstrate a higher level of competence on every sub-area of planning. They were particularly strong on planning tasks for particular purposes and in conceiving of appropriate presentation strategies. Both groups were very clear about planning pupil learning, and both were weakest on preparation of materials and understanding what difficulties pupils might have with the tasks set.

Students were asked to reflect on and evaluate their lesson in the same categories as for their planning. Table 10.4 also sets out these data.

The differences are even wider here where again the musicians demonstrate higher levels of competence in each sub-area. Another repeat pattern is the relative weakness of both groups in the sub-areas of materials and difficulties. In the additional category of strengths and weaknesses, the musicians were much more adept at reflecting on the whole lesson and suggesting strategies for improvement.

Finally, judgements were made of task appropriateness. The ability to develop classroom tasks in the light of planned intentions, which are suitably differentiated for the range of pupil capability in the class, and present them with suitable instructions or explanations and supporting materials, demands several knowledge bases – of content, curriculum, children's learning and pedagogy. It is therefore uncertain, *a priori*, what relationship might exist between subject specialism and levels of appropriateness.

The findings are presented in Table 10.5 which shows that the musicians' chosen tasks were better linked to purposes, and were more appropriately presented. Differentiation was very good in both groups. Indeed, students were most proficient in the area of differentiation, and least so in presentation. This may be a pattern specific to music lessons however. Differentiation was high because many lessons involved whole-class singing and the like, which most pupils were capable of performing at their own level.

Summary

The differences in the performances of musicians and non-musicians are very clear and consistent. Musicians devote much more time to intellectual

Table 10.5 Levels of appropriateness by musicians and non-musicians (per cent)

	Purposes		Presentation		Differentiation	
	Mus.	Non-mus.	Mus.	Non-mus.	Mus.	Non-mus.
Appropriate	75	50	59	50	84	100
Partly appropriate	25	50	41	25	16	0
Not appropriate	0	0	0	25	0	0

aspects of teaching, mainly in the didactic mode. They perform at consistently higher levels of competence, and are more skilled in making appropriate links between purposes and tasks, and between tasks and their presentation. They spend much less effort on the logistical or management aspects of teaching, and substantially less of their talk is devoted to issues of classroom order.

Finally, their performances in the interactive aspects of teaching are matched by those in planning and evaluation where they consistently performed to higher levels of competence.

Mathematics

Twenty-nine lessons were analysed, sixteen by the mathematics students and thirteen by students from non-mathematicians (hereafter called 'others'). Tables 10.6 and 10.7 set out the proportions of talk concerning the intellectual and logistical aspects of teaching.

Table 10.6 Didactic and interactive intellectual talk (per cent)

| | | Didactic | | Interactive | |
| | | *Management* | | *Management* | |
	Intellectual	*of input*	*Monitoring*	*of input*	*Monitoring*
Mathematicians	68.4	18.2	14.6	24.3	11.3
Others	71.0	28.3	16.8	16.3	9.6

Unlike the findings in music there is no difference in the balance between talk relating to pedagogical content knowledge and the general pedagogical knowledge. Also unlike the music findings there is a much more even balance between didactic and interactive approaches. There are few differences between the two groups of students in their amount of talk related to monitoring, but considerable differences in the management of input in the two teaching modes. Mathematicians give more emphasis to interactive teaching and others to the didactic mode.

There was little difference between the two groups in their proportion of talk devoted to the logistical or management aspects of teaching. When these are broken down into their constituent categories, as in Table 10.7, the two groups are virtually indistinguishable.

Table 10.7 Differences in logistical aspects of talk (per cent)

| | | Didactic | | | Interactive | | |
| | | *Management of* | | | *Management of* | | |
	Logistical	*Activities*	*Order*	*Materials*	*Activities*	*Order*	*Materials*
Mathematicians	31.6	16.8	3.8	1.7	4.8	0.2	4.4
Others	29.0	18.0	3.1	1.9	5.0	0.2	0.8

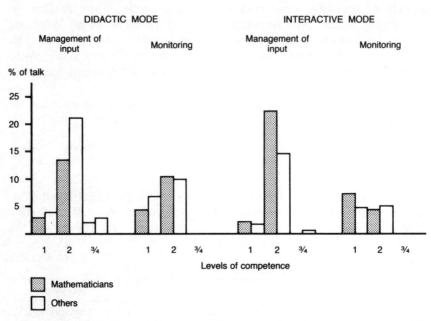

Figure 10.3 Levels of competence in mathematics and others (intellectual mode)

Figure 10.3 shows at what levels of competence these teaching patterns were achieved in intellectual aspects of teaching. In monitoring, the levels of competence are virtually identical in both teaching modes. However, the non-mathematicians more often attained levels 2 and 3/4 in managing input in the didactic mode, whereas the mathematics students more often reached level 2 competence in the interactive mode.

When levels of competence are considered within each of the logistical categories there are again very few differences. The only one to occur was in didactic, management of activities, where the non-specialists attained level 2 more often, but did not attain level 3 as often as the mathematics students.

Planning and reflection

Differences between the mathematics students and others are not large in planning and preparation, as Table 10.8 shows. It is only in the area of planning tasks that the mathematicians show a sizeable superiority, otherwise the differences are slight and not significant.

The differences in reflection and evaluation are also slight overall, but interestingly it is the non-mathematics students who perform at a consistently higher level in most areas. Thus the superiority of mathematicians in the area of task planning is not paralleled by the quality of their evaluations. Additionally, the non-mathematicians appear slightly

Table 10.8 Differences in planning and reflection/evaluation

	Planning		Reflection/evaluation	
	Mathematicians	*Others*	*Mathematicians*	*Others*
Task	2.7	2.2	2.4	2.5
Purposes	2.4	2.2	2.1	2.0
Presentation	2.1	1.9	2.2	2.1
Materials	1.4	1.5	2.0	2.3
Organization	1.4	1.3	2.0	2.1
Learning	2.4	2.2	2.0	2.3
Assessment	1.6	1.5	2.2	2.2
Difficulties	1.7	1.5	1.5	1.8
Strengths/ weaknesses	–	–	2.1	2.8
Average	2.1	1.8	2.1	2.2

Table 10.9 Levels of appropriateness by specialists and non-specialists in mathematics (per cent)

	Purposes		Presentation		Differentiation	
	Maths	*Others*	*Maths*	*Others*	*Maths*	*Others*
Appropriate	82	49	59	46	54	46
Partly appropriate	12	28	28	39	32	46
Not appropriate	6	8	13	15	13	8

more adept at reflecting on the strengths and weaknesses of the whole lesson.

The pattern of findings on appropriateness in mathematics are quite different from those in music, as Table 10.9 shows. If concern is limited to those tasks which were totally appropriate then the mathematicians display higher levels of proficiency in each index. Other students have a much higher proportion of partly appropriate ratings. Interestingly, however, the mathematicians present more tasks which are inappropriately differentiated.

Summary

The pattern of findings in mathematics teaching is totally different to that in music. There is no difference in the balance of intellectual and logistical aspects, although the mathematicians tend to emphasize interactive more than didactic approaches. There are few differences in the levels of competence reached by the two groups in either mode of teaching. In short, there is virtually nothing to distinguish mathematicians and others in teaching mathematics.

Science

Twenty-three science lessons were observed, sixteen by science students and seven by others. Tables 10.10 and 10.11 present the balance between the intellectual and logistical aspects of teaching.

Table 10.10 Differences in intellectual aspects

| | | Didactic | | Interactive | |
| | | Management | | Management | |
	Intellectual	of input	Monitoring	of input	Monitoring
Scientists	67.7	28.8	14.0	17.9	7.0
Others	60.2	19.3	8.8	22.1	10.0

The balance observed in science is a little different from that in mathematics in that the scientists emphasize more the intellectual aspects of teaching. However, the emphasis is by no means as marked as that in music. Neither is it sustained across both teaching modes. There is significantly more talk by specialists in the didactic mode, both in the management of input and in monitoring. The reverse is true in interactive teaching. The overall pattern then is for the science students to be more didactic, and the others more interactive, in a curriculum area in which inquiry approaches tend to be prescribed. This pattern is mirrored when competence levels are considered. Scientists emphasize and achieve higher levels of competence in didactic teaching (e.g. 24.3 per cent level 2 compared to 11.7 per cent) whereas the others emphasize interactive teaching and are more competent in it (e.g. 19.6 per cent level 2 compared to 12.7 per cent).

A greater proportion of non-science students' talk was in logistical aspects. Table 10.11 shows that the increased level of management talk among non-scientists is almost entirely in the interactive mode, and in particular in the amount of talk devoted to the management of materials. Otherwise there is little to differentiate the two groups.

Table 10.11 Differences in logistical aspects

| | | Didactic | | | Interactive | | |
| | | Management of | | | Management of | | |
	Logistical	Activities	Order	Materials	Activities	Order	Materials
Scientists	32.2	16.8	3.6	3.4	6.1	0.3	2.1
Others	39.8	19.2	3.3	3.2	7.5	0.4	6.2

This is also true when competences in the management area are considered. Very few differences exist, neither group managing very often to break through to levels 3 or 4. Indeed in the management of order, and of materials categories the great majority of their talk is at level 1.

Planning and reflection

The science students appear to plan at a consistently higher level than the others (Table 10.12). This shows particularly in the preparation of materials, of classroom organization, and of assessment. They are also better able to conceive of the difficulties which pupils will have with the tasks planned.

Table 10.12 Differences in planning and reflection/evaluation

	Planning		Reflection/evaluation	
	Scientists	Others	Scientists	Others
Task	2.1	1.9	2.3	2.3
Purposes	2.5	2.3	1.7	2.9
Presentation	2.3	2.0	2.0	1.9
Materials	1.8	1.3	1.8	1.7
Organization	1.8	1.1	1.8	1.7
Learning	2.5	2.1	2.1	2.0
Assessment	1.9	1.4	1.9	1.7
Difficulties	1.7	1.1	1.7	1.6
Strengths/ weaknesses	–	–	2.5	2.6
Average	2.1	1.7	2.0	1.9

The pattern for planning does not extend to the quality of students' reflections and evaluations however. Here the specialists and non-specialists are virtually indistinguishable.

Levels of appropriateness are shown in Table 10.13. The striking pattern here is that in two of the three indices the non-science students perform better. The link between tasks and purpose is substantially better in their lessons, and their presentations are marginally better. One quarter of the science students' lessons were marred by poor presentation. In differentiation, however, they presented a higher proportion of suitable tasks, but also a higher proportion of unsuitable ones.

Summary

In science teaching the pattern of findings is mixed. Science students emphasize intellectual aspects of teaching slightly more, but strangely

Table 10.13 Levels of appropriateness in science (per cent)

	Purposes		Presentation		Differentiation	
	Scientist	Others	Scientist	Others	Scientist	Others
Appropriate	56	100	41	43	75	57
Partly appropriate	31	0	34	57	6	43
Not appropriate	13	0	25	0	19	0

operate more in the didactic mode in a subject which is supposedly inquiry-based. They are more competent in the didactic mode than the others, but the latter are more competent in the interactive mode. The others also have the edge in levels of appropriateness. The science students plan and prepare their lessons better but appear no better able to reflect on, and evaluate, their teaching performances.

CONCLUSION

Three groups of student-teachers were studied to gain an indication of the relationship of subject knowledge for teaching-to-teaching performances. One group, the musicians, had comparatively high levels of music knowledge and experienced a specialist music curriculum course as well as general curriculum courses. Two groups of students, the mathematics and science groups, had comparatively only average levels of knowledge for teaching their subject. They too experienced a specialist curriculum course in their subject as well as general curriculum courses. The argument advanced was that if subject-matter knowledge for teaching was a more powerful influence than specialist curriculum courses on teaching performance, then the music students should teach music to higher levels of competence than other students, but that the mathematics and science students would not.

The data provide clear strong support for this position, and accord with recent studies in the United States. Nevertheless, the representativeness of the student-teacher sample, and of the tasks observed, is unknown, and further studies are needed before such patterns can be generalized. They are nonetheless of great interest, and potential importance, for the education of teachers. As such, and in an attempt to gain a greater understanding of how knowledge bases for teaching are enacted in the classroom, the next chapter puts flesh on the quantitative 'skeletons' presented in this, by portraying six case studies chosen to highlight differing performances and their implications.

Chapter 11

Case studies in learning to teach

Neville Bennett and Rosemary Turner-Bisset

The patterns and trends established in the last chapter, although clear, are abstractions, based on averages across performances. As such they give little flavour of the reality of learning to teach. In order to capture this reality more firmly, and to elaborate on the nature of the links between knowledge bases and teaching performances, three sets of comparisons are presented, one in each subject area. The selection of the case studies was informed by the models of task processes, and pedagogical reasoning, detailed in Chapter 1. As such they highlight issues in comprehension, transformation and implementation.

In the first comparison, two student-teachers, a music specialist and a science specialist are compared teaching the same topic – an idea taken from their music tutor on clapping rhythms. The interest here is on how each specialist transformed the content knowledge into an actual teaching event.

In the second comparison, two student-teachers on the science specialist course have been selected to highlight differential competence in classroom management and control. The contrast also emphasizes the importance of the comprehension and transformation stages of pedagogical reasoning, as well as the role of context in supporting or otherwise, beginning attempts at teaching.

In the last comparison, a student-teacher following the mathematics specialism, although a history graduate, is compared with a music specialist when both are teaching a similar lesson on shape. This contrast highlights the problems that can occur when student-teachers attempt to model, or imitate, an activity by their tutor, without having the appropriate competence to do so. The important issue of context is again raised in this comparison.

A COMPARISON OF TWO MUSIC LESSONS

The student-teachers

Melanie was a member of the music course and was aged 21 at the time of the study. She had a good honours degree in music, and A levels in

English, history and music. She enjoyed sport, though not competitively, and outdoor pursuits. Attending concerts and the theatre took up much of her free time.

Sybil was a member of the science course and was also aged 21. She had an honours degree in psychology, with a biology subsidiary. Her A levels were in English, history and biology. She had been head girl at school, and won prizes for public speaking and drama. She also enjoyed swimming, dancing and work with children.

Sybil's music lesson

Planning

Sybil's intention for the lesson on rhythm was to give the children practical experience at clapping out and playing rhythms on musical instruments. She expected that the children would learn about different rhythms and practice experimenting with their musical instruments. She stated the task vaguely: 'music based on rhythms' and was no more specific in her planned presentation: 'I will introduce the children to basic clapping rhythms'.

Teaching performance

She took a group of twenty-five 7- to 8-year-olds to the specialist music room and settled them on the carpet in a circle. She started the lesson by demonstrating the task and describing what the children had to do. Sybil anticipated problems of order by setting up an explicit rule.

> T: But before I go any further I want to tell you what the sign for stop is. If I put my finger on my lips you've all got to do it straight away and the last person . . .
> P: is out.
> T: Is out; so you've all got to look and watch very carefully.

She clapped some rhythms to the children and then invited individual children to create rhythms. However, she soon ran into difficulties. She found that she could not recall the rhythms which she had originally clapped, or that she had repeated them wrongly; the children corrected her repeated rhythms and she had to reprimand them:

> T: Christopher, I'm doing the lesson.

After the clapping, it took a long time, eleven minutes, for each child to collect his or her chosen instrument. Much talk was expended on this change of activity, interspersed with talk for management of order:

> T: Who would like to play a tambourine? Right then Oliver, could you go and sit over there please. I said don't touch the instruments, put

them down! Mark, sit down please, I'm sorting this out. Mary, what would you like to play?

This pattern of talk continued for the eleven minutes, but the children were patient and made very little noise. After twenty-four minutes the children used their chosen instruments to mimic particular rhythms created by Sybil, one group at a time. Sybil gave no input during this time, but organized each group to play in turn, reprimanding those who played out of turn. At the end of the lesson everyone joined in the playing of *all* instruments to particular rhythms. Throughout, the children were involved and very well-behaved.

Melanie's music lesson

Planning

Melanie's intentions for her lesson on rhythm were to develop abilities to listen carefully to rhythms, and to discuss and describe the music heard. She wished them to learn how to play 'Switch', how to isolate rhythm in a musical performance, and to gain an understanding of general points about Indian music: the tala, raga and drone. These intentions were to be fulfilled through a clapping game called 'Switch'. She planned to play a simple version of the game, in which the class changes the rhythm when the teacher does so; and the more difficult version, in which the class continues with the old clapping rhythm against the teacher's new one, until the teacher says 'Switch'. This second version creates a situation in which children must clap one rhythm while hearing another. After playing both versions of 'Switch', Melanie planned to give a general introduction to Indian music: playing and discussing pre-taped musical examples. The children would play 'Switch' again to finish.

Teaching performance

Melanie introduced the lesson exactly as planned, with ten 9-year-olds sitting in a circle in the hall. They played both versions of 'Switch' as a warm-up to the listening activity, but also for other purposes as became apparent later. She regrouped them in a semi-circle on the floor using the organization as a role-play for the next activity. The children represented the Indian audience around the performers:

> T: The audience doesn't sit on chairs. They sit on the floor and they sit in a semi-circle around the performers, right? You're the audience and I've got the tape-recorder.

She monitored at level 2 for previous knowledge of Indian music and instruments:

T: Now what do the drums play?
P: Rhythms.
T: That's right. They play the rhythms and that's what we are especially looking at today, but we'll see that later.

During this, the children were shown photographs of Indian instruments and told to listen for the rhythms in the music. The three extracts of music were very short, one minute each. After each one she monitored their listening and understanding; then used the monitoring to pace her explanations:

T: What about the rhythms? Are they simple or are they like what you'd expect?
P: They like waver up and down.
T: That's right.

The pupils listened carefully to the taped extracts, and responded well to the questioning, making connections between the 'Switch' game and the Indian rhythms:

P: In the 'Switch' we were doing rhythms like that.

This independently-made observation reflects the quality of the selection and editing of materials by the student-teacher. It enabled children to link the rhythms in the music with the rhythms in the game.
After the tapes she summed up:

T: That's the style of the Indian music, that's what Indian music does. It got more complex, didn't it, the rhythms got more complicated as they went on!

They digressed briefly on to Eastern and Western music, moving to look at a map in the hall to locate India and Europe. Melanie quickly regrouped them in a circle to play 'Switch Mark 2' again. She stopped them at a significant moment to explain why they all went wrong when the leading child changed rhythms:

T: Good and then Emma changed, didn't she? She went one two three, one two three, one two three, so while we were counting four she was counting three and it all got very confused, and that is cross-rhythms, and that is exactly what you have been listening to for the last fifteen minutes. That is what happens. They get threes against fours and twos against threes and then it all sounds very mingled, doesn't it, and it all sounded very complicated and that's just what happens. You've just done that yourselves.

Melanie emphasized the important point that they had been playing the same sort of cross-rhythms as they had heard in the Indian music. The lesson ended with a variant of 'Switch'. The children loved it and were on task throughout the lesson.

Analysis of lesson transcripts: music lessons by Melanie and Sybil

From the foregoing accounts of teaching performance, it would appear that both lessons were reasonably effective with the children being interested, involved and well-behaved. But in what ways, if at all, did Melanie's specialist knowledge manifest itself? The outcomes of the analysis of the transcripts of the two lessons are shown in Figures 11.1 and 11.2.

The contrasts are dramatic. In Melanie's lesson there is four times as much intellectual input than logistical, whereas that for Sybil is almost exactly the reverse. This is seen particularly in the amount of input that Melanie provides – almost half of the lesson, and at all four levels of competence. Melanie also carries out nearly three times as much monitoring as Sybil, much of it at level 2. In Sybil's lesson only about one quarter of this activity is at level 2, i.e. limited to a simple checking that children can carry out the work.

Almost 80 per cent of Sybil's lesson is devoted to management of activities and to the management of order – largely a result of a lengthy period involving giving out musical instruments, and the necessary reprimands during that phase of the lesson. All Sybil's substantial logistical talk is at the first two levels of competence. Melanie had much less talk of this nature, indeed there was virtually none relating to the maintenance of order, and the talk covered all four levels.

Perceptions of teaching performance: reflection and evaluation

How did Sybil and Melanie perceive their own performances?

Sybil

Sybil felt that the children got plenty of experience. She was happy with the presentation. She thought the children had learnt about different rhythms, and enjoyed the lesson. She commented that some aspects of organization had been weak, such as length and timing of activities. She felt that she had not catered for differing abilities. She also recognized her own difficulties in reproducing rhythms. She stated that she had no subject knowledge in music; the lesson was 'loosely based on stuff done in the course'. When asked what she would change about the task, she responded 'less rhythm work as it began to get tedious'. She would change to a more creative activity.

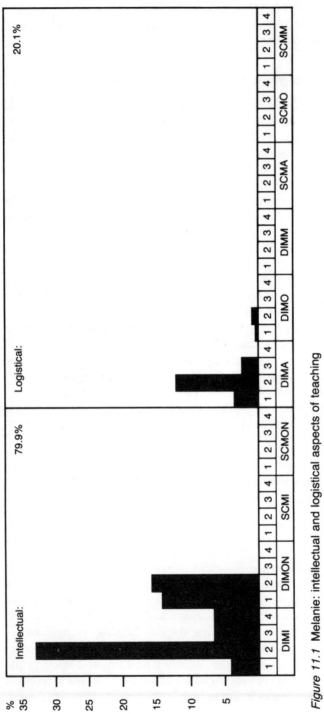

Figure 11.1 Melanie: intellectual and logistical aspects of teaching

Key to lesson transcript analysis graphs (for Figures 11.1–11.6)
Vertical axis – percentage of total talk for the lesson
Horizontal axis– teaching competence categories + levels
DIMI – direct instruction management or input
DIMON – direct instruction monitoring
SCMI – structured conversation management of input
SCMON – structured conversation monitoring

DIMA – direct instruction management of activity
DIMO – direct instruction management of order
DIMM – direct instruction management of materials
SCHMA – structured conversation management of activity
SCMO – structured conversation management of order
SCMM – structured conversation management of materials

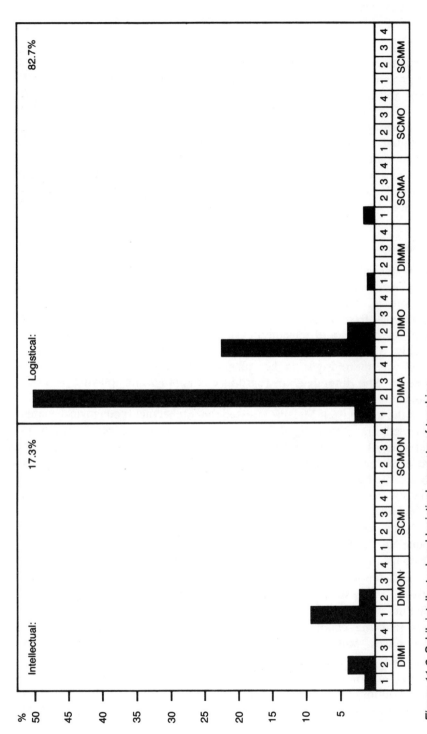

Figure 11.2 Sybil: intellectual and logistical aspects of teaching

Melanie

Melanie tended to be hypercritical of her own performance, but felt that the presentation was good, in that children helped to explain the 'Switch' game and the introduction to Indian music was not too long or detailed. She was content with the task and felt it catered for differing abilities. Her organization was suitable and effective in the way that they had emulated an Indian audience. Melanie criticized her digression on to Eastern and Western music as unprepared and not very clear. She also thought that the last game of 'Switch' had gone on too long. She felt that her subject knowledge of rhythm was crucial, since the concept of rhythm is difficult to understand and explain.

Summary

Both student-teachers took an idea from the music course and used it in a well-managed, orderly lesson. There are, however, important differences. Melanie planned and prepared thoroughly, taking subject knowledge from several sources, choosing representations of the concept of cross-rhythm, and selecting musical extracts of appropriate length and quality. She reached level 3 in most areas of planning and preparation. Sybil was more vague in her planning, reaching only level 1 in most aspects. She intended to reproduce clapping and playing activities modelled in the course.

In the lesson itself Melanie stressed the intellectual (pedagogical content knowledge), whereas Sybil focused on the logistical (general pedagogical knowledge). Sybil agreed that she had no appropriate knowledge; she mainly organized pupil performances. This lack of subject knowledge meant she had no resources, in the broadest sense of the word, on which to draw, to provide input for lessons on rhythm work.

Melanie on the other hand, used her knowledge to weld the intellectual and logistical aspects of the lesson in a sophisticated way. The game of 'Switch' acted as a physical representation of the cross-rhythms in Indian music, more powerful than an analogy, since the game functioned simultaneously as a 'warm-up' and 'wind-down' to the lesson, and also as an active learning metaphor for the Indian cross-rhythms. That this representation was successful can be seen by the fact that the children made the link between the two activities for themselves. Melanie's subject knowledge enabled her to add a potent representation to her instructional repertoire, even as a beginning teacher; in the words of McDiarmid, Ball and Anderson (1989), Melanie had 'more options for connecting pupils with subject matter'. Sybil, in contrast, could only reproduce an item from someone else's repertoire without transforming it.

In the post-lesson evaluation, Melanie reached mainly level 3; Sybil achieved an average of level 1. These ratings illustrate the fact that Melanie was able to reflect on both the content knowledge and organizational aspects of the lesson, whereas Sybil, lacking the subject knowledge, found herself concentrating mainly on organizational aspects.

CASE STUDIES IN SCIENCE

The contrast presented here centres on the quality of pedagogical reasoning; how, in practical science lessons, the initial intentions become transformed into competent teaching actions.

The student-teachers

Sybil has already been described in the comparison of music lessons. Here she was observed teaching science, specifically a topic in biology, which was one of her A level and degree subsidiary subjects.

Paula, aged 22, was another psychology graduate from the science course, with A levels in biology, chemistry and psychology. She was keen on sport and had worked with children as part of her Duke of Edinburgh Gold Award. She was observed here teaching a topic in physics.

Sybil's science lesson

Planning

Sybil planned her lesson as part of a scheme of work on: 'Ourselves: our bodies'. Her intentions were three-fold: to develop the practical skills that allow children to explore their environment; to give the children experience in following written instructions; and to give experience in recording experimental results, interpreting observations and reporting back to others.

The presentation was planned to start with a discussion on 'touch', prior to a recap of previous work on the senses. The sixteen 9-year-old children would then be put into two groups of eight, and work in pairs within these groups. Group 1 was to tackle the 'core' activities first ('feely' box and pin probes), whilst group 2 completed associated questions in a worksheet. They would then exchange tasks. In addition, extension activities were planned for the more able children in order to stretch them sufficiently.

Teaching performance

Sybil started the lesson with a very brief recap on previous work on the senses, moving rapidly on to touch:

T: Now today we are going to have a look at touch which is one of our senses, and it's very important. Can anyone tell me why it's important, what touch serves, what things it helps us do?

After this monitoring for previous knowledge, she explained the tasks:

T: I'm going to let you explore touch by feeling things only and having your eyes closed and trying to guess things with those feely boxes over here.

and the organization:

T: Right! The others are doing the science activity: so could you get into pairs pretty quickly please. Work with who you like.

Sybil made sure the children doing the activities were occupied with the taped-down instructions before giving direct instruction to the worksheet group:

T: I'd like you to think of objects, anything you like, anything outside or inside that is smooth, rather sticky, – these are the different groups – and put them in there. The second activity is think of things in the house which we mustn't touch because they will hurt us.

Sybil moved swiftly back to the practical group:

T: The science activity people: can you just look over here a minute please?

She explained the touch-probe activity and monitored at level 2 to ensure that all the children knew what the different parts of the body were:

T: Tell me where the back of the hand is, David. Right, the palm of the hand, Catherine.

Once she was sure they could start the experiment, she moved on to the two pairs doing the 'feely boxes'. She did not scan the class, but helped children with what they were doing. She monitored at level 2 for their understanding of the concept of sensitivity, and why some parts of the body are more sensitive than others:

T: Why do you think some parts are more sensitive than others?
P: Because you are using them more.
T: Yes, you could try that.

Sybil was positive in her response to the child's answer, leaving it open, for there was clearly more to find out.

At thirty-seven minutes, she efficiently attracted the attention of all sixteen children.

T: Right can everyone put their pencils down and stop please what they are doing now. Philip can you put the materials back in the box now please.

The pairs reported back to the class about their experiments. The children showed interest, not only in the 'feely boxes', but also in the pin-probe testing the sensitivity of different parts of the body. Sybil let the children explain and demonstrate; then summed up important points. Overall the review was concise and effective; the children spoke as much as the student-teacher. There was absolute quiet while the children listened to each other. The observer commented that the flow, organization and commitment reflected a well-planned and effective lesson.

Paula's science lesson

Planning

Paula's lesson was part of the school's scheme of work on 'Transport'. Her intentions were rather more vaguely stated: to continue with the topic of transport, with the introduction of the idea of force; and to encourage the children to work out solutions to problems as a group effort. The children would 'hopefully learn the basic concept of force, although not to a great level'. She also expected them to begin to write experimental results in a table, and that faster groups would progress to constructing bar-charts of results. Paula was vague about what the task was and how she would present it. She claimed to have thought of other experiments, but these had nothing to do with force.The lesson was to be with the whole class of thirty-one 7-year-olds. They were to be grouped into mixed-ability groups of four children in order to avoid those with writing difficulties falling behind.

Teaching performance

Paula was nervous and wanted to get the children started as soon as possible:

> T: Right, we're going to carry on doing transport, but we're going to look at the cars you brought in today. Now can anybody tell me what a force is?

She accepted examples of kicking or forcing a door open:

> T: If you were going to force the door open what would you do? James, what do you think?
> P: Ram it.
> T: You'd ram it; now why would you ram it? Why don't you just stand near it and ram it?
> P: So that you get more power.
> T: You'd get more power to open it up, wouldn't you, so force is a sort of power.

Either Paula is using the terms 'force' and 'power' colloquially here, or she has a misconception of what power is. Further attempts at ad-lib were not effective either. She asked a child to knock a ruler off a desk; then monitored to see if they understood why it fell:

> T: That's right. Now what was the force that made it land on the floor, Jenny? Where did the force come from?
> P: The floor.
> T: Well it's Mark who made the force isn't it because he tipped the table didn't he? Now, why did the ruler fall off when he tipped the table, Joanne?
> P: Because it wasn't stuck to the table.
> T: That's right. If it had been stuck on with glue it would have stayed there, wouldn't it, because the glue would have acted as a force and kept it on the table.

She rejected Joanne's answer 'the floor', but stated somewhat misleadingly that it was Mark who *made* the force. In fact, Mark *applied* the force by tipping the table. The force here is gravity, which Paula did not mention. Her response to the answer about glue is correct at a molecular level, but perhaps not very helpful in this context.

She moved on to the amount of force required to move an object:

> T: Why would a pencil move?
> P: It's not strong.
> T: Another word instead of strong? Don't all try it! Wait! Mark, sit down. All of you pick up your pencils and put them back on the table.

Paula did not make it clear how the children were expected to make connections between the presentation and the practical activity, speaking as she did in incomplete, disjointed sentences:

> T: Right, we're going to try this afternoon with your cars that you brought in as long as you are all sensible. If anybody starts being silly or makes too much noise they can go and do some writing somewhere else and we're going to work in groups of four and I am deciding the fours.

The children moved noisily into groups to read the prepared worksheets. At this point she realized that she had not prepared all the resources:

> T: Now who can look on their instruction sheet and see what they are missing? Tell me what you need on your instruction sheet that we haven't got at the moment, James?
> P: Stopwatch.

She had also relied on the children to bring in toy cars. Fortunately, one boy brought in fifteen cars or she would not have been able to do this activity. She also had to leave the room with a few children to find the ramps, leaving an embarrassed girl in front of the class to report back misbehaviour.

On her return Paula started to monitor the groups, but realized that she had not told them what to do. The worksheets were too difficult for them to read; so she had to explain the task.

> T: Right, all of you stop. Some of you are working very well and some people are just making a lot of noise. You can do the same thing but do it more quietly and the sheet that has just come round has got a table on it for you to fill in like a chart. If you haven't got one, one will be coming in a minute.

Here she missed an opportunity to explain the task to everyone at once.

The children were told to carry on, but they still did not know what to do. The activity was conducted with much noise and excitement. Some children moved from group to group and ran around aimlessly. Cars were thrown and there was almost no attempt to time their progress down the ramps. There were too few watches with second-hands and no stopwatches. In any case the ramps were too short to allow accurate timing. Results were thus highly inaccurate or imaginary. The lesson lasted seventy-five minutes, but there was little attempt to bring it all together. When the children were questioned in a group in the last few minutes, it became clear that they had little, if any, idea of the activity, the results, or the idea of force. Graphs could not be made.

Analysis of lesson transcripts

Coincidentally, the same observer reported on both science lessons. It would appear, from these accounts of teaching performance, that there were marked differences in quality in the two lessons. What specific factors were responsible? The analysis of the lesson transcripts provides some indications of these. Figures 11.3 and 11.4 show the distribution of talk and levels of competence in each category.

Sybil gave somewhat more emphasis to intellectual aspects, with talk relating to pedagogical content knowledge being 64 per cent compared to Paula's 57 per cent. This difference is largely a consequence of Sybil talking more in the interactive mode, stressing in particular monitoring children's achievements. Paula engages in substantially less of this activity – 13.8 per cent to Sybil's 31 per cent.

Sybil achieved the higher levels of competence in three dimensions, Paula in only one. In addition, Paula was exceptional in the sample in the proportion of talk (25 per cent), which was inappropriate or inaccurate, as, for example, when she stated that force was a sort of power.

In the logistical aspects nearly all of Sybil's talk relates to the manage-

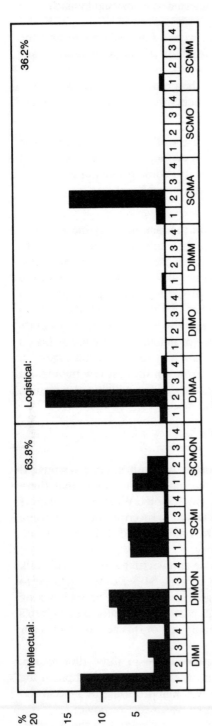

Figure 11.3 Sybil: intellectual and logistical aspects of teaching

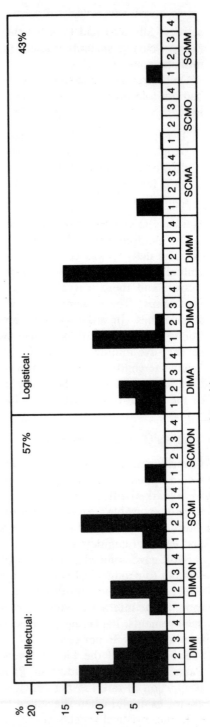

Figure 11.4 Paula: intellectual and logistical aspects of teaching

ment of activities, the great majority of it being level 2, and sometimes higher, reflecting the managing of various activities like 'feely' boxes, pin-probes and worksheets. She devotes not one word to the management of order. Paula, on the other hand, expends a much higher proportion of talk in managing order and in managing materials, most of it at level 1. This too reflects the lesson and the difficulties she experienced with these aspects of her teaching.

Perceptions of teaching performance: reflection and evaluation

What were Sybil's and Paula's own perceptions of their performance?

Sybil

Both Sybil and the observer felt that her intentions had been fulfilled. She was happy with the presentation, but admitted forgetting some of it. She thought that her strengths were good organization, detailed planning and thorough preparation of materials. The children had worked well in a friendly but controlled atmosphere.

With regard to pupil learning she listed four achievements: about the sensitivity of different parts of the body; that some familiar objects are easy to identify by touch alone; but just using touch alone can be difficult; and that touch is an important sense, particularly from the point of view of safety. She had made these assessments through a consideration of written work combined with questioning and observation.

When asked about the role of subject knowledge she admitted to reading some thirty books on 'our bodies' to find appropriate detail on touch, and had then used her wider scientific knowledge to forge this into workable activities. She admitted that her basic approach was based on that learned in the training institution, i.e. good preparation, giving children first-hand experiences, matching tasks to children's abilities, and work in small groups.

Paula

Paula admitted the weaknesses in her lesson. She stated that it had been mayhem: her organization was unsuitable and so were most of her resources. Children had found the worksheets too difficult. Neither was she happy with her presentation. The task was inappropriate for the children and they had not learned about the notion of force. She felt however that they had learned something about cooperating in groups and that toy cars travelled at different speeds. She said that she had observed their results, but admitted that some children simply copied from others. Paula had not predicted such poor behaviour and her problems with control. She identified as additional weaknesses her poor preparation and explanations. Although she claimed to have used her scientific knowledge in the lesson and its preparation, it was evident that her understanding of concepts of force, energy and gravity was insecure.

Summary

There were stark contrasts in these two lessons. Sybil's thorough planning of activities and organization and her meticulous preparation of worksheets and materials resulted in a well-run, orderly lesson, in which conditions were suitable for learning to occur. Paula's lack of planning and preparation, and ill-thought-out management of activity led to a situation which she herself described as 'mayhem' and 'a riot'.

A crucial aspect of planning is the appropriateness of the representation selected to illustrate a concept. In Sybil's case the 'feely boxes' and touch-probes were wholly appropriate to convey notions of touch and sensitivity. At no point in Paula's planning did she make it clear how learning would occur, or how the toy cars activity would illustrate concepts of force. Whatever understanding Paula had of the concepts, she failed to share it pedagogically with her pupils. Sybil received an average rating of 3 for her planning, but Paula averaged only 1. Sybil's perceptions of her lesson were validated by the observer; she received an average rating of 3 for her evaluation. Paula admitted her many weaknesses but clung to the belief that the children had learned something about speed and working in small groups, in spite of evidence to the contrary from the observer and the lesson transcript. She received a level 2 rating for her evaluation.

It should be added that the contexts in which Sybil and Paula taught were very different. Sybil taught sixteen 9-year-olds and had a supportive cooperating teacher who made helpful suggestions. In contrast Paula taught thirty-one 7-year-olds and had a non-supportive cooperating teacher who provided very little advice or feedback. She was also attempting to change a very traditional classroom organization into one supportive of more active learning. The children were not used to such a teaching approach and difficulties in control may, in part, be due to that. On the other hand, it could be claimed that Paula should have been alert to this and planned accordingly. What does seem clear is that the differences in quality of these two lessons were attributable to both intellectual and logistical aspects of teaching.

CASE STUDIES IN MATHEMATICS

Two student-teachers are compared teaching similar lessons on shape, which were influenced by the approach in their training institution. Both lessons focused on the drawing, cutting out and naming of shapes, with groups of a similar size. The interest lies in the extent to which each student-teacher was able to transform material and approach from maths course work into representations for the lessons.

The student-teachers

Jackie was 22, had a good honours degree in music and was a member of the music course. She had two A levels, in music and geography. She enjoyed a variety of musical hobbies, as well as sport and outdoor pursuits. She had achieved the Duke of Edinburgh's Gold and Queen's Guide awards.

Helen was 30, a mature student married with two children. She has a good honours degree and an MA in history. Her A levels were in English, history and geography. She was a member of the local archaeological society, an ex-playgroup leader, and ran her own business prior to entering teaching.

Jackie's maths lesson

Planning

Jackie was instructed by the cooperating teacher to do shape with a group of 9- to 10-year-olds. She did not know in advance which ability group she was to teach; hence she decided that the main purpose of the lesson was to determine how much the children already knew through the identification of shape names and features. This was to be achieved via sorting shapes into sets. Her presentation was to start with each child drawing shapes; she would then put shapes into sets on criteria unknown to the group, who would then have to decide the criteria used.

Teaching performance

Jackie began:

> T: Right, today we're going to do some shapes in maths. I want each of you to draw three shapes for me.

When they had finished, she selected certain shapes to go in a set in the centre of the group of tables. She asked:

> T: Right Nicola, what have they all got?
> P: Circles.
> T: They're all circles.

She repeated this selection procedure asking:

> T: If anyone thinks they've got a shape that can go in with this . . . then put theirs in.

Jackie next asked individuals to make the selection of shapes; the rest were to guess the selection criteria. After one child had had a turn at this, she compromised the idea underlying the activity by saying:

> T: Right. You think of something that's going to be really hard; that's going to catch them out. You could do something like the initials on the front of the page or if they've got their full names on.

A child did follow Jackie's suggestion, thereby sending the group off on a tangent, and an opportunity for genuine mathematical discussion was missed. Jackie repeated the activity, using a more relevant criterion. She monitored that they knew the terms 'quadrilateral', 'trapezium', 'hexagon' and 'polygon', then issued a challenge:

> T: So are all these hexagons do you think?
> P: No.
> P: They're polywatsicons.
> T: They're all polygons but they're six-sided shapes. Are all six-sided shapes hexagons?
> P: No.
> T: Why not, James?

She did not pursue the point about regular polygons, but monitored for knowledge of shapes with more than six edges. Finally, she moved on to twelve-edged figures:

> T: What do you think the proper geometric shape should be for a twelve-sided shape?
> P: A polygon.
> P: A twelver.
> T: No. What would it look like?
> P: A polygon.
> T: No. What would it look like?

Clearly, at least some of the group did not understand the question. This was not surprising, as she did not make it clear whether the shape was to be regular or irregular. She found it difficult to draw the shape:

> T: It's very hard to draw a proper twelve-sided shape.

There was no discussion of regular or irregular polygons, no guidance for the less able on how to draw a twelve-edged shape, nor any reference to what was happening to the shape as the number of edges increase. The lesson ended with a puzzle: to draw a certain shape, like an open envelope, without taking their pencils off the paper. There was no summary, simply a demand that they prepare for some language work.

Helen's maths lesson

Planning

Helen planned her lesson as part of a scheme of work on shape. Her purposes were to reinforce learning about shape and to consider the relationship between polygons and circles. She expected them to learn that as the number of sides increase in shapes they become more like a circle; and to learn how to create a hexagon or octagon from a circle. She intended to present the task by discussing it with them, and then demonstrating it. She thought that the open nature of the task should allow for differing abilities. Helen was to teach a mixed-ability group of nine 8- to 9-year-olds, while the other two groups in the class did different activities. In the event, the cooperating teacher was absent and Helen had to manage the whole class.

Teaching performance

Helen began briskly:

> T: Right. On the board are the groups for the next half an hour. We're going to have the blues doing English. You all remember what we're going to do and it's up on the board if you've forgotten.

Once the class was swiftly organized, she monitored her group to check recall of previous work:

> T: What did we do? What shapes did we look at?
> P: Octagon, hexagon, pentagon.
> T: Do you remember how many sides the octagon had?
> P: Eight.
> T: And how many sides did the hexagon have?
> P: Six.
> T: And how many sides did the pentagon have?
> P: Five.

She began directing them towards the idea of a relationship between various shapes and circles:

> T: Can anybody be really clever and tell me what that shape looks a bit like?
> P: A round circle.
> T: Well done, Christian. Yes, it looks like a circle, doesn't it?

She asked:

> T: Do you think if we put more sides on the shape it looks more like a circle?

From here Helen moved to the practical activity of using circles to make hexagons and octagons:

> T: Right. What have I got now then? Let's fold it in half.
> P: Yes.
> T: Now, the more difficult bit. Well, I'm going to fold it into quarters. Are you watching?

Having made an octagon, she made a mistake in her attempt to produce a hexagon:

> T: So what did I do wrong? How did I do an octagon, Louise?
> P: You've done eight sides.
> T: I folded it wrong, didn't I? I didn't fold it in three. I folded it in four again. Shall we see if I can get it right this time?

She utilized this error to check the children's understanding of the activity; at the same time creating an ethos in which it was perfectly acceptable to make mistakes. Once she was sure the group could manage she moved away to monitor the project group working on 'History through bicycles' and the language group. On her return to the maths group she shows her knowledge of learners by reassuring those who made mistakes and praising the ones who did well:

> T: You clever thing! You did a hexagon first time. How about you, Stacey?
> P: I did a square.
> T: Never mind. Try again. I did a square as well first time.

Helen moved the more able on to the next stage of making several hexagons and octagons to tessellate. This did not go well; the activity required more time, perhaps a separate input session. Throughout this time she was dealing with requests for help from the other two groups.

Analysis of lesson transcripts

The foregoing descriptions of teaching performance indicate that in general terms both were reasonably effective, if not inspired, performances. Although Helen was a member of the specialist mathematics course neither had qualifications in the subject. So did subject-matter knowledge, or lack of it, manifest itself?

Figures 11.5 and 11.6 (pages 186 and 187) show the distribution of talk and levels of competence reached in each teaching dimension. Overall, the differences in the intellectual dimensions are not marked, with 66 per cent of Helen's talk being in pedagogical subject knowledge compared to Jackie's 57 per cent. The graphs reflect differing teaching styles. Jackie does comparatively little didactic input, tending to use the interactive mode for this. She monitors the whole group in the didactic mode, using the lesson to ascertain previous knowledge. In contrast, Helen does some didactic monitoring at level 2 to check recall of previous work. Most of her input is didactic; then once the group is working she again monitors, this time interactively with small groups. Helen's management of activity is more effective than Jackie's, reaching level 3 for a comparatively large proportion of the lesson. She thus leaves herself space to do more level 2 monitoring, in which she is diagnosing individual pupil's difficulties. Finally, Helen has more than twice as much talk at levels 3 and 4 than Jackie.

Perceptions of teaching performance: reflection and evaluation

Jackie

Jackie thought that her diagnostic purposes had been fulfilled, but she doubted whether the children had understood her real purposes. She considered that she had catered for differing abilities and provided learning about shape, but this perception was not validated by the observer, who stated that the children already knew the shapes. Jackie's perceived weaknesses included lack of planning and organization, lack of structure in the activities, and inadequate materials. She also commented on her poor presentation: she was very nervous, did not speak loudly or clearly enough, and had not planned what to say. She rushed them into practical activities. Jackie felt she had mathematical knowledge; the problem was communicating it. She did agree that her knowledge needed some revision.

Helen

Both Helen and the observer agreed that her purposes had been fulfilled. Helen was content with the presentation. She felt that the children had learned about the relationship of different shapes to circles and, incidentally, manual skills, and the need for accuracy in folding and cutting. She thought that the children had enjoyed it; the activity put across a basic concept well and that she had been competent in her relationships with the children. She saw as weaknesses the fact that she had not stretched the more able and that her materials had not been ready to hand. She added that they had not really understood the concept of tessellation; this needed to be covered in a separate lesson. She also reflected on the classroom organization, which was not hers. She preferred to teach maths in ability groups and have the whole class working on the same curriculum area. Helen did not consider that she had specialist knowledge in maths.

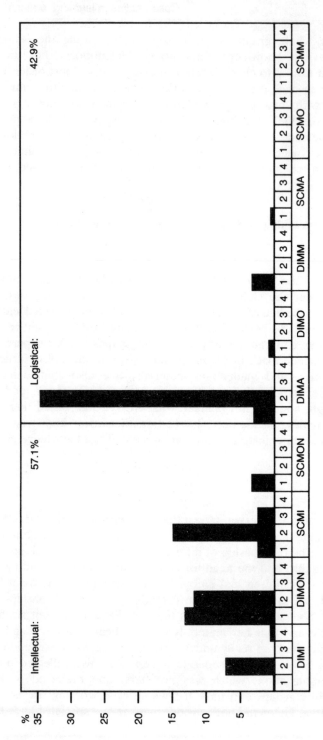

Figure 11.5 Jackie: intellectual and logistical aspects of teaching

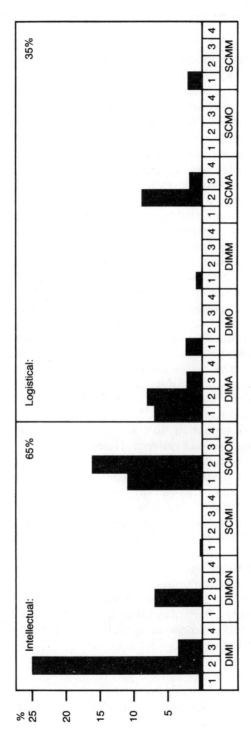

Figure 11.6 Helen: intellectual and logistical aspects of teaching

Summary

Both Jackie and Helen modelled their lessons on input from the training institution, but in Jackie's case it was imitation without expertise. Her mathematical knowledge required revision, and she had not comprehended the topic sufficiently to transform it into activities suitable for the particular group of learners. Her purposes were diagnostic, constrained as she was by her cooperating teacher's lack of communication. Her planning, necessarily tentative, was at level 1 in most areas. Helen reached level 2 in planning. Her purposes were superficially more limited, but conceptually richer, in that she wanted children to become aware of what happens when the number of edges of a shape is increased. The making of shapes from circles functioned as an active learning metaphor for the concept of that relationship. Helen's modelling of input from the course was at the level of principle, i.e. doing something practical, tactile and fun as a starting-point. She also read around the topic to find the activity. The result was an amalgamation of content, pedagogy and subject-specific pedagogy in an activity which served several phases of learning. The less able could learn how to make shapes accurately and practice doing so. The more able could consider the relationships between shapes; this conceptual enrichment would lead eventually to the geometry of circles and work on angles.

Helen's evaluation shows her reaching level 3 in more areas than Jackie. Helen is already thinking in terms of relating her whole classroom organization to her purposes of what she wants to achieve as a teacher. She dutifully abides by her cooperating teacher's constraints, doing so very effectively, but in private reveals her own beliefs on how a primary classroom should be organized. In contrast, Jackie is still thinking about how to organize one group of children. Helen did not accept that because all the children enjoyed the task, that it catered for differing abilities. She could see in her own thorough individual monitoring that she ought to have provided other extension activities for the more able, apart from tessellation, which was best tackled in a separate lesson. It is also significant that in terms of classroom organization, Helen was already operating at a standard which left plenty of time for individual diagnosis; the activities had been structured to allow for this.

Both Jackie and Helen worked under fairly severe constraints however. Jackie's planning was compromised by lack of information from the cooperating teacher and Helen found herself teaching a whole class after planning to teach only a third of it. Despite this, the root of the differences in these particular performances is essentially in the differing sophistication of their pedagogical reasoning.

CONCLUSION

A number of points emerge from these studies. The first is that lack of subject knowledge appears to exhibit itself in less intellectual input and more management. The importance of the latter should not be denied however. High quality teaching is not possible without high quality management. What is required is an appropriate balance between the intellectual and logistical aspects of teaching. Secondly, the studies high-light the constraints under which student-teachers learn to teach. The cooperating teachers were extremely variable in the support they offered. They also impose their own organizational framework within which students are forced to work. Such frameworks may be antithetical to the student-teachers' own conceptions of organization. There are also many variables, such as group size and school ethos, which have to be taken into consideration. As McDiarmid, Ball and Anderson (1989) remind us: 'teachers' reasoning takes place in concrete, dynamic situations, inherently fraught with dilemmas'.

The third and most significant trend illustrated in these studies is the clear operation, amongst some of these student-teachers, of pedagogical reasoning. Both our own model of task processes and Shulman's model of pedagogical reasoning implicate the role of subject knowledge in how lessons are conceived and implemented. These views were supported, in general terms, in the last chapter, and are confirmed in more specific case-study terms in this. The contrast of Melanie and Sybil demonstrated clearly how Melanie's knowledge informed her intentions, the task chosen, its representation and organization, and not least the quality of reflection and evaluation. On the other side of the coin it highlighted how lack of appropriate knowledge crippled Sybil's ability to develop or elaborate the theme.

Contrast Sybil's attempt at imitation without comprehension in her music lesson, to her performance in a subject where she did have some expertise. The quality of planning was substantially higher, as was the representation, where she had created her own pin-probe equipment to test skin sensitivity. Here too her organization and control were good, as was differentiation of tasks, assessment and evaluation.

Jackie too tried to model without the appropriate knowledge and thus failed to comprehend the impact of the tasks on her particular group of learners, or her own role in that process. This, incidentally, is not to deny the value of modelling, particularly when it is combined with structured attempts at reflection and evaluation. Nevertheless it would argue that it is likely to be more successful in areas where the imitator has the necessary subject knowledge base.

An appropriate knowledge base would appear to be necessary, but not sufficient, for competent teaching performances. However, the nature and level of that knowledge is unclear. Paula, for example, studied science at A level and was following a specialist science course. Despite this it was clear that her own knowledge of force was insecure, and this, combined with a lack of general pedagogical knowledge, particularly of organization and order, led to the self-confessed mayhem. What appears to be emerging is that competent performances of the intellectual aspects of teaching require both a secure background of substantive knowledge together with a revisiting or active procurement of what some have called episodic knowledge, i.e. that required by the particular curriculum demands. This kind of revisiting or active procurement is illustrated in the planning of Melanie's music, Sybil's science and Helen's maths lesson. It is lacking in the other three lessons, where the student-teachers did not have the background of content knowledge, and did not revisit or acquire requisite knowledge. The capability, and motivation, to constantly revisit one's knowledge or seek out additional knowledge, is obviously an important aspect of a teacher's continuing professionalism.

The evidence from the case studies and elsewhere shows that modelling alone is not enough:

> Providing beginning teachers with ready-made repertoires would not ensure that they could effectively connect their pupils with subject matter. Teachers must be able to appraise the pedagogical content of an available representation and determine how well it fits the context.
>
> (McDiarmid *et al.*, 1989)

The most effective student-teachers observed seemed to have embarked already on the process of pedagogical reasoning, on transformation and adaptation of content knowledge via appropriate and sometimes powerful representations.

Chapter 12

The first year of teaching

Clive Carré

INTRODUCTION

There are many references in the literature which equate learning to teach with going on a never-ending journey. Copa (1991) for example argued,

> Each new teacher enters the classroom more or less as a stranger in a strange land. The suitcases he or she carries are filled with articles from the old country, the familiar land just left.

This chapter considers the way newly qualified teachers learn to teach, with suitcases filled with understandings gleaned from the initial training programme and knowledge of the enabling conditions in school that help teaching and learning. They are also filled with other experiences of life. As one said: 'It's very hard for me to tell what I've actually assimilated from my course at the School of Education and what I had before from my previous experience.'

What we know about the process of beginning to teach is limited. Research has been characterized by descriptive investigations, identifying the experiences of beginning teachers, or explanatory studies that have attempted to identify and categorize the needs or problems of new teachers. Investigators document critical problems and comment on the feelings of frustration, anxiety and doubt brought on as beginning teachers learn to teach (Dow, 1979; Fullan, 1982; Olson and Osborne, 1991).

Some of the problems appear to lie with an inability to fit into a school's sociological system (Zeichner, 1983) whilst others appear to centre on concerns about self-image (Goodman, 1987); many other problems are understandably associated with classroom routines, discipline, management issues and dealing with the individual needs of children (Veenman, 1984). It is reported that, in general, teacher-training courses do not prepare teachers appropriately; it is more demanding and more exhausting than anticipated. Difficulty with management is often perceived as a lack of control; to maintain discipline, beginning teachers may react by shifting from their liberal ideals to authoritarian approaches.

Many overplan in reaction to feeling inadequate, and become very tired in the process (Lacey, 1977). Handling time effectively is a major problem for them, and there is a perceived dilemma in balancing the delivery of the curriculum and the desire to 'really educate' (Goodman, 1987). Many of the concerns and problems described for beginning teachers can be explained as having their origins in the lack of application of information and skills, from a sound pedagogical knowledge base (Copa, 1991). The HMI (DES, 1988a) survey of first-year teachers, for example, indicated that three-quarters of lessons were at least satisfactory on overall quality of teaching, and in the vast majority of lessons the teachers had established good, or at least satisfactory, relationships with their pupils. Nevertheless there were aspects of performance of new teachers which were identified as unsatisfactory, as was indicated in Chapter 1. HMI comments on provisions made for first-year teachers indicated that only half were well or reasonably well satisfied with their induction programme. The support from local education authorities was judged to be very low, and often fell short of what schools saw as desirable; newly trained teachers not only needed support and close monitoring, but were entitled to it.

THE FOLLOW-UP STUDY

From the random sample of twenty-four student-teachers, thirteen volunteered to take part in the follow-up study, through their first year of teaching. The intention was to describe the way they felt they developed as teachers; to identify their perceptions of strengths and weaknesses, elicit what they thought about theory–practice links, and to find out how classroom incidents were resolved or made sense of, through private understandings of theory (cf. Elbaz, 1983; Clandinin, 1986). Data were collected by face-to-face and telephone interview. The four points of data collection were:

1 Telephone interview at the end of their first week of teaching.
2 First visit to school, mid-autumn term.
3 Second visit to school, mid-spring term.
4 Telephone interview at the end of the school year.

In addition, information was collected on the nature of support given throughout the year. Headteachers were interviewed on both school visits. All interviews were recorded on tape and transcribed for analysis. The interviews were semi-structured and informal in nature. The questions were common but sufficiently open to enable the expression of personal understandings within the classroom contexts they knew. In the analysis transcripts were read and re-read, and a running list of characteristics was made that provided the recurrent and common issues inferred for the group. Their first teaching appointments were in different parts of the country; two schools were in inner-city areas, seven in large towns or cities, three in small or rural towns and one was a small village school.

There are three major sections to the chapter: firstly, preparing for the new job and the first week in school; secondly, developing competences; and thirdly, support from mentors and the school. Three summary profiles of progress end the chapter.

ARRANGEMENTS BEFORE TAKING UP APPOINTMENT

Detailed guidance was given by the Department of Education and Science (DES, 1990) to local authorities and schools on the induction of new teachers, their treatment and assessment. Part of the arrangements for newly appointed teachers is that they receive information about the school; its organization, staff, resources, curriculum documents and 'adequate notice of the timetable to be taught'. In addition, research into beginning teachers' learning to teach (e.g. Busher, Clarke and Taggart, 1988) points to the importance of communicating 'the norms and expectations of the school'. To what extent did the schools provide for these needs, indeed the rights of the newly qualified teachers?

Only one did not have the opportunity to visit the school and meet the staff prior to taking up her appointment. Most visited for one day, although one was invited to visit on five separate occasions. The majority met their future class but, surprisingly, fewer than half received pertinent information about the children they would be teaching. One was told that they were 'a rowdy lot with attitude problems', and others received a similar lack of information, with no records of ability. One was even given wrong information and told to plan for children 'heading for level 4', whereas they were only at level 2. Only two reported that the information provided on their future class had been full and helpful, and included details of achievements and behaviour.

Only half the group received the school handbook and school curriculum policies so information on general school routines was often lacking; for example, one relied only on that which she had received verbally at interview. Some schools did not provide timetables and this hindered preparation before school started. One had to wait until just before half-term and was in despair: 'so we spent the first five weeks without a timetable . . . very very difficult it was.'

Although everyone planned to some degree before school started, the amount of time spent on it varied. One described only 'planning the topic in general terms of skills and concepts, but not in detail . . . no activities'. Others valued the cooperative effort of meeting with teachers in the school during the vacation and 'did half-termly forecasts, covering all aspects of the curriculum'. The value of a well-organized school was appreciated by one who found the detailed structure for planning gave a sense of security:

It was structured. . . . The school asked for aims and objectives for the whole term on a form . . . list all the statements of attainment from the National Curriculum . . . then plan in detail in two-week blocks. I used this planning straight away.

The experience of three was less than satisfactory. Two described how the school had given them the wrong topic for planning, resulting in a great deal of unnecessary and irrelevant work during the vacation. Probably the worst experience was that which described continued futile attempts to negotiate with a teacher (her year partner) who could not make up her mind on a topic. Eventually, 'three or four days before term, she told me to plan on my own'.

For those who had been given guidance about planning, finding suitable resources created problems. Only two commended the school for being well-resourced, therefore most relied on making and using their own material. Local libraries provided books and magazines for information and ideas, and the National Curriculum was used as a major resource. Published curriculum schemes in maths and science were specifically mentioned as being useful in planning, but few mentioned university course notes as being helpful.

In summary, it was clear that, before taking up a post, anxiety was heightened when there was little information about: timetable arrangements and overall plans, detailed records of children's capabilities, the whereabouts of resources, expectations of the school routines and organization.

THE FIRST WEEK IN SCHOOL

At the end of the first week in school the teachers were telephoned at home to see how well they had fared. Their responses gave a vivid picture of coping with a blitz of stimuli, establishing classroom routines and settling in. It was as one described it, 'absolutely mind-boggling, but OK'.

The majority expressed feelings of being very tired, perceived by some to be the consequence of 'finding where things are and how things are done normally' and by others the stress of coping with children. Some initial class encounters were difficult, because 'The children are extremely rude and disrespectful . . . and the boys fight.' For others, with no experience of working in an open-plan system, the challenge was of a different kind:

a hectic beginning . . . difficult to get used to the system, the children seem to be going here, there and everywhere. Bit panicky at first.

However, the general feeling was one of optimism and feeling happy. In part this was the result of the teacher's perception of their new class. Nine out of the thirteen made positive statements about their children, particularly about having 'no behavioural problems at all'. Only two felt disheartened and disillusioned as one explained: 'I've twenty-two boys in my class and most are really naughty so I've been quite hard.'

If problem children were mentioned it was a minority group of *boys* which caused trouble. Individually pleasant, but as one described them in class, they were 'the little horrors . . . five or six . . . quite a handful, kicking, swearing and throwing things.'

With such diverse experiences, relationships with children were perceived differently. Behind non-committal comments such as 'so far, alright', were elaborated feelings about the struggle to overcome one of the most important dilemmas of their practice. As one said, she 'tried hard to get the balance right between being in control and not making them frightened', and another expressed his desire for an atmosphere 'happy, friendly but disciplined'. The teachers were aware of the cliché advice, 'not to smile before Christmas' and statements reflected this sentiment; for example, 'I've been quite hard on them so far . . .' and 'clamping down a lot'. In developing this balance early on one said she wanted, 'to be friendly but more of a stand-off person'. Others described their strategy by 'generally sounding each other out', and being 'partly authoritarian in establishing the rules.'

To be in authority yet not authoritarian, to be friendly and have this reciprocated and not abused, were concerns which probationers needed to address. They tried to resolve these dilemmas about relationships through the establishment of routines and class rules, but some thought it wise simply to adopt those in operation. Over half the group discussed with the children the need for rules and negotiated class routines.

Others extended the dialogue and 'negotiated a job list for different individuals about responsibilities', and a few even negotiated routines associated with ways of working; children were introduced to organizing their own work and planning work schedules.

With such sensible intent and useful interaction, what were the self-perceptions of these beginning teachers so early in their careers? How adequate did they feel?

Only one person described her feelings as being 'very adequate'. The large majority of the group expressed a tentativeness about their feelings. As one put it, 'Most of the time I feel adequate, but sometimes realize that with so many things to do that it is impossible, and I feel inadequate'. 'Feelings fluctuate,' as another put it, 'this morning I feel quite adequate and this afternoon I felt totally inadequate.' The reasons expressed for feeling much better than when on teaching practice were associated with being alone, and not 'looking for approval from another teacher'. An appropriate analogy was drawn by one,

> I feel like I've just passed my driving test and in the car on my own. I couldn't be myself on teaching practice because I didn't feel like the

class-teacher. Now it's my class . . . and I'm excited and wanting to do the best I can, realizing the constraints.

The main reasons given for feeling inadequate were associated with the difficulty to equate bright ideas of training with the realities of classrooms, class discipline and resource organization. To probe these views further, they were asked about the adequacy of their training. No obvious teaching skill was perceived as missing, and their general feelings were tinged with realism, as one expressed: 'No one can really be totally prepared for having full responsibility of your own class.'

During that first week, staff were often described as 'wonderful'. They valued the welcome received from everyone, as one said, 'from the caretaker, cleaners, cooks and staff'. Without exception these beginning teachers perceived their colleagues as friendly and helpful; in both professional and social aspects the staff made it easy for them to begin their new roles.

Almost everyone agreed that they had been made to feel part of the school and that, 'everyone's willing to help if you ask'. Little things count and the feeling of acceptance was heightened for one probationer when the head 'even introduced me at assembly'.

Besides the general reaction of friendliness and support there were no formal, arranged meetings to offer advice during the first week. The LEA adviser had not contacted anyone and school subject coordinators had made minimal contact. Most agreed that the first two 'training days' of term were restricted to the basic, if necessary, 'getting classrooms ready', and not to teacher training. The general impression was that these in-service days were not taken very seriously. A typical comment was that, 'Days one and two were not training days, just getting sorted out because the place was like a tip.' Only two commented on useful in-service provision, one on developing a reading policy and the other on computer work.

DEVELOPING COMPETENCES DURING THE YEAR

When asked during the first few months about how they thought they had developed as teachers the main issue that was talked about was their feelings of increasing confidence. Understandably they made reference to their teaching practice experiences and in general their comments were tinged with feelings of uncertainty. Even though they differed in age, were in different schools and working with different aged children, there was a commonality in their perceived professional development.

The following categories emerged from the interview transcripts, as issues impinging on their feelings of confidence:

(a) Improving confidence and learning by success/failure. The main reasons given were:

  (i) better discipline and control of the class;
 (ii) trying out different teaching roles;
(iii) better classroom organization;
(iv) better at using subject matter appropriately with children.
(b) Understanding links between theory and practice.
(c) Changes in relationships with children, parents and colleagues.

Each is discussed in turn below.

(a) Improving confidence and learning by success/failure

(i) Better discipline and control of the class

In the first term there were frequent references to feeling more confident than when on teaching practice. One reason put forward was that as a student-teacher the class-teacher diminished their confidence, by being over-protective or by devaluing their ability. Another reason for feeling confident was the way they had learned to gain more control, as one said:

> I think I tackle difficult children differently. I used to shout all the time. I think they were more frightened of me then. They're not very frightened in my class. I don't like the idea that the only reason they're working is because they're frightened. I'd rather they did it because they wanted to do it. So I've been trying to be more persuasive.

However, the feelings of being in control and the confidence that gave were, for the majority, *tentatively* expressed, as, for example:

> To start with it was more or less mob control, then just trying to get the children to calm down and to get on with some work. So I think probably control might be more of a strength now. I think I've learnt how to deal with some of the discipline problems a little bit better. I mean, sometimes I still think, Oh, what shall I do now?

They were unsure about their ability to control the exuberance of the class and mentioned in particular the struggle to balance disciplining children, while still appearing friendly.

During the second term everyone mentioned feeling more confident; some were able to add, 'and more happy'. In general, there were fewer expressed feelings about anxiety. For the majority, discipline and control was still at the forefront of their minds; it was the first thing mentioned in reply to the question on how they thought they had developed as a teacher. For example, one said how it was such a relief for her to walk into the classroom and feel that she was in control, even if it meant, 'at times being stubborn, putting your foot down and even being quite nasty!'

At the end of the year almost everyone mentioned that they had gradually developed more confidence and felt more in control of the class's behaviour. Their professional development was seen by many as an ability to control children through understanding them better.

(ii) Trying out different teaching roles

There was an obvious overlap of statements about controlling behaviour and teaching effectively; learning to control adequately to enable one to teach in different ways. Initially many resolved the conflict by using previously tried-out lesson plans from teaching practice. At the first-term interview only one felt sufficiently confident and in control to express her willingness to take risks. Teaching for her was not seen as a one-shot affair:

> Probably I'm not afraid of making mistakes. I know it's not that important. Having my own class makes me feel that this isn't the only chance we'll get to do this. It's a gradual wearing away – it's like the drip, drip, drip on the stone – it's not going to be this wonderful lesson that I do that is going to have them all understanding. It won't, it'll be over a period of time.

During the second term there was more mention of feeling confident to stand back and try out different teaching roles, controlling children through their learning. By the end of the school year there was less expressed tentativeness about trying out ideas and more definite perceptions of competence. Some talked of learning 'to know what worked and what didn't'; a trial-and-error procedure of controlling discipline on the one hand and meeting their role responsibility to achieve academic successes on the other. The dilemma involved risk, of which many were now aware. One saw his realization of success as a teacher not merely in the control of the class, but in a responsibility to help them learn:

> I think that I have gained confidence over the year and a bit of experience so that I worry a lot less about tackling new ideas. I am more prepared to take on challenges and I don't worry so much about what will happen if things go wrong, because I know that I can cope. I don't mean discipline kind of control, I can deal with that. It's going wrong with the children not understanding.

There were associated comments about motivating children, at last being able to, 'get children interested in what they were doing', whereas at the beginning of the year as one said, 'everything we did was seen as boring, no matter what it was. They don't ever say that any more.' Professional strengths over the year were therefore seen in terms of developing confidence to control the class in a less tight way and then feeling sufficiently secure to, 'step back a bit from what's going on, trust them and then do some adventurous things'. Trying out new roles meant improving organization skills, as the next section shows.

(iii) Better classroom organization

During the first term, organization was seen as a problem and some indicated that it took them time to offer children opportunities to work in groups, or to let some classwork be done with minimal supervision. For the majority, development was seen in learning to manage children in different ways, i.e. developing a repertoire of organizational strategies.

Many reflected on trying out the most effective ways to organize a new class, and the feelings of inadequacy when for example their ideas of developing autonomy did not come up to expectations. A commonly expressed anxiety lay in the consequences of trying out new styles of representation; getting the balance right between direct teaching and child-centredness and helping children to adjust to a new teacher's expectations. Inevitably successes and failures were felt as children tried to accommodate. One said:

> I came in and was very disappointed that they couldn't do things that I thought they should be able to do, and I've had to change. I think that that's something that needs to be consistently developed throughout. You've got to set your sights at a certain place; I didn't have sights on really what I thought they should be able to do, not what they can do; I think I've developed in that way.

Apart from these concerns, particularly about judging children's ability, many talked about the vital necessity to teach the children their expectations about organization.

> I've now got books set out so that they can easily be found, and I've had felt-pen tins labelled clearly. Certainly with these children, you can't just say we'll tidy up . . . you have to say, the scissors go in this, this goes here and you have to say it every time that you do it. But I think I have developed.

During the second term they expressed a much greater degree of confidence about such matters, generally, for example in 'organizing their movements around the class' and much easier management of children's teaching and learning. Some saw the benefits of detailed planning as the key, 'the structure actually making it easier for learning to take place and easier for progression'. By the end of the year management was not referred to as a problem, and resources were not mentioned as being difficult to locate or to use. Display work was felt to be better presented. In general they felt much more at ease, and were more confident in organizing themselves in teaching and the children in different learning strategies.

(iv) Better at using subject matter appropriately with children

'Getting things across' to children, i.e. the best form of representation to use when teaching a particular topic, was mentioned by many as a concern in the first term. They felt it involved learning to make judgements about the appropriateness of a task or presentation, and then diagnosing its success or otherwise. These two extracts make the point:

> It's more with the maths I think, when you've got a basic idea of a right angle, I mean some of them didn't know what a right angle was, which I was really surprised at for third-year juniors. Just the basic concept, a square I was thinking of you see, a corner, but then squares are made of right angles. So that was no good to them really either. It's just what basic things they ought to know.

> I still feel my ability to assess is not terrific and I do worry that I'm not getting things across that they should know, because I'm not very good at sort of evaluating what's going on I suppose.

Matching tasks and presenting them appropriately were only part of the concerns expressed about handling subject knowledge. Others talked of the problems of planning for progression, when there was a lack of feeling secure in subject-matter knowledge, for example:

> I still feel quite weak in teaching maths and progression. We don't have a maths scheme here, which means that I actually have to sort everything out and decide where the children are going for myself. . . . How well I am actually putting the subject over is on me . . . it's actually – the progression of the children's work and sorting out where they're going I find I'm not really sure about.

In the second term there was much more confidence expressed about the ability to match and to plan for progression, and a third of the group mentioned matching as an important attribute in their development. Others still felt concern about knowing enough about a subject to get children to understand, 'getting the level right, getting it low enough with the basic principles'.

By the end of the school year very positive statements were expressed about their handling of subject-matter knowledge, enabling children's learning. They were proud of their achievements as these two extracts show:

> I had some children at the beginning of the year who really hadn't begun reading. . . . They are all quite strong readers now, so I feel that the reading methods that I've used got them on their way.

> You can see the numberwork developing. . . . Now they are able to count to ten and do the correspondence that goes with it and some of them are doing addition and being able to add quite happily up to ten. Their emergent writing . . . they are suddenly, from doing a few squiggles on a page, now able to write sentences, which is fantastic.

Perceived strengths in teaching subject-matter knowledge were talked about in terms of being more aware of the outcomes of their teaching; and many felt that they were learning concepts themselves in order to prepare their lessons. As to weaknesses, they were quick to say that they would probably never stop learning and everything they did could be improved. As a group, they were self-critical! However, the humanities were most frequently mentioned as a perceived curriculum area where support was still needed, and confidence was low. As a consequence, a few felt their presentation was poor, and their children did not learn as well.

(b) Understanding links between theory and practice

By the end of the first term most had not made much sense of the links between theory and practice. Their reasoning was the lack of time to reflect and to get to know the children. One said:

> If I had time to think about it, I think I could recognize the links. Behaviour and positive reinforcement, things like that – I can see a definite link there. Also this idea of level of attainment rather than levels of ability. I think my experience this term has kind of reinforced my support of that idea.

Others were more blunt and said the theory they had learned about in training they found impossible to put into practice.

By the end of the second term the question about theory–practice links was still not readily understood. Responses were of two types; those referring to theoretical ideas met on the course, and those describing practical theorizing.

(i) Theory–practice links

Many gave some examples of connections between 'real' (i.e. abstract, formal) theory and its application to their class setting. These included behaviour techniques, special educational needs, cognitive development, positive reinforcement, matching, ownership in writing, and mixed-ability grouping. In struggling to dredge appropriate topics from the back of their minds it was apparent that there were no *obvious* connections being made. It was as if the text-book theory was compartmentalized and had been 'done', and as one honest reply indicated, 'I don't think very hard about the theory really'. Incongruously they did! For example, one said:

> Like if I think specifically about our language course and the way we read – we talked about teaching children to read and write. I use a lot of that. It's theory I believe in, and I do use the practical help they've suggested. But I've also made up my own ways of doing it, but the theory came from initial training.

And in doing so, illustrated what the group as a whole was becoming aware of; probationers could talk in some detail about making sense of theory in their own terms, what worked for them, as the next section indicates.

(ii) Practice–personal theory links

Most were able to give examples about their developing personal theories; a basis for action. Some were not articulated further than tentative hypotheses. As for example in talking about matching, one said, 'If you get the right level of work, you've often got less trouble.' Another said, 'you can actually assess a child just by talking to them, talking maths – talk with them to find out where they are.'

In describing personal theorizing, there was considerable evidence that, as one said, 'formal theories have become so practical I think they've lost their identities'. Another corroborated this view:

> I don't really see that much as theory any more, it's more a practical way of doing it. Like the idea of how children learn. . . . It's suddenly stopped being such a kind of text-book, black-and-white theory and it's turning into reality. So because I haven't much time to actually read a lot and to look back on my notes, the actual line between theory and practical has got very blurred.

These interviews gave an indication of one of the ways probationers reflect. In essence they gave a picture of views in transition, a concern for a better understanding of pedagogy, by trying things out and evaluating *what worked for them in their particular set of circumstances*. So reflecting on action involved putting personal theory to the test, and proceeding on a trial-and-error basis, i.e. 'finding out what I think works . . . this doesn't, so I'll do it again'. This seems to conform to Gunstone and Northfield's (1992) view of meta-cognition which they define as 'having an informed and self-directed approach to recognizing, evaluating, and deciding whether or not to reconstruct.'

By the third term, theory–practice links were in general seen as the development of personal theories. For a year they had been in the business of making sense of classroom behaviour to find out what worked for them. What they described included, for example, their own ideas about organizing science practical work, so that children learned about process in helping to plan and select materials: about providing choice 'for children to do it *their* way', which may conflict with a teacher's idea of the product in mind; organizing groups in different ways for different activities and teaching 'holistically through cross-curricular themes, to make working out progression easier'. Many had personal theories about control and discipline. One said of her strategy for her new class next year:

It was a bit of a culture shock when I first came here. I'm not going to be as friendly with them as I have been with this class because they have taken advantage of that. I can control them, but it takes a lot of hard work. So I know that I am going to go in there with a stricter attitude and maybe not smile and laugh so freely.

The 'idealistic theory' of training gave expectations that in general were found difficult to work in *their* contexts and this frequently caused concern. Anxiety was relieved when success was observed, justification for a continued belief in one's personal theorizing and pragmatism.

(c) Changes in relationships

Part of the image of being a teacher is to be recognized as one in the eyes of the children. Many made this point: 'I think the children take me as their teacher, they don't know I'm a probationer either'.

In the first term there were many expressed feelings about 'belonging' to a class, and the need 'to get on with the children', together with the desired expectations of being liked. Most thought their relationships were informed and friendly:

> I've got a very warm, friendly relationship with the children. . . . I have very firm rules which the children understand and as long as they stick within those rules then they and I get along fine.

Comments in general indicated that they were in the business of trying out the degree of friendliness or strictness necessary to achieve a workable, balanced relationship. Explanations as to why relationships with children were better than when on teaching practice included the sense of achievement in seeing change in children's learning and behaviour, and the increased feeling of responsibility that went with being the class-teacher. There was a genuine feeling of ownership of the class and the pride that went with it:

> I feel quite protective towards them. They're MY class and I feel quite proud when all three classes, for example, are in here watching television and mine aren't making any noise! And I feel very pleased for them when they do anything that's good.

In the second term some described their relationships improving through being more relaxed and by developing mutual respect. The reciprocal needs of liking and being liked was seen by a few to be so important that it was made explicit when dealing with discipline problems:

> I can be quite firm. I think they think that I like them, and I'm quite kind and I do say to them well it's your behaviour that I don't like in this situation and not you. I think some of them felt reassured about that.

At the end of the school year good relationships with children and seeing their progress were the main reasons given for having enjoyed the year. On reflection they had enjoyed helping children to learn and as one said: 'sort of growing with the kids. They've grown and I've grown as well you know. I've adjusted to them and they to me.' And in doing so, many commented on their increased sense of responsibility, a more holistic perspective:

> In a way you are responsible for them for everything they do . . . like an all-round relationship . . . you see them progressing and get to know them a lot better . . . and you get to know the family and any problems that they have . . . some of the time we're working with parents.

Awareness of a child's background was considered to be very important and thus relationships with parents were fostered. A few reported parents coming into school, to help with supervision of small groups, in cooking, art, technology and computer work. However, others were not so fortunate. There were reports of very few attending parents' evenings and parents coming into class to help which made learning for pupils and organization for the beginning teacher more difficult.

Even at the end of the year, relationships with parents were reported with mixed feelings: for some there were accounts of productive cooperative efforts; for others, parents were seen as a problem, a threat or as an 'undesirable influence in class'.

The large majority described relationships with colleagues as friendly, open and supportive. They were made to feel accepted both socially and professionally. In general, they appreciated the staff's willingness to be supportive, with location of resources, timetable difficulties and so on, to be behind them in times of crisis with parents and difficult children, but above all to allow them to be themselves. That feeling of being allowed to experiment to find one's own style and role orientation, within a context of supportive colleagues, was thought to be an ideal.

At the end of the school year their comments were again positive. Mention was made about increased feelings of belonging to the school, but there was also appreciation of genuine professional interest in them and their perceptions. For example, interest in the progress the children had made under their guidance, and help that many beginning teachers had given in their specialist areas, in computer work and in music. Some relationships were so well developed that they not only shared ideas with staff, but felt comfortable to comment on what colleagues were doing in their own classrooms. There was only one instance where the relationship with staff was thought to have hindered progress: one teacher was reluctant to cooperate in organizing a parallel class.

Relationships with headteachers throughout the year were for most good, and were described as friendly and supportive. Some were protective of the over-enthusiastic:

> He's supportive in that he doesn't want me to do too much. I was all keen to start a choir, start this, that and the other, and he said, 'Look you'll kill yourself if you do too much, so just slow down a bit', so he's quite understanding.

Even though it was recognized that headteachers were very busy, it was appreciated when they found time to keep in touch with their progress and took a personal interest in their planning of work and general settling-in. They appreciated the reduction of timetable time, the organization of visits and the way they were supported from the top when dealing with difficult children. However, their influence was not always seen as positive.

A few complained that relationships with their headteacher were strained. One thought the headteacher was remote and difficult to communicate with because he felt that a beginning teacher should work all the time, 'all week-end' and didn't appreciate that there was 'life after school, even if you love your job'. Another felt there wasn't any feeling of personal interest, no support when needed, and he was seen as a factor hindering development.

There was only one person who felt that the headteacher had been unfair in giving her a curriculum responsibility in a subject area where she felt her knowledge to be inadequate, and another who felt a legitimate grievance that her head had not given her beginning teachers' privileges.

INDUCTION

The mentor's role

Although the first year of teaching is designed to be a settling-in period, it is an apprenticeship with a difference; from the start beginning teachers are thrown into the deep end and it is expected that they take full responsibility for a class. Schools are required to help them do this, and the DES (1990) sets out that they should be able 'to seek help and guidance from a nominated member of staff'. One question at interview was to find out if a mentor had been appointed, what role that person had taken, and what help had been given.

The relationship between the beginning teachers and their mentors by the end of the second term had remained very much the same as that in the first term. Two reported that no one had specifically been appointed as mentor. The remainder perceived their mentor's influence as being of tremendous value and the comment frequently expressed was that 'I don't know what I would have done without one really'. Their appreciation of support was understandable when research (e.g. Olson and Osborne,

1991) clearly indicates that the first year of teaching is filled with un-certainty, frustration and high levels of anxiety. Among the types of help offered to the majority of probationers, whether the mentor relationship was on a structured, regular basis or not, were:

1 General help (e.g. 'if I'm in doubt about what's going on in school, or how do I handle parents at parents' evening').
2 Practical advice (e.g. 'really useful ideas about classroom management and how to keep order, looks at my displays and comments').
3 Discipline help (e.g. 'ask for help on how to deal with those particularly difficult children').
4 Counselling (e.g. 'If I'm feeling fed up or if I've come to the end of my tether she's been there for me to cry on her shoulder').

The perceived role of the mentor was thus varied but, as Hogben and Lawson (1984) have pointed out, an underpinning factor is guidance which gives a feeling of being accepted, both personally and professionally.

Four patterns of mentoring were described. The most popular method mentioned by more than half the group, was the 'open-house' arrange-ment. Mentors were under pressure and beginning teachers soon realized that with the best will in the world, intentions to make regular meetings were not realized. The onus was in general placed upon them to seek help, and to find out a time when their mentors were free to see them. The 'open-house' system worked for most, but as one said:

> I've generally been left to get on with it by myself and if I have any problems I know that I can go and ask. However, it might have been nice for her to have shown more interest perhaps. She's only come into my classroom once since I've been here.

The second arrangement described a 'model' role, especially made possible in team teaching. The mentor was described as giving advice, saying 'what he likes and doesn't like' and explaining by example 'how to deal with problem children'. Having an experienced teacher so close to hand had disadvantages too; one said that because he was 'so set in his teaching ways that it's quite difficult to get my own way with anything, and my ideas taken on'.

The third arrangement of 'many-mentors' operated for two. Although both had a designated mentor, the staff acted as a supportive whole. One said, 'I just go to whoever I think will be able to help me . . . certainly not always the same person'. The fourth pattern, the 'listening and discussing' role, was described by two in glowing terms, of being a very supportive and very constructive relationship. These mentors were per-ceived as being good at listening, discussing problems and giving feedback; in particular a specific aspect of professional development could be focused upon at a time, which one probationer called a 'zone of development':

She advises me really and watches several lessons a term and writes a report to me and sits down and discusses this with me and we agree a zone of development . . . she's not interfering in any way, just shows me how to get on and makes suggestions, and is around to talk to whenever I need.

Whatever the style of mentor supervision, the support was appreciated. It was particularly so when they took the time to work alongside, to empathize with specific classroom dilemmas. One described such an instance, dealing with less-able readers; visiting her class, 'she knew what I was talking about'.

The mentor role is a complex one, and as Anderson and Shannon (1988) have pointed out, effective mentoring programmes require a clear conceptual foundation, including the essential functions of the mentor and their activities. More is required than the notion of a 'helper-friend'.

School support

The large majority of schools provided a programme of support for beginning teachers. Arrangements varied, some more structured than others, but for most it appeared that the schools were acting within the spirit of the requirements of the Administrative Memorandum (DES, 1990).

For the majority, by the middle of the second term provision had been made for them to

- have a reduced teaching load (half a day a week for most);
- observe other teachers teaching (informal basis);
- visit other schools (up to five for some);
- attend meetings for probationers (organized by the local education authority).

The value of the visits to school was to 'see an expert in action' and to 'just be a fly on the wall, not to be involved'. Many emphasized that they didn't want to be given things to do, for they didn't know the children or the context. What they did appreciate was to compare classroom organization and see children learning in the same aged class as they taught. As one said, 'it's quite reassuring'. Besides 'picking up ideas', mention was also made, by most, of the value of seeing an experienced teacher manage a class with a theoretical idea in mind; 'organizing good role-play' was one mentioned, and 'seeing good emergent writing in reception' was another. Some referred enthusiastically to seeing 'language policies in action' and others appreciated learning more about what they perceived as 'weaknesses' in subject knowledge. For example:

I chose to go to this school because they teach the arts well. They have this kind of integrated way of teaching, using the arts as a basis. I feel that one of my weaknesses is definitely the arts, and I felt that I could learn a lot by actually seeing good practice.

In contrast to the perceived value of school visits, meetings organized for newly qualified teachers by the local education authority were generally thought of as poorly organized, unproductive and a waste of time. As one pointed out, she 'had better things to do', for what was requested (i.e. 'things like discipline, dealing with children with special needs') were not provided. For some the content was thought to be more relevant to secondary teachers, or was similar to what had been done already in training. In general the only value of these meetings was seen as opportunities to meet other new teachers and to share common problems.

Very few observed colleagues teaching, and only one described this imaginative arrangement:

The teacher in Year 6, she's very good at dance and we've arranged that I'm going to watch her take her class next week for a dance lesson. Straight after that she's going to take my class for a dance lesson, so I get to watch both, so that's good.

In general, opportunities were missed by not organizing visits *within* the school, to observe colleagues in action. Ironically it is this aspect of school support which they said they would value greatly.

SUMMARY PROFILE SKETCHES OF THREE PROBATIONERS

Schaffer, Springfield and Wolfe (1990) conclude that two important factors contributing to professional development in teacher induction programmes were support and specific feedback. However, even when these were provided they found that 'new teachers required time to develop the complex repertoires of behaviour necessary to succeed in classrooms'. Data from this study suggest that the rate at which development takes place varies with the individual and progress was often limited or accelerated because of school influences. Detailed examination of the progress of individuals illustrated different patterns of development. A summary of three profile sketches is given of three beginning teachers who taught 9–10-year-olds and were in schools where staff were friendly and helpful.

Case 1 – steady improvement

Sonia settled in quickly having organized her classroom before school started and prepared plans of work to half-term. The headteacher had provided detailed information about the school and children she was to teach. The picture was one of competent preparedness on both sides.

She was confident and gradually learned not to over-organize. She explored different teaching strategies and balancing whole-class teaching, group work and individual work. She was a thinking person and willing to learn through trial and error which approaches were best for her and the children. As she became less 'flustered and panicky to get everything sorted out', her relationship with the children improved and she no longer needed to nag them!

Her relationship with staff was good. Her mentor was supportive and she received well-informed feedback throughout. At no time had there been any problems; the headteacher thought she had shown gradual improvement and was much more professionally aware at the end of the year.

Case 2 – downhill progress

Anthony felt exhausted and stressed at the end of the first week. On the first day he realized that his efforts of planning and collecting resources had been in vain. Not only had the school not communicated the topic he was to teach but he had no general school information, school policies or curriculum outlines. He had serious problems settling in, exacerbated by the conflict between what the school wanted and his complying with those expectations. For example, his idealistic views about teaching maths for meaning, were in conflict with the school's insistence on 'a clear focus on National Curriculum requirements and evidence in children's books'.

He was confident, enjoyed the children but found 'an awful lot of pressure from different directions'. There were expressions of concern about organization and control and his naive views on theory and practice. Feedback about his performance was minimal; his façade of confidence made people reticent to help. He said 'my self-esteem went down and down, as I got more and more busy.' His good days were good and his bad days were 'real black bits'. The school indicated that he had 'improved radically in his display work and relationships with children'. He realized that he had to get a lot right in teaching subject matter, especially getting children to understand mathematical ideas.

Case 3 – slow to start, rapid acceleration

It is hard to dismiss the real difficulties which Felicity had to establish herself on equal terms with her experienced team-teacher. She had planned conscientiously before term started, along guidelines given by the school. Her problem was to try to establish herself alongside a teacher who was set in his ways and could handle any disciplinary problem with ease, when she was facing, 'the worst class in the school . . . a rowdy lot of little devils with attitude problems'.

Unintentionally her team-teacher, also her mentor, inhibited her from making her mark and she felt superfluous. She said 'really he's the teacher and I hardly say a word'. After the second term the picture changed dramatically. She became more confident, took advantage of the mentor's modelling to learn more about matching, management and control. In the third term they shared ideas in planning, she was frequently in sole charge of the sixty children and she introduced and established music as an important part of the curriculum. It was thought by the headteacher that they had over the year forged a productive working relationship and that Felicity with determination 'had developed a strong professional awareness'.

CONCLUSION

It is clear that the arrangements made before taking up appointments varied widely, and there were instances where they bore little resemblance to DES (1990) requirements. In general, the reaction to the newly qualified teachers on arrival was warm and supportive. The school induction programme, for example visits to other schools to see model practice, and reduced teaching loads were much appreciated. However, the area meetings for new teachers were thought to have little value.

Many described the year as an intense learning period, exhaustingly hard work, demanding, but in retrospect enjoyable. Besides the will to survive and stamina to do so, what were the main pointers to indicate professional development?

Associated with feelings of increasing confidence were common themes which reflected their varied experiences. Beginning teachers became more confident and felt that a major development was their improved control of children, often through getting to know them better. In turn this enabled them to try out different teaching strategies and eventually to take risks to do so. Classroom organization improved and with it the planning for progression. They got better at handling subject-matter knowledge; representing ideas, making judgements about the appropriateness of tasks, then diagnosing their success or otherwise and planning accordingly.

In this study, four different roles for mentors were described. The quality and type of support varied and was lacking in two instances. Developing relationships within the school was an all-important aspect of the year. For some fitting in with the norms of the school necessitated compromise and this caused tension and anxiety. However, most reported that relationships with staff and with children were good. In terms of the former there were associated deep feelings of being affiliated, being accepted and respected by the school, and with their classes a developing feeling of responsibility and ownership.

The research of Elbaz (1983) and Clandinin (1986), for example, focused on the importance of a teacher's practical knowledge, and Connelly and Clandinin's (1987) review sought to clarify its meaning; although there was an apparent commonality in researchers' language it was difficult to cross-reference research. In this study the intention was to identify the relationship of knowledge to action, the kind of thinking that guided practice. It is clear that the majority of beginning teachers perceived links between theory and practice in terms of personal theorizing, as one described, 'the practice and the theory all get blown together . . . it's not an isolated thing that you read about in books, it actually seems like a real thing'. They were able to theorize on classroom practicalities, based on explanations of their actions rather than capricious ideas. Thinking about these actions involved putting them to the test, and they were in general tentatively expressed. Personal theories were described in the context of decision-making about practical dilemmas arising from their teaching. The self-doubt and anxiety which this often generated can be seen as an important element in their professional development.

Chapter 13

Learning to teach

Neville Bennett, Clive Carré and Elisabeth Dunne

The study set out to achieve enhanced understandings of some central issues in the training of primary teachers, i.e. the extent to which, and how, knowledge bases for teaching develop through training, the relationship of these knowledge bases to teaching performance, and the impact of the first year of teaching. Each of these issues has important policy and practical implications for the preparation of teachers, particularly at a time when conceptions and criteria for training are being reconsidered.

In order to address these issues it was necessary to assess what knowledge and beliefs student-teachers brought with them to the course, and if, and how, they had changed as a consequence of it: as Barnes (1989) has argued, 'Too often, in considering what beginning teachers need to know, we have failed to consider what novices think they already know.'

Changes in subject-matter knowledge for teaching were limited to English and music. In science and mathematics there was no significant change; in both, the student-teachers showed only a basic understanding of many of the topics they are obliged to teach in the National Curriculum. Interestingly the misconceptions they displayed in these subjects were similar to those found in primary school children. There was, however, some improvement in English and music. Their knowledge about language improved, but not their understandings of the structure of language, especially grammar. All groups improved their knowledge of music, although most started from a very low base.

Students' knowledge about the structure, and ways of knowing the disciplines, even that which they had recently graduated in, was poor. This is of some concern since, as Grossman, Wilson and Shulman (1989) argue, a teacher's knowledge of these substantive structures has important implications for how and what teachers choose to teach.

The specific areas of most improvement in these assessments was, not surprisingly, where subject knowledge was associated with pedagogical issues. Thus, in mathematics, most improvement was apparent in their ability to diagnose pupil errors on routine tasks; in English, it was linked to knowledge of language functions, and the use of language in a variety of contexts; in music, improvements were evident in increased knowledge of, for example, children as composers, and in science, in the practical and procedural aspects of the subject.

Changes in attitudes towards subjects were more clearly visible. In their attitudes towards the nature of science there was a tendency to perceive it less as a fixed and rigid set of facts and laws, and more as tentative inquiry influenced by social and personal attributes. Although this shift was not massive it was associated with their changing perceptions towards science teaching as being a problem-solving approach incorporating constructivist principles. Similarly, beliefs about the nature of mathematics shifted towards a more relativistic stance, from a restricted to a more open, flexible view. Associated with this change was a greater feeling of liking and confidence about the subject. In English they left the course thinking more of language as a process – a learning tool rather than a set of skills to be acquired – and held a more holistic view of literacy learning. Finally, although there was little change overall in attitudes to music, their responses indicated a flexible and liberal attitude to music in school, even if one does sing out of tune!

Changes in beliefs and attitudes to teaching and to educational issues were slight. They appeared to be well formed on entry but were not, as American studies often seem to suggest, antithetic to the course aims. What shifts did occur were in relation to the realities and constraints of classroom life, reflecting a move from idealism to pragmatism, and a greater understanding of how beliefs relate to practice.

The manner in which changes in knowledge, skills and beliefs are related to aspects of the course are evident through the eyes of student diaries, from interviews, and the observations of their teaching. Their reflections, and evaluations of, their curriculum courses provide extensive evidence of perceived learning about curriculum and pedagogy. In addition there was some evidence of enhanced understandings of subject knowledge, not generally through incremental change, but through the enrichment and restructuring of knowledge already held.

The diary entries regarding the more theoretical course on children's learning similarly showed clear evidence of perceived learning. Here they developed their interpretations based on constructivist principles, and related these to classroom practice. Work on such issues as children's responses, teaching skills, classroom grouping models and task matching, gave them both a vocabulary to describe and explain classroom action, and a vision of what was pedagogically possible. This input also supported and extended their beliefs about the purposes, and roles, of teaching and teachers.

These diaries also pointed to issues which teacher-educators ensure student-teachers are made aware of, yet rarely consider themselves in relation to their own courses, i.e. the range of knowledge and skill in groups of learners, and how to plan for, and execute, a differentiated curriculum.

One point of concern in student reactions to their courses was the marked change in course evaluation at the end of the second, and third terms. On the earlier occasion, 85 per cent gave a very positive response, yet one term later, after the longer, final, teaching practice, only 37 per cent did so. As detailed earlier there are many interpretations of this phenomenon, but unfortunately it can too easily be accepted as a condemnation of the quality of teacher training.

The course on children's learning was closely linked to the first school experience of one day per week. As a consequence, perhaps, the focus for writing on these occasions was clearly on the child as learner. Little was written in diaries about the teacher, and even less about the tutor. However, this focus changed radically during their two later teaching practices. Here the quality of the relationship with the cooperating class-teacher was all-pervading. The influence of the class-teacher was very strong. Where the teacher was helpful and generally supportive the student-teacher gained in confidence and enjoyment; where the help and support was lacking it led to feelings of resentment and abandonment.

The majority of teachers in this study were supportive, but it was apparent that they had no agreed, common mission, and no appropriate training. This could equally be stated of the supervisors. Their interest and expertise in supervision varied considerably. Although some had a coherent, and clearly explicated, view of their role, there appeared to be no institutionally agreed role or set of purposes. This in part could explain the differential attention paid to the ambassadorial role by supervisors.

The fact that an agreed set of criteria for teaching competences had not been fully implemented meant, with the exception of the experimental group, that neither teacher, supervisor nor student had satisfactory means for considering student-teacher development over teaching practices. Neither did the student-teachers have a coherent basis for self-reflection. It is of interest in this context that the requirement of the research team for a pre-lesson pro forma and a post-lesson interview in the observation stage was regarded by the students as being very helpful in the development of their self-reflection.

It was hypothesized that subject knowledge for teaching would show itself in students' teaching performances. Within the limitations of the sample this was shown to be the case. The group with high levels of appropriate knowledge, i.e. the music group, taught music at consistently higher levels of competence than other students, both in the preactive and interactive aspects of teaching. This finding was supported, in a negative sense, by the mathematics and science groups who exhibited only average levels of appropriate knowledge and taught their subjects no better, on average, than other students.

The case studies illustrated more vividly the ways in which subject knowledge for teaching was related to all aspects of pedagogical reasoning, from the framing of intentions, through task design and representation, to evaluation and reflection. They also characterized the implications for teaching of lack of, or partial knowledge, for example, in the inability to develop or extend a theme, and failure to model a lesson. Sybil is of particular interest in this context in demonstrating how her lack of knowledge in music crippled her attempts to frame or fulfil her intentions, whereas in science her knowledge for teaching underpinned a successful lesson.

But these studies also showed clearly that subject-matter knowledge is a necessary but not sufficient ingredient for competent teaching performances, by illustrating the powerful role of context and how that context is managed.

Managing the learning context was high on the agenda of these former students in their first year of teaching. Many of the dilemmas raised were context dependent, e.g. the issue of authority versus being authoritarian; dependence versus autonomy; and sticking to the known versus experimentation. As they gained confidence, and matured as classroom managers, they became less tentative and more willing to take risks. Their relationship with children improved, as did their personal practical knowledge.

Their experiences in the first year of teaching did however raise issues of concern in such crucial areas as school planning, school expectations, the amount and quality of mentoring, sloppy appraisal practices and the generally poor quality of induction training.

LEARNING TO TEACH

The two models which informed this study – of task processes, and of pedagogical reasoning – both have their limitations. The former does not deal explicitly with transformation processes, nor specifically with the role of reflection in action. The latter suffers from lack of consideration of teacher intent and purposes and of lesson implementation. Neither are adequate to explain the processes of development in learning to teach since they are based on the performance of experienced teachers. The only indication of how student-teacher development could occur in the model of pedagogical reasoning, for example, is learning from experience via reflection.

However, in the beginning stages of teacher training most students have had little direct experience of participating in primary classrooms for at least a decade, and then only as learners. They thus have little real experience to reflect on, and very little knowledge to bring to bear on their reflections. These are therefore likely to be limited to discrete events (Borko and Livingston, 1989), or lack connections between specific activities and broader goals of education (Feiman-Nemser and Buchmann, 1987). Reynolds (1992), in reviewing this area, concluded that student reflections are less focused than those of experienced teachers, and that they have difficulty zeroing in on what is instructionally important for reflection because of the lack of developed schemata for organizing information about classroom experiences.

McIntyre (1992) has also argued that reflection is a much more central means for learning for experienced teachers than it can or need be for beginners. He believes that student-teachers' first steps in teaching need conscious deliberation and planning. Competence is thus achieved through conscious control; they do not need to reflect in order to be conscious of what they have been trying to do and know. He proposes three levels of reflection: the technical, the practical and the critical. In the early days of student teaching reflection is at the technical level, where their major task is the attainment of given goals: e.g., basic criteria of teaching such as achieving and maintaining classroom order, gaining pupils' attention, etc. They progress later to practical reflection where the emphasis is on articulating their own criteria, and evaluating and developing their own practice. Critical reflection concerns wider ethical, social and political issues, and is, according to McIntyre, rarely practised even among experienced teachers. His view is therefore that there is a limited role for reflection in initial training as a means to learning, even though learning to reflect must be an important goal.

These conceptions generally accord with the experiences of student-teachers in this study. It is clear from their diaries, and the case studies of teaching, that their early attempts at teaching were characterized by modelling, or imitating, activities either suggested by tutors, or which they had personally experienced on the training course. As such there were few attempts at transformation of content. They did, however, generally have a clear idea of what they wished to achieve, but these intentions did not necessarily involve a comprehension of the content to be taught. Finally, they deliberated, or technically reflected, on their intentions and goals, and the extent to which the lesson 'worked' or not.

A model of pedagogical reasoning based on these early teaching experiences is therefore not well elaborated. This is signified in Figure 13.1 which contains only three elements – intention, instruction (where tasks are modelled) and deliberation.

Modelling can have unforeseen, and sometimes unfortunate, outcomes as the case studies show. Nevertheless it does appear to have value in stimulating reflection, and in building up a repertoire of teaching activities and actions. Modelling of routines underpins Schon's (1987) notion of the reflective practicum, and might, as Calderhead (1991) avers, be an essential stage in the process of becoming a reflective teacher.

Modelling, and the associated notion of apprenticeship, are congruent

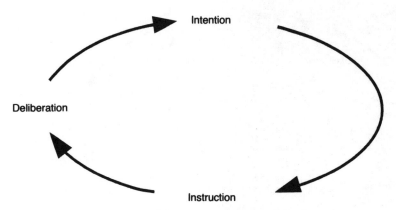

Figure 13.1 A model of early pedagogical reasoning

with recent work in the field of situated cognition. The underlying premiss of this work is that thinking is inextricably interwoven with the context of the problem to be solved. It draws on Vgyotsky's model of cognitive development through social interaction – 'development builds on the internalization by the novice of the shared cognitive processes, appropriating what was carried out in collaboration to extend existing knowledge and skills' (Rogoff, 1990). From this perspective cognitive development is an apprenticeship occurring through guided participation in activity.

The use of modelling, although having theoretical validity, is but a stepping-stone to more informed and independent practice. This requires more experience, more confidence and a shift, in McIntyre's terms, from technical to practical reflection. A model of the second stage of learning to teach is thus much more elaborated than the first, as Figure 13.2 indicates.

All the core elements are now in place; each element requiring particular combinations of knowledge bases. Transformation, for example, demands subject-matter knowledge for teaching, pedagogical content knowledge, knowledge of curriculum and of learners. The implementation element, on the other hand, relies more on general pedagogical knowledge.

The third stage of the model would be characterized by developing teaching competences in each element through improving knowledge bases and skills, together with a move towards critical reflection. This stage of development will ideally be characterized by the kind of personal theorizing so evident in Chapter 12, leading to more coherent and cohesive personal belief structures about teaching and its wider purposes. As Feiman-Nemser and Buchmann (1985) argue, the process of clarifying and developing awareness of the relationship between beliefs and practice is critical to development.

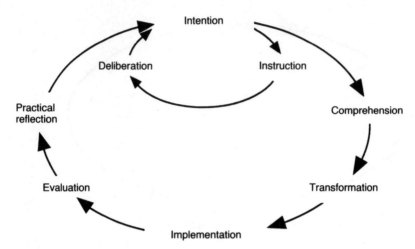

Figure 13.2 A model of the second stage of learning to teach

IMPLICATIONS

Several major implications flow from the foregoing analyses. Of these the most important appear to be the training environment, the content of training and the role of competences. The role of reflection is writ large both in student-teacher accounts, and in the wider research literature. Reflection is, unfortunately, a much over-used and abused term, and here the terminology of cognitive science is useful where, as von Wright (1992) succinctly puts it, reflection 'provides declarative access to procedural knowledge'. The critical question for training is what kind of process underpins the development of reflection, and how can it be best achieved?

Von Wright (1992) believes that self-reflection is more a skill than a capacity: it can be learned and trained through the development of meta-cognitive skills and knowledge. It is these skills that regulate and modify the progress of cognitive activity. He argues that social interaction should be emphasized in such training, on the grounds that social contexts elevate thinking to an observable status (Glaser, 1991). The reflective processes of participants then become apparent, providing the opportunities for understanding and shaping them. Focusing on context also directs attention to the fact that knowledge is always 'situated'.

Such an approach has been built into some teacher preparation programmes. In describing their programme Gunstone and Northfield (1992), for example, assert that 'the development of metacognitive skills and knowledge must be in the context of learning tasks perceived by learners to be appropriate and valuable'. Vonk (1991) too reports training procedures involving problem-discussion strategies based on systematic reflection. The implications are that training environments should be as similar as possible to the environment in which the knowledge and skills are to be used. This in turn appears to argue for a substantial proportion of training to be classroom-based, initially at least, within an apprenticeship model.

However, there is a fundamental dilemma here since our data, and other research, indicate that although this is likely to lead to improvements in some aspects of teaching, it will seriously neglect others – most noticeably the development of subject knowledge for teaching. As it is, understandings of subject matter rarely figure prominently in teacher preparation. 'Constrained by limits of time, teacher educators tend to take prospective teachers' subject-matter knowledge for granted, focusing instead on pedagogical knowledge and skills' (McDiarmid, Ball and Anderson, 1989). Alexander, Rose and Woodhead (1992) present an identical analysis, arguing that training courses are overcrowded, but that beginning teachers require specialist subject knowledge. Thus the knowledge bases to be acquired must be reduced, or aspects of training must be postponed. Kennedy (1992) perceives this to be an enduring dilemma and concludes that there is a need to shift our conceptions from teacher knowledge as a problem to be solved, to a dilemma that must be managed. One way out of this dilemma is, she believes, to assume teacher learning as a continuous process, and to search for ways of facilitating that development.

Alexander *et al.* (1992) have set out on that search, no doubt guided by the latest advice of HMI (1991) in this regard, that 'it would be unreasonable to suppose that initial training could prepare all teachers for all aspects of their professional work and for schools to expect that they will receive fully-fledged practitioners'. Alexander *et al.* thus argue strongly that initial training should be a preparation for the early years of teaching, and a foundation on which subsequent training and development can build. So, for primary teacher training to become more effective, 'there must be a clearly understood division of labour between the initial, induction and Inset stages, and a formal obligation laid on those responsible for each to deliver their part of the training process'. This would seem to be a critical obligation since our findings on the generally poor quality of induction are very similar to those of HMI (1988). They found that the quality of arrangements for induction varied widely, and were poor or unsatisfactory in one-third of the local education authorities visited.

Notions of continuous teacher learning need a baseline from which to work, and towards which to aim. Alexander *et al.* assume a model of core, broad-based, teaching competences much along the lines adopted in this study. This would provide each teacher with a competency profile achieved on exit from the initial training programme, and on which further training would be based. Such a system could also fruitfully integrate continuing teacher development and modes of teacher appraisal. A competency system is also necessary to delineate which aspects are to be targeted at each phase of training.

However laudable, those proposals do not address the problems of the lack of subject knowledge of beginning teachers in the short term. There is no doubt that teacher educators must now overtly address this issue and implement more flexible programmes to allow, for example, self-diagnosis and evaluation of subject knowledge, and independent learning units, addressing the knowledge required for teaching different levels and areas of the National Curriculum.

Work will also need to continue on developing an acceptable set of core-teaching competences both for the purposes outlined above, and, as crucially, for informing the design and implementation of training courses. Our data show very clearly that an agreed set of competences and levels bind student, teacher and supervisor to a common, understood, mission. It is equally clear that any form of apprenticeship requires adequate training of the cooperating teacher/mentor, and the supervisor alike. Little is yet known about what characterizes effective mentoring, and some commonsense assumptions, for example, that good teachers make good mentors, have been disputed. Studies in this area thus need to address what models of mentoring exist, their conceptual underpinnings, effectiveness in practice, and their impact on those involved.

The paucity of models of learning to teach, and lack of systematic data on such central issues as teaching competences and mentoring, highlight the lack of a sound empirical base from which to develop teacher education. The resultant conceptual void has, in recent proposals for reform, thus been filled by political polemic in the absence of empirical evidence. As teacher educators we must take some responsibility for this, and learn by the experience. In future we must be as reflective of our own practice as we expect teachers to be of theirs.

Appendix

A.1 PLANNING AND PREPARATION

Student code

TEACHING EXPERIENCE: STUDENT SHEET
(To be completed prior to observation)

SUBJECT AREA:
IS THIS YOUR SEMI-SPECIALISM? YES/NO
NUMBER OF CHILDREN YOU PLAN TO TEACH:
IS THIS WHOLE CLASS/PART CLASS?
APPROX. LENGTH OF LESSON:

1 (a) Describe the content of the task/activity you are planning.
  (b) Was this task chosen by you/by the teacher?
  (c) Did you/the teacher consider alternative ways of teaching this topic?
      If so, what were they?
      Why did you/the teacher choose this particular way?

2 (a) What is the purpose of this task?
  (b) Is this your decision/the teacher's?

3 (a) How will you present the task to the children?
  (b) Is this your decision/the teacher's?
  (c) How will you cater for differing abilities?

4 (a) What materials will you use? (e.g. own/commercial/teacher's)
  (b) Is this your choice/the teacher's?

---

5 What did the children learn from the task?
  What aspects of the work did they not understand?
  Were you aware of any general misconceptions about the content of the task?

---

6 How did the student ascertain what the children learned or understood?
  How did he/she assess the pupils' work?
  How did he/she feed this information back to the children?

---

7 Did any of the predicted difficulties arise? If so, what?

---

8 When you review the lesson as a whole, what do you think were:
  (i) the main points of strength?
  (ii) the main points of weakness?

A.2 POST OBSERVATION INTERVIEW

1 (a) Did you actually do the task you had planned?
      Probe: If not, why not?
  (b) Would you change it if you did the same task again?
      Probe: If not, why not? If yes, in what ways?

2   Do you think your purposes were fulfilled – well/adequately/poorly?
    Which ones were not fulfilled and why?

3.   Were you happy with the way you presented the task?
     Probe: If yes, what was good about it? If no, why not?

4.   Were the materials adequate/appropriate?
     Probe: If yes, why do you think so? If no, why not?
     What improvements could have been made?

5 (a) Was your classroom organization suitable to fulfil the purposes of the task?
      Probe: If yes, what was it that was good about it? If no, what was wrong?
  (b) What alternatives could you have used?

6   What did the children learn from the task?
     What aspects of the work did they not understand?
     Were you aware of any general misconceptions about the content of the task?

7   How do you know what the children learned or understood?
     How did you (or will you, if lack of time) assess the pupils' work?
     How did you (will you) feed this information back to the children?

8   Did any of your predicted difficulties arise? If so, what?

9 (a) When you review the lesson as a whole, what do you think were:
      (i) the main points of strength;
      (ii) the main points of weakness.
  (b) Would you do anything differently if you taught the same lesson again?
      Probe: If yes, what and how? If no, do you think this was a 'perfect' lesson?
  (c) Which of the teaching skills you used during the lesson did you feel most competent about/least competent about?

10   Did you use your specialist knowledge during this lesson?
     Probe: If so, what area of knowledge was it? In what ways?

11   What parts of this lesson (if any) were a direct result of what you have learned in the School of Education?

A.3 TRANSCRIPT ANALYSIS CATEGORIES

Pedagogical content knowledge

This is a complex amalgam of content knowledge, curriculum knowledge, knowledge of learners and their characteristics, and general pedagogical knowledge.

Direct instruction – management of input

Characteristics The teacher provides and controls the input and steers the class firmly in her intended direction. Techniques may be instruction, question and answer, explanation and various forms of representation.

1 Attract children's initial interest; introduce some content knowledge; be able to demonstrate and describe tasks; use appropriate visual aids.
2 Sustain interest; pace explanation in light of children's responses; convey enthusiasm with appropriate verbal behaviour; use language at the appropriate levels in instructions/explanations.
3 Choose concepts with both subject matter and children's interests in mind; use a range of language, examples and aids to meet diversity of children's attainments; summarize key issues.
4 Choose appropriate examples, analogies and metaphors; make explanations efficient and concise; choose examples for their power in the subject; concise effective review of input.

Direct instruction – monitoring

Characteristics The teacher uses this with the whole class to check understanding of input, recall of previous input, to adjust pacing and level of explanation/review.

1 Check children can follow and understand instructions just given; check children can follow and complete the work set; give appropriate feedback.
2 Check recall and understanding of previous work through questioning and feedback which confirms/extends understanding; simple diagnosis.
3 Use monitoring to create hypotheses about children's difficulties; attempt to analyse and test hunches; use monitoring to inform adjustments of teaching.
4 Create time for and attempt deeper diagnosis of children's responses to tasks.

Structured conversation – management of input

Characteristics The teacher interacts with the children, eliciting input and responding to input from the class/group/individual. Most usually seen with small groups/individuals, but occasionally with the whole class.

1 Listen carefully to what children are saying and respond supportively; ensure children's engagement with the content of the task; use appropriate visual aids.
2 Attempt to elicit children's responses; recognize and attempt to analyse difficulties; use range of examples and ideas in conversational form to focus children's thinking and generate response.

3 Focus on challenging children's ideas by drawing attention to and providing conflicting ideas; by asking for examples and supporting children in reporting their thinking.
4 Adopt a chairperson's role in fostering thoughtful consideration of appropriate concepts and issues.

Structured conversation – monitoring

Characteristics   The teacher monitors the class or group as small groups or individuals once the main input is complete and activities started. Would then be seen throughout lesson.

1 Check children can follow and understand instructions just given; check children can follow and complete the work set; give appropriate feedback.
2 Check recall and understanding of previous work through questioning and feedback which confirms/extends understanding; simple diagnosis.
3 Use monitoring to create hypotheses about children's difficulties; attempt to analyse and test hunches; use monitoring to inform adjustments of teaching.
4 Create time for and attempt deeper diagnosis of children's responses to tasks.

Planning and preparation

1 Plan with some purpose; prepare basic resources for children working on a given activity; select content and activities to suit purpose. Some thought given to differing abilities.
2 Plan with clear purposes; plan and prepare specific activities to engage either practical or one or two intellectual skills and processes; ensure activities meet purposes and range of ability; pay attention to organizational matters such as time, safety, resources and transition between activities. Clearer ideas on catering for differing abilities.
3 Plan with clear purposes to engage a variety of intellectual skills and processes including enquiring, imagining, connecting, hypothesizing, theorizing, planning, recalling, creating, re-creating, evaluating, learning appropriate vocabulary and concentrating, through a range of structured activities. Detailed specific plans to cater for differing abilities.
4 Plan programmes of work to engage a balance of identified skills and intellectual processes with clear reference to policy guides, continuity and progression, demonstrating a sound grasp of appropriate subject and curriculum knowledge. Plan to allow for flexibility and adaptability with clear reference to careful management of the teacher's time.

Evaluation and reflection

1 Give some account of own performance, tending to be content with basic levels of achievement and behaviour by the children. Give some consideration to the reactions of children of differing abilities.

2 Provide valid descriptions of own performance and children's performance of tasks. Offer some analyses of own performance, especially with respect to appropriate use of resources and materials.

3 Offer justifiable evaluations of own performance and children's performances. Use these evaluations to plan future work with reference to own activities in lesson, and children's activities. Use experience to plan more specifically for children with differing abilities.

4 Relate evaluation to broader curriculum planning seeing, for example, the necessity for re-planning schemes. Reflect on evaluations to conceptualize personal model of teaching; challenge own assumptions about subjects, curriculum, organization.

General pedagogical knowledge

This encompasses the broad principles and strategies of classroom management and organization that appear to transcend subject matter. It includes also some knowledge of learners and their characteristics.

Characteristics

1 In Direct Instruction, this is talk relating to the management of activities, materials and order for the whole class, or whole group if the teacher is giving an input to a group rather than a whole class.

2 In Structured Conversation, this is talk relating to the management of activities, materials and order for small groups, pairs or individuals.

Management of activities

The teacher introduces the lesson, organizes the class/group and implements the planned structure of the lesson. Management of activities includes talk relating to the details of organization, and the ending of the lesson, which may or may not include reorganization for a review.

1 Attract initial attention. Organize suitable seating/working arrangements for an activity. Ensure children are all on task. Organize children effectively for group/pair work. Give general instructions. Attempt to end lesson.

2 Reorganize suitable seating/working arrangements for a series of linked activities with minimum attention loss between activities. Give more complicated instructions clearly and concisely. Inform clearly of end of

lesson, instruct class/group to tidy/collect in work/materials. Establish good routines.

3 Organize appropriate seating/working arrangements for an activity or series of activities bearing in mind the characteristics of children. Sustain interest through pacing. Make some attempt to pull lesson together. End lesson effectively.

4 Maintain appropriate arrangements for activity/series of activities, bearing in mind children's characteristics, with no disruption to task/flow of lesson. Pull class together for summing up/reporting back/reading. Organize efficient shared tidying.

This encompasses the broad principles and strategies of classroom management and organization that appear to transcend subject matter. It includes also some knowledge of learners and their characteristics.

Management of order

The teacher operates procedures for management of order so that activities may proceed and learning may take place. Talk ranges from a brief reprimand to a situation in which a high level of management of order is present. Level 4 is not necessarily revealed in the transcripts except negatively, i.e. through an absence of reprimands.

1 Attempt to operate some procedures for orderly activity.
2 Anticipate problems of order, attempt to meet these with a clear system of rules through explicit teaching.
3 Anticipate the need for and identify own set of rules and procedures; work at teaching these rules and procedures; attempt to secure appropriate role for children; persist in trying to assimilate disruptive children to the class community; use a variety of approaches with disruptive children whilst maintaining a sense of proportion.
4 Achieve a situation in which order is endemic to the work system. Give few or no reprimands.

Management of materials

The teacher prepares, provides, selects or designs materials, resources and visual aids. Talk mainly reveals levels 1 and 2; the high levels are found in the pre-lesson and post-lesson data, as they relate to design and selection.

1 Provide and manage materials translated directly from course work; check availability and accessibility of required materials; ensure proper use of those materials; manage appropriate use, including sharing and subsequent collection.

2 Use available materials imaginatively and creatively.
3 Experiment with and use materials which improve on available items.
4 Design, produce or adapt and select purposeful materials and use effectively.

Music knowledge for teaching

The instrument to assess subject knowledge for teaching in music comprised three sections – composing, performing and listening. The pre-test scores of all students, and of the study sample, are presented in Table 10.1. This showed that the music group had substantially, and significantly ($p > 0.0001$), higher scores than each of the other groups in total, and in each of the sections. There were no statistically significant differences between the scores of the maths, science and early years groups.

Table A.1 Change in music knowledge for teaching

Curriculum group	Pre-test mean per cent	Post-pre-test	p
Mathematics	27.5	9.6	0.0008
Science	23.9	8.5	0.0002
Music	45.3	6.4	0.0023
Early years	27.4	13.6	0.0001
Total	31.1	9.5	0.0001

Table A.1 shows the pre-test per cent scores for each of the strands together with the mean change pre- to post-test. It is apparent that significant improvements occur in each group, these being highly significant. The music group improves least but this is not surprising given the substantially higher baseline level. This improvement occurs in each sub-section of the test, but least in Performing.

References

Alexander, R.J. (1984a) *Primary Teaching*, London: Holt, Rinehart & Winston.
Alexander, R.J. (1984b) 'Innovation and continuity in the initial teacher education curriculum', in Alexander, R.J., Craft, M. and Lynch, J.H. (eds), *Change in Teacher Education: Context and Provision since Robbins*, London: Holt, Rinehart & Winston, 103–60.
Alexander, R., Rose, J. and Woodhead, C. (1992) *Curriculum Organization and Classroom Practice in Primary Schools*, London: HMSO.
Anderson, C. (1991) 'Policy implications of research on science teaching and teachers' knowledge', in Kennedy, M. (ed.), *Teaching Academic Subjects to Diverse Learners*, New York: Teachers College Press.
Anderson, E.M. and Shannon, A.L. (1988) 'Leadership: towards a conceptualization of mentoring', *Journal of Teacher Education*, 39, 1, 38–41.
Ashton, P. (1991) 'A teacher education paradigm to empower teachers and students', in Katz, L.G. (ed.), *Advances in Teacher Education*, vol. IV, Norwood, NY: Ablex Publishing Co.
Ashton, P., Kneen, P., Davies, F. and Holley, B.J. (1975) *The Aims of Primary Education: A Study of Teacher Opinions*, London: Macmillan.
APU (1985) *A Review of Monitoring in Mathematics 1978 to 1982*, London: DES
Ausubel, D. (1968) *Educational Psychology: A Cognitive View*, New York: Holt, Rinehart & Winston.
Ball, D. (1990a) 'With an eye on the mathematical horizon: dilemmas of teaching elementary school mathematics'. Paper given at the annual meeting of the American Educational Research Association, Boston, 1990.
Ball, D. (1990b) 'The mathematical understandings that prospective teachers bring to teacher education', *The Elementary School Journal*, 90, 4, 449–66.
Ball, D. (1991) 'Teaching mathematics for understanding: what do teachers need to know about subject matter?', in Kennedy, M. (ed.), *Teaching Academic Subjects to Diverse Learners*, New York: Teachers College Press.
Baratz-Snowden, J. (1990) 'The NEPTS begins its research and development program', *Educational Researcher*, 19, 19–24.
Barnes, H. (1989) 'Structuring knowledge for beginning teaching', in Reynolds, M.C. (ed.), *Knowledge Base for the Beginning Teacher*, New York: Pergamon.
Battista, M.T. (1986) 'The relationship of mathematics anxiety and mathematical knowledge to the learning of mathematical pedagogy by preservice elementary teachers', *School Science and Mathematics*, 86 (1), 10–19.
Bennett, N. (1976) *Teaching Styles and Pupil Progress*, London: Open Books.
Bennett, N. (1988) 'The effective primary school teacher: the search for a theory of pedagogy', *Teaching and Teacher Education*, 4, 19–31.

Bennett, N. (1992) *Managing Learning in the Primary Classroom*, Association for the Study of Primary Education: Trentham Books.

Bennett, N. and Dunne, E. (1992) *Managing Classroom Groups*, Hemel Hempstead: Simon & Schuster.

Bennett, N. and Kell, J. (1989) *A Good Start: Four Year Olds in Infant Schools*, Blackwell: Oxford.

Bennett, N., Desforges, C., Cockburn, A. and Wilkinson, B. (1984) *The Quality of Pupil Learning Experiences*, London: Erlbaum Associates.

Bennett, N., Wragg, E.C., Carré, C.G. and Carter, D.S.G. (1992) 'A longitudinal study of primary teachers' perceived competence in, and concerns about, National Curriculum implementation', *Research Papers in Education*, 7 (1), 53–78.

Ben Peretz, M., Browne, R. and Halkes, R. (1986) *Advances in Research on Teacher Thinking*, Swets and Zeitlanger: Lisse.

Berliner, D.C. (1987) 'Ways of thinking about students and classrooms by more and less experienced teachers', in Calderhead, J. (ed.), *Exploring Teachers' Thinking*, London: Cassell.

Bloor, T. (1986) 'What do language students know about grammar?', *British Journal of Language Teaching*, 24 (3), 157–60.

Borko, H. and Livingston, C. (1989) 'Cognition and improvisation: differences in mathematics instruction by expert and novice teachers', *American Educational Research Journal*, 26, 473–98.

Borko, W., Livingston, C., McCaleb, J. and Mauro, L. (1988) 'Student teachers' planning and post-lesson reflections: patterns and implications for teacher preparation', in Calderhead, J. (ed.), *Teachers' Professional Learning*, Lewes: Falmer Press.

Brandt, R. (1991) 'On teacher education: a conversation with John Goodlad', *Educational Leadership*, 49, 11–13.

Brownjohn, S. (1980) *Does it have to Rhyme?*, Sevenoaks: Hodder & Stoughton.

Brownjohn, S. (1982) *What Rhymes with Secret?*, Sevenoaks: Hodder & Stoughton.

Busher, H., Clarke, S. and Taggart, L. (1988) 'Beginning teachers' learning', in Calderhead, J. (ed.), *Teachers' Professional Learning*, Lewes: Falmer Press.

Calderhead, J. (1988) 'Introduction to *Teachers' Professional Learning*', Lewes: Falmer Press.

Calderhead, J. (1991) 'The nature and growth of knowledge in student teaching', *Teaching and Teacher Education*, 7, 531–6.

Calderhead, J. and Robson, M. (1991) 'Images of teaching: student teachers' early conceptions of classroom practice', *Teaching and Teacher Education*, 7, 1–8.

Chandler, P., Robinson, W. and Noyes, P. (1988) 'The level of linguistic knowledge and awareness amongst students training to be primary teachers', *Language and Education*, 2 (3), 161–74.

Clandinin, D. (1986) *Classroom Practice: Teacher Images in Action*, Lewes: Falmer Press.

Clarke, C.M. and Peterson, P.L. (1986) 'Teachers' thought processes', in Wittrock, M. (ed.), *Handbook of Research on Teaching*, New York: Macmillan.

Cohen, D.K. and Peterson, P.L. (1990) *Effects of State-level Reform of Elementary School Mathematics Curriculum on Classroom Practice*, Research Report 90–14. National Centre for Research on Teacher Education. Michigan State University, East Lansing, Michigan.

Connelly, F.M. and Clandinin, D. (1987) 'Teachers' personal knowledge: what counts as "personal" in studies of the personal', *Journal of Curriculum Studies*, 19 (6), 487–500.

Copa, P.M. (1991) 'The beginning teacher as theory maker: meanings for teacher education', in Katz, L. (ed.), *Advances in Teacher Education*, vol. 4, Norwood, NY: Ablex Publishing Corporation.

Copeland, W. (1980) 'Student teachers and cooperating teachers: an ecological relationship', *Theory into Practice*, 28, 194–9.

Cremin, L.A. (1961) *The Transformation of the School: Progressivism in American Education 1876–1957*, New York: A.A. Knopf.

Crowther, H.I.G. (1978) 'Self-image confidence, and perception of the learning environment in relation to science in primary preservice teacher education.' Unpublished doctoral dissertation, University of Exeter.

Deford, D.E. (1985) 'Validating the construct of theoretical orientation in reading instruction', *Reading Research Quarterly*, 20, 351–67.

DES (1982) *Mathematics Counts*, Report of the Committee of Inquiry chaired by Sir W. Cockcroft, London: HMSO.

DES (1983) *Teaching Quality*, London: HMSO.

DES (1984a) *Initial Teacher Training: Approval of Courses*, DES Circular 3/84, London: HMSO.

DES (1984b) *English from 5 to 16*, London: HMSO.

DES (1985) *Science 5–16: A Statement of Policy*, London: HMSO.

DES (1988a) *The New Teacher in School: A Survey by HM Inspectors in England and Wales 1987*, London: HMSO.

DES (1988b) *Report of the Committee of Enquiry into the Teaching of English Language*, London: HMSO.

DES (1989a) *English for Ages 5 to 16*, London: HMSO.

DES (1989b) *Initial Teacher Training: Approval of Courses*, Circular 24/89, London, HMSO.

DES (1989c) *National Assessment: The APU Science Approach*, London: HMSO.

DES (1989d) *Science in the National Curriculum*, London: HMSO.

DES (1990) 'Administrative Memorandum 1/90'. The treatment and assessment of probationary teachers, London: HMSO.

DES (1991a) *Science in the National Curriculum*, London: HMSO.

DES (1991b) *The Orders for Mathematics (Revised National Curriculum)*, London: HMSO.

DES (1992a) *Curriculum Organisation and Classroom Practices in Primary Schools, A Discussion Paper*, Alexander, R., Rose, J. and Woodhead, C., London: HMSO.

DES (1992b) *Reform of Initial Teacher Training: A Consultative Document*, London: HMSO.

Dow, G. (1979) *Learning to Teach: Teaching to Learn*, Melbourne: Routledge & Kegan Paul.

Driver, R., Guesne, E. and Tiberghien, A. (1985) *Children's Ideas in Science*, Milton Keynes: Open University Press.

Dunn, J., Styles, M. and Warburton, N. (1987) *In Tune with Yourself*, Cambridge: Cambridge University Press.

Dunne, R. (1992) 'The acquisition of professional activity in teaching', in Harvard, G. and Hodgkinson, P. (eds), *Action and Reflection in Teacher Education*, Norwood, NY: Ablex Publishing Co.

Dunne, R. and Harvard, G. (1990) 'Teaching practice criteria', mimeo, University of Exeter.

Dunne, R. and Harvard, G. (1992a) 'Competence as the meaningful acquisition of professional activity in teaching', in Saunders, D. and Race, P. (eds), *Developing and Measuring Competence*, London: Kogan Page.

Dunne, R. and Harvard, G. (1992b) *The implications for course design and assessment in initial training of a competence-based programme*. Paper presented at HMI hospitality conference on competence-based teacher education, Bromsgrove, Worcs, 9–10 March 1992.

Edwards, A.D. and Furlong, V.J. (1978) *The Language of Teaching: Meaning in Classroom Interaction*, London: Heinemann.

Edwards, D. and Mercer, N. (1987) *Common Knowledge: The Development of Understanding in the Classroom*, London: Methuen.

Elbaz, F. (1983) *Teacher Thinking: A Study of Practical Knowledge*, New York: Nichols Publishing.

Ernest, P. (1988) 'The attitudes and practices of student teachers of primary school mathematics', *Proceedings of XIIth International Psychology of Mathematics Education Conference, Volume 1*, Veszprem, Hungary: OOK.

Ernest, P. (1989) 'The knowledge, beliefs and attitudes of the mathematics teacher: a model', *Journal of Education for Teaching*, 15 (1), 13–33.

Ernest, P. (1991) *The Philosophy of Mathematics Education*, London: Falmer Press.

Feiman-Nemser, S. (1983) 'Learning to teach', in Shulman, L.S. and Sykes,G. (eds). *Handbook of Teaching and Policy*, New York: Longman, 150–70.

Feiman-Nemser, S. and Buchmann, M. (1985) 'Pitfalls of experience in teacher preparation', *Teachers College Record*, 87, 53–65.

Feiman-Nemser, S. and Buchmann, M. (1987) 'When is student teaching teacher education?', *Teaching and Teacher Education*, 3, 255–73.

Fullan, M. (1982) *The Meaning of Educational Change*, Toronto, Ontario: OISE Press.

Galton, M., Simon, B. and Croll, P. (1980) *Inside the Primary Classroom*, London: Routledge & Kegan Paul.

Gilbert, J. and Watts, D.M. (1983) 'Concepts, misconceptions and alternative conceptions: changing perspectives in science education', *Studies in Science Education*, 10.

Glaser, R. (1991) 'The maturing of the relationship between the science of learning and cognition and educational practice', *Learning and Instruction*, 1, 129–44.

Goodlad, J.I. (1984) *A Place called School*, New York: McGraw-Hill.

Goodlad, J.I. (1991) 'Why we need a complete re-design of teacher education', *Educational Leadership*, 49, 4–6.

Goodman, J. (1986) 'Making early field experiences meaningful: a critical approach', *Journal of Education for Teaching*, 12 (2), 109–22.

Goodman, J. (1987) 'Factors in becoming a proactive elementary school teacher: a preliminary study of selected novices', *Journal of Education for Teaching*, 13, 207–29.

Gore, J.M. and Zeichner, K.M. (1991) 'Action research and reflective teaching in pre-service education: a case study from the United States', *Teaching and Teacher Education*, 7, 119–36.

Grossman, P.L., Wilson, S.M. and Shulman, L.E. (1989) 'Teachers of substance: subject matter knowledge for teaching', in Reynolds, M.C. (ed.), *Knowledge Base for the Beginning Teacher*, New York: Pergamon.

Gunstone, R.F. and Northfield, J. (1992) 'Conceptual change in teacher education: the centrality of metacognition', Paper presented at American Educational Research Association Conference, San Francisco.

Hacker, R.J. (1984) 'A typology of approaches to science teaching in schools', *European Journal of Science Education*, 6 (2), 153–67.

Harlen, W., Black, P. and Johnson, S. (1981) *Science in Schools Age 11; Report 1*, London: HMSO for the Assessment of Performance Unit.

Harste, J. and Burke, C. (1977) 'A new hypothesis for reading teacher research: both the teaching and learning of reading is theoretically based', in Pearson, P. (ed.), *Reading: Theory, Research and Practice*, New York: Mason.

Harvard, G. (1992) '*An integrated model of how student-teachers learn how to teach and its implications for mentors*'. in Harvard, G. and Hodgkinson, P. (eds), Reflection and Action in Teacher Education. Norwood, NY: Ablex Publishing Co.

Harvard, G. and Dunne, R. (1992) 'The role of the mentor in developing teacher competence', *Westminster Studies in Education*, 15, 33–44.

HMI (1978) *Primary Education in England: A Survey by HMI of Schools*, London: HMSO.

HMI (1982) *The New Teacher in School*, London: HMSO.

HMI (1985a) *Mathematics from 5 to 16*, London: HMSO.

HMI (1985b) *Education 8 to 12 in Combined and Middle Schools*, London: HMSO.

HMI (1987) *Quality in Schools: The Initial Training of Teachers*, London: HMSO.

HMI (1988) *The New Teacher in School*, London: HMSO.

HMI (1991) *The Professional Training of Primary School Teachers*, London: HMSO.

Hogben, D. and Lawson, M.J. (1984) 'Trainee and beginning teacher attitude stability and change: four case studies', *Journal of Education for Teaching*, 10, 135–53.

Holmes Group (1986) *Tomorrow's Teachers*, East Lansing: MI.

Howey, K. (1983) 'Teacher education: an overview', in Howie, K. and Gardner, W. (eds), *Teacher Education: A Look Forward*, New York: Longman.

Johnson, S. (1989) *National Assessment: The APU Science Approach*, London: HMSO.

Joyce, B. (1975) 'Conceptions of man and their implications for teacher education', in Ryan K. (ed.), *Teacher Education*, 74th Yearbook of the National Society for the Study of Education, Chicago: University Chicago Press.

Kennedy, M. (1991) 'An agenda for research on teacher learning', NCRTL Special Report, Michigan State University.

Kennedy, M. (1992) 'Merging subjects and students into teaching knowledge', in Kennedy, M. (ed.), *Teaching Academic Subjects to Diverse Learners*, New York: Teachers College Press.

Kruger, C. and Summers, M. (1989) 'An investigation of some primary teachers' understandings of changes in materials', *School Science Review*, 71, 17–27.

Kruger, C., Summers, M. and Palacio, D. (1990) 'INSET for primary science in the National Curriculum in England and Wales: are the real needs of teachers perceived?', *Journal of Education for Teaching*, 16 (2), 133–46.

Kuhn, T.S. (1962) *The Structure of Scientific Revolutions*, Chicago: University of Chicago Press.

Lacey, C. (1977) *The Socialization of Teachers*, London: Methuen.

Lampert, M. (1985) 'How do teachers manage to teach? Perspectives on problems in practice', *Harvard Educational Review*, 55, 178–94.

Lanier, J. and Little, J. (1986) 'Research on teacher education', in Wittrock, M. (ed.), *Handbook of Research on Teaching*, New York: Macmillan.

Lawlor, S. (1990) *Teachings Mistaught: Training in Theories of Education in Subjects?*, London: Centre for Policy Studies.

Lawson, A. (1991) 'What teachers need to know to teach science effectively', in Kennedy, M. (ed.), *Teaching Academic Subjects to Diverse Learners*, New York: Teachers College Press.

Leinhardt, G. and Feinberg, J. (1990) *Integration of Lesson Structure and Teacher*

Subject Matter Knowledge. Centre for the Study of Learning, LRDC University of Pittsburgh.

Lortie, D.C. (1975) *Schoolteachers: A Sociological Study,* Chicago: University of Chicago Press.

McDiarmid, G.W. (1990) 'What do prospective teachers learn in their liberal arts classes?', *Theory into Practice,* 29, 21–9.

McDiarmid, G.W. and Wilson, S.M. (1991) 'An exploration of the subject matter knowledge of alternate route teachers: can we assume they know their subject?', *Journal of Teacher Education,* 42 (2), 93–103.

McDiarmid, G.W., Ball, D.L. and Anderson, C.W. (1989) 'Why staying one chapter ahead doesn't really work: subject specific pedagogy', in Reynolds, M.C. (ed.), *Knowledge Base for the Beginning Teacher,* New York: Pergamon.

McIntyre, D. (1992) 'Theory, theorizing and reflection in initial teacher education', in Calderhead, J. (ed.), *Conceptualizing Reflection in Teacher Development,* London: Falmer (in press).

Millar, R. and Driver, R. (1987) 'Beyond processes', *Studies in Science Education,* 14, 31–62.

NCC (1991) *The National Curriculum and the Initial Training of Students, Articled and Licensed Teachers,* York National Curriculum Council.

NCTM (1989) *Curriculum and Evaluation Standards for School Mathematics,* Reston, Virginia: National Council of Teachers of Maths.

Neale, D. and Smith, D. (1989) 'Implementing conceptual change teaching in primary science', Paper presented at the Annual Meeting of the American Educational Research Association, San Francisco.

Newby, M. (1987) *The Structure of English,* Cambridge: Cambridge University Press.

Olson, M.R. and Osborne, J.W. (1991) 'Learning to teach: the first year', *Teaching and Teacher Education,* 7 (4), 331–43.

Osgood, C.E., Suci, G.J. and Tannenbaum, P.H. (1957) *The Measurement of Meaning,* Chicago: University of Illinois Press.

Perry, W.G. (1970) *Forms of Intellectual and Ethical Development in the College Years: A Scheme,* New York: Holt, Rinehart & Winston.

Reynolds, A. (1992) 'What is competent beginning teaching? A review of the literature', *Review of Educational Research,* 62, 1–36.

Rogoff, B. (1990) *Apprenticeship in Thinking. Cognitive Development in Social Context,* Oxford: Oxford University Press.

Ross, D. (1979) 'The role of teachers' beliefs in teaching practice.' Paper presented at the annual meeting of the American Educational Research Association, San Francisco.

Russell, T., Bell, D., McGuigan, L., Qualter, A., Quinn, J. and Schilling, M. (1992) 'Teachers' conceptual understanding in science: needs and possibilities in the primary phase', *Evaluation and Research in Education,* 6 (2 & 3), 129–43.

Schaffer, G., Springfield, S. and Wolfe, S. (1990) 'Two-year effects on classroom interactions of a sustained beginning teacher induction program.' Paper presented at the annual meeting of the American Educational Research Association, Boston.

Schofield, H.L. and Start, K.B. (1978) 'Mathematics attitudes and achievement among student teachers', *The Australian Journal of Education,* 22 (1), 72–82.

Schon, D.A. (1987) *Educating the Reflective Practitioner,* San Francisco: Jossey-Bass.

Schwab, J. (1964) 'The structure of the disciplines: meanings and significances', in Ford, G. and Purgo, L. (eds), *The Structure of Knowledge and the Curriculum,* Chicago: Rand McNally.

Schwab, J. (1978) 'Education and the structure of the disciplines', in Westbury, I. and Wilkof, N.J. (eds), *Science, Curriculum and Liberal Education*, Chicago: University of Chicago Press, 229–72.

Shulman, L.S. (1986a) 'Paradigms and research programmes in the study of teaching: a contemporary perspective', in Whittrock, M.C. (ed.), *Handbook of Research in Teaching*, 3rd edn, New York: Macmillan.

Shulman, L.S. (1986b) 'Those who understand: knowledge growth in teaching', *Educational Researcher*, 15, 4–14.

Shulman, L.S. (1987a) 'Knowledge and teaching: foundations of the new reforms', *Harvard Educational Review*, 57, 1–22.

Shulman, J. (1987b) 'From veteran parent to novice teacher: a case study of a student teacher', *Teaching and Teacher Education*, 3, 1, 13–27.

Smith, D. and Neale, D. (1989) 'The construction of subject matter knowledge in primary science teaching', *Teaching and Teacher Education*, 5 (1), 1–20.

Stanley, J.C. and Hopkins, K.D. (1972) *Educational and Psychological Measurement and Evaluation*, Englewood Cliffs, N J: Prentice-Hall.

Stodolsky, S.S. (1988) *The Subject Matters*, Chicago: University of Chicago Press.

Stoessiger, R. and Ernest, P. (1992) 'Mathematics and the national curriculum: primary teachers' attitudes', *International Journal of Mathematical Education in Science and Technology*, 23 (1), 65–74.

Tabachnick, R.R. and Zeichner, K.M. (1984) 'The impact of the student teaching experience on the development of teacher perspectives', *Journal of Teacher Education*, 29, 28–36.

Teel, K. and Hollingsworth, S. (1988) 'Learning effective classroom management: a study of perservice teacher change', Paper presented at the Annual Meeting of the American Educational Research Association, New Orleans.

Thompson, A.G. (1984) 'The relationship of teachers' conceptions of mathematics and mathematics teaching to instructional practice', *Educational Studies in Mathematics*, 15, 105–27.

Tobin, K., Butler Kahle, J. and Fraser, J. (1990) *Windows into Science Classrooms: Problems Associated with Higher Level Cognitive Learning*, London: Falmer Press.

Veenman, S. (1984) 'Perceived problems of beginning teachers', *Review of Educational Research*, 54, 143–78.

Vonk, J.H.C. (1991) 'Becoming a teacher, brace yourself'; in Ho Wah Kam and Ruth Y. Lo Yong (eds), *Improving the Quality of the Teaching Profession*, Singapore: ICET, 63–81.

von Wright, J. (1992) 'Reflections on reflection', *Learning and Instruction*, 2, 59–68.

Whitty, G. (1991) 'Competence-based teacher education: approaches and uses', *Cambridge Journal of Education*, 21 (3), 309–18.

Wilson, S.M., Shulman, L.S. and Richert, A.E. (1987) '150 different ways of knowing: representations of knowledge in teaching'. in Calderhead, J. (ed.), *Exploring Teachers' Thinking*, London: Cassell, 104–25.

Wragg, E., Bennett, N. and Carré, C. (1989) 'Primary teachers and the National Curriculum', *Research Papers in Education*, 4, 17–37.

Wray, D. (1988) 'The impact of psycholinguistic theories on trainee-teachers' views of the teaching of reading', *Journal of Reading Education*, 14 (1), 24–35.

Wubbels, T., Korthagen, F.A.J. and Broekman, H. (1991) *Pedagogical subject matter knowledge in secondary mathematics teacher education: characteristics and strategies for change*. Paper presented at the Annual Meeting of the American Educational Research Association, Chicago.

Zeichner, K.M. (1980) 'Myths and realities: field-based experiences in preservice teacher education', *Journal of Teacher Education*, 31, 237–44.

Zeichner, K.M. (1983) 'Individual and institutional factors related to the socialization of teaching', in Griffin, G.A. and Hukill, H. (eds), *First Years of Teaching: What are the Pertinent Issues?*, R & DCTE Report No. 9051, pp 1–59). Austin, TX: University of Texas at Austin, pp. 1–59.

Zeichner, K.M. (1992) 'Conceptions of reflective practice in teaching and teacher education', in Harvard, G. and Dunne, R. (eds), *Westminster Studies in Education*, vol. 15.

Zeichner, K.M. and Liston, D.P. (1987) 'Teaching student-teachers to reflect', *Harvard Educational Review*, 57 (1), 23–48.

Index